THE COMPLETE
GUITAR
MANUAL

THE COMPLETE
GUITAR
MANUAL

LONDON, NEW YORK,
MUNICH, MELBOURNE, DELHI

Project Editor	Ed Wilson
Senior Art Editor	Michael Duffy
Production Editor	Joanna Byrne
Production Controller	Mandy Inness
Creative Technical Support	Adam Brackenbury
Cover Designer	Mark Cavanagh
Managing Editor	Stephanie Farrow
Managing Art Editor	Lee Griffiths
US Editor	Liza Kaplan
Americanizer	Rachel Bozek

Produced for Dorling Kindersley by

cobaltid

The Stables, Wood Farm, Deopham Road,
Attleborough, Norfolk NR17 1AJ

Editors
Marek Walisiewicz, Louise Abbott,
Maddy Edwards, Sarah Tomley

Art Editors
Paul Reid, Darren Bland, Lloyd Tilbury

www.cobaltid.co.uk

DVD videography
Martin Holmes

DVD authoring
Adam Crute

First American Edition, 2011
Published in the United States by
DK Publishing
375 Hudson Street
New York, New York 10014

11 12 13 14 15   10 9 8 7 6 5 4 3 2 1

001—177869—May/2011

Published in Great Britain by
Dorling Kindersley Limited.

A catalog record for this book is available
from the Library of Congress

ISBN 978-0-7566-7553-0

DK books are available at special discounts when purchased in bulk for sales
promotions, premiums, fund-raising, or educational use. For details, contact:
DK Publishing Special Markets, 375 Hudson Street, New York, New York 10014
or SpecialSales@dk.com.

Printed and bound in Singapore by Star Standard Industries

Discover more at
www.dk.com

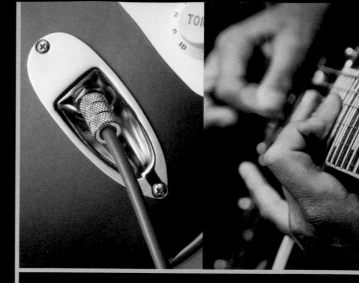

CONTENTS

INTRODUCTION

Like no other instrument, the guitar opens up a vast world of musical possibilities. It welcomes everyone from casual strummers to studious technicians, and is ideal if you want to join a band to accompany a singer, or if your desire is to bask in the limelight as a soloist. It offers countless choices of expression—from sensitive fingerpicked acoustic playing all the way through to loud, distorted electric guitar sounds—and is suited to almost any genre of music. Then there is the magnetic appeal of guitar icons and their music: the desire to learn the guitar is often driven by emulation. Perhaps you are enthralled by Jimi Hendrix, Bob Dylan, Steve Vai, or Wes Montgomery—with the guitar, you are never short of inspiration.

What matters most is the relationship you develop with the guitar. The longer you play, the more of its secrets will unfold—it may be a new technique, a new chord, an effects pedal sound, or a lead lick from a

song that had always eluded you. Whatever it is, the guitar will always keep providing musical pleasure for as long as you play.

This book and its accompanying DVD is a practical guide to the guitar. It includes guidance on choosing the right instrument, maintaining your guitar, and becoming a musician. At its heart is a step-by-step instructional guide to playing, based around 10 learning sessions. In each of these sessions, you will learn and develop new skills and techniques through short, specially written musical exercises and build a sound knowledge of theory. Of course, there will be moments of frustration when you seem to hit a brick wall in your development, but this is common to every guitarist—you will learn to appreciate that barre chord or string bending hurdles have been experienced by countless others before you. They overcame them and so, with the help of this book, will you.

"... if you feel that you're not getting enough out of a song, change the instrument—go from an acoustic to an electric or vice versa ..."

THE **KIT**

THE GUITAR

An amazingly versatile instrument, the guitar has some of the percussive qualities of a drum, the melodic beauty of a cello, and the utility of a piano—and yet it retains a character distinctly its own. It can be relatively cheap to buy and simple to maintain, and it can be used to produce chords and melodies with equal ease. It is also kind to mistakes, so even the most hesitant beginner can produce decent tunes with a little practice.

EARLY BEGINNINGS

The guitar's history spans four centuries. Early 17th-century examples made in Venice were highly ornate and had four or five sets of gut strings. The design of the modern acoustic guitar developed later in 19th-century Europe and the US.

THE INSTRUMENT

This chapter gives you the information you need to choose and buy the right guitar for you. It explores the basic construction of both acoustic and electric guitars, and explains the principles by which they produce sound. It examines a range of models—acoustic, semi-acoustic, and electric (*see pp.18–25*)—but of course, this is only a fraction of the huge number of designs available. You may pick, or aspire to, a particular model because it's played by a musician you admire, but remember that when it comes to guitars, however flashy the design or big the manufacturer's name, the tone of the instrument is what counts.

Tone is determined by the complex interplay between the a guitar's build and components (*see pp.26–29*); it is therefore essential to try before you buy. Make a good music shop your first port of call; it will probably soon become one of your favorite places.

Jack White Front man of the White Stripes, Jack White developed his distinctive raw sound with old, relatively cheap guitars, teamed with an array of effects pedals.

Eric Clapton One of the most influential guitarists of all time, Clapton developed several distinctive guitar sounds through his solo career and with the Yardbirds and Cream.

AMPS AND ELECTRONICS

If you're buying an electric guitar, you'll also need an amplifier to produce any meaningful sound. You don't need to spend a lot—a small and basic "practice" amp can be surprisingly affordable—but, as with your guitar, make sure you test before you buy. Bring your own guitar with you to a shop (or choose the guitar closest to your model) and plug it into a few amplifiers to test the tones it can produce. Pages 34 to 37 of this book will guide you through the different types of amps available.

You'll doubtless also be tempted by the amazing number of sound effects units you can bolt onto your basic kit. This is a world of jargon—and while you may already have an idea

Solid bodies The form and tone of today's electric guitars owes much to talented players who worked closely with manufacturers in the 1950s and 1960s to develop new instruments. Modern electronics continue to shape the instrument.

of what "reverb" and "overdrive" sound like, this chapter contains a guide to the range of effects you can use to shape your guitar sound (*see pp.38–39*). Understanding how the various types of amps enhance your sound, and how sound is modified when you press an effects pedal, will help you make confident choices when buying.

This chapter also includes information on the evolving possibilities of digital sound enhancement: while this is exciting for some, for others it is no substitute for the raw sound of a Fender Telecaster or the stage presence of the Marshall stack. By all means take inspiration from your guitar icons, but experiment, too, to develop your own sound.

Joe Satriani Guitar virtuoso Satriani has played with most of rock music's greats. He has worked closely with guitar company Ibanez on the development of new guitar models.

Bo Diddley Rhythm and blues legend and technical innovator Bo Diddley had a key role in the evolution of rock and roll, earning him the nickname "The Originator."

ANATOMY OF AN ACOUSTIC GUITAR

Acoustic guitars are the perfect tool for songwriting and impromptu performances, and the best examples have a vibrancy and complexity of tone that can be matched by few other instruments. While the vast majority of guitars are built in factories, there are luthiers (guitar-makers) in nearly every nation. If you get the chance to try a handmade acoustic guitar, you'll notice it has an extra richness of tone that you won't find in many factory-built guitars. The attention to detail that goes into such instruments comes at a price, but if you do decide to invest in one, it will give you a lifetime of superb service.

Neck

Hardwood back

Body shape
The shape of the guitar and its constituent woods help define its sound.

Rear view   Side view

Neck joint
The neck typically joins the body at the 12th or 14th fret; an internal metal truss rod helps give it rigidity.

Saddle

Bridge

Soundboard

Pickguard, or scratchplate

BRIDGE
This shallow block of hardwood, attached to the "bridgeplate" inside the guitar, spreads the load of string tension across the soundboard. The strings pass over the saddle (*see right*) and enter the body of the guitar, held in place by six bridge pins.

SADDLE
Inset into the bridge is a bar that forms a counterpart to the nut (*see opposite*) at the top of the neck. The distance between saddle and nut determines the "scale length" of the guitar—the zone within which the strings can vibrate freely.

STRINGS
The standard guitar has six strings but 12-string guitars (*see p.19*) are a popular alternative for acoustic players. Originally made from gut, strings are now made from nylon polymers or metal alloys ("steel strings") for a bright sound.

SOUNDING OUT

When an acoustic guitar is strummed, the vibration of the strings is transmitted from the bridge into the soundboard. The broad, flexible surface of the soundboard vibrates in sympathy with the strings and sets the air around the guitar into motion, generating sound. The other parts of the guitar's boxlike body also help to project the sound. For this reason, an acoustic guitar produces a louder sound than an unplugged electric guitar (which has a solid body and requires amplification).

CONSTRUCTION

The body of an acoustic guitar is essentially a hollow box. The top, or soundboard, is made of strong, light wood, typically sitka spruce for steel-string acoustic guitars. Its job is to resonate freely and generate sound (*see box, left*).

The back of the guitar and its curved sides have a different job to do: instead of being light and flexible, they must provide structural strength and reflect sound outward toward the listener. For these reasons, they are usually made of a strong, dense hardwood, such as rosewood or mahogany. The guitar's neck is usually attached to the body with a glued dovetail joint, although some makers favor a bolt-on design. The necks of nearly all modern acoustic guitars contain a slender, adjustable metal rod, known as a truss rod. It is used to induce a slight bow shape in the neck that makes playing easier.

Headstock   Tuning keys

Nut

Fretboard

Fret markers

Strings

Truss rod cover
This hides the end of the metal truss rod that runs the length of the neck.

Frets These thin bars of nickel-silver wire divide the fretboard.

Machine heads

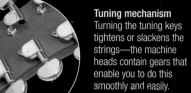

Tuning mechanism
Turning the tuning keys tightens or slackens the strings—the machine heads contain gears that enable you to do this smoothly and easily.

FRETBOARD

This shallow strip of hardwood forms a cap over the upper surface of the neck and has a subtle edge-to-edge convex curve or "radius" to enhance playability. Set into the fretboard's surface are 18–20 frets—metal bars positioned at carefully calibrated intervals.

NUT

This bar of dense material (traditionally bone) has evenly spaced notches in which each string sits. When correctly tensioned, the strings pass over the nut and run down along the length of the fretboard, held taut slightly above its surface.

HEADSTOCK

This angled plate of wood is glued to the top section of the neck with a long, tapering joint known as a scarf. Its main function is to mount the machine heads. These translate rotation of the tuning keys into fine adjustments in string tension.

ANATOMY OF AN ELECTRIC GUITAR

In comparison to a hand-crafted acoustic guitar, the electric guitar is a relatively simple instrument. Like the acoustic, it has a wooden neck, but its body is usually solid rather than hollow, and typically made from a dense, durable hardwood (*see p.24*)—although some instruments feature metals or plastics. The tone produced by the best electric guitars can be every bit as complex and nuanced as that of acoustic instruments.

Neck

Back plates

Body shape
The electric guitar has a slim profile. Plates on the back allow access to the wiring for the pickups.

Rear view　　**Side view**

Pickup selector

Strap button

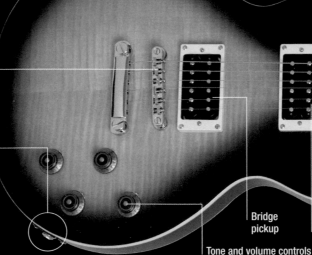

Bridge and saddles

Cutaway
Contouring at the neck improves access to the upper frets.

Bridge pickup

Neck pickup

Tone and volume controls

Output socket A standard ¼in socket connects the guitar to an amp, via a cable.

BRIDGE AND SADDLES
The bridge usually mounts six grooved saddles that form the lower end point of the guitar's scale length (the zone in which the strings can vibrate freely), with the nut forming the other end. Most designs are adjustable for height and intonation.

TONE AND VOLUME CONTROLS
The tone control adjusts the amount of treble; in most models, treble is reduced by turning it counterclockwise. The volume control adjusts the strength of the guitar's output. In most guitars, volume reduction also has the side effect of damping treble response.

PICKUPS
As many as three magnetic pickups (*see box, above right*) may be fitted between the neck and bridge, each producing a different tone from bassy (neck) to hard and sharp (bridge). The pickup selector allows the player to switch between, or blend, pickups.

HOW IT WORKS – IN A NUTSHELL

Lacking a hollow, resonating body, a solid-body electric guitar cannot produce a clearly audible tone on its own. Instead, one or more magnetic "pickups" are mounted on the top surface of the body, between the fretboard and the bridge. An electrical signal is generated by the pickups when the guitar strings vibrate; this current is carried through the guitar lead to the amplifier, or amp (*see pp.34–37*), which transforms it into audible sound. Effects units that modify the sound, such as fuzz and wah-wah pedals (*see pp.38–39*), can be positioned between the guitar and the amp, or the amp may incorporate a variety of effects that can be controlled via a foot switch.

PICKUPS

A pickup is a magnet wrapped in a coil of fine copper wire. When the strings move, the magnetic field is disturbed, inducing electric voltage in the copper coil. Early single-coil pickup designs had a bright, clear tone, but generated unwanted noise or "hum" when near other electrical devices. In the mid-1950s, Gibson engineer Seth Lover developed a pickup configuration that eliminated this effect, calling it the "humbucker."

TYPES OF PICKUP

Single-coil These are associated with bright tone. Six polepieces, usually made of Alnico (aluminium, nickel, and cobalt alloy), focus the magnetic-field effect on individual strings, ensuring that each is heard in the overall sound.

Humbucker These pickups have a hum-cancelling effect and are associated with a thicker tone and a higher output than single-coil pickups. The most famous design is Gibson's PAF.

Piezo-electric Some electric guitars, such as the Parker Fly, also have this nonmagnetic, vibration-sensitive pickup in the bridge; it allows the player to emulate the tone of an acoustic guitar.

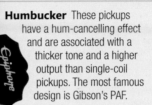

Strings

Machine heads

Fretboard

Frets

Nut

Tuning keys

Fret markers These indicate key positions on the neck; designs range from simple plastic dots to ornate mother-of-pearl inlays.

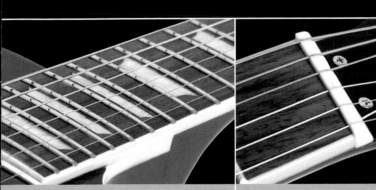

FRETBOARD
Rosewood, maple, and ebony are favorite choices for guitar fretboards, and each has a subtly different tone. Electric guitar necks usually have either 22 or 24 frets, with the neck typically joining the body around the 18th fret.

NUT
A bar made of bone, graphite, brass, or plastic, the nut holds the strings up and away from the fretboard. There may be a "string tree" to guide the strings from the tuning posts (*see right*) to the nut at an angle that will ensure optimum contact between the two.

HEADSTOCK
The headstock mounts the machine heads, used to adjust the tension—and so also the pitch—of the strings (*see p.58*). The six tuning posts rotate when the machine heads' tuning keys are turned, winding (tightening) or unwinding (loosening) the string.

ACOUSTIC GUITARS

Today's acoustic guitars are descended from small, gut-stringed instruments built in 19th-century Europe. Along the way there have been a few evolutionary leaps. In 1918, the Martin guitar company in the US developed a loud new design, called the Dreadnought, which pioneered a square-shouldered, large-bodied shape that remains with us today. Meanwhile, some makers simply enlarged the hourglass shape of earlier designs to increase volume: Gibson's Super Jumbo 200, as used by Elvis, is a classic example. Archtop guitars achieved greater loudness with their convex tops and revised construction—while resonator guitars made use of metal parts for the same effect. Today, many acoustic guitars are fitted with built-in pickups, which means that they can be more easily heard by large audiences.

LANDMARK ACOUSTIC GUITARS

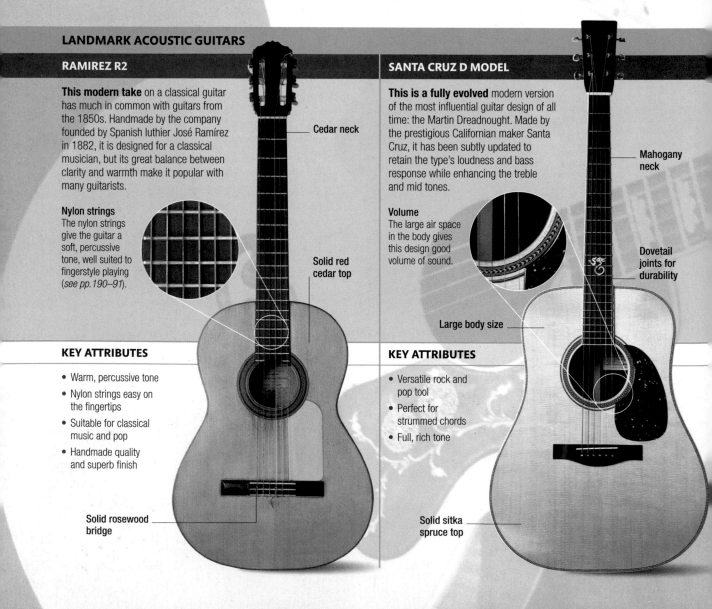

RAMIREZ R2

This modern take on a classical guitar has much in common with guitars from the 1850s. Handmade by the company founded by Spanish luthier José Ramírez in 1882, it is designed for a classical musician, but its great balance between clarity and warmth make it popular with many guitarists.

Nylon strings
The nylon strings give the guitar a soft, percussive tone, well suited to fingerstyle playing (*see pp. 190–91*).

Cedar neck

Solid red cedar top

KEY ATTRIBUTES

- Warm, percussive tone
- Nylon strings easy on the fingertips
- Suitable for classical music and pop
- Handmade quality and superb finish

Solid rosewood bridge

SANTA CRUZ D MODEL

This is a fully evolved modern version of the most influential guitar design of all time: the Martin Dreadnought. Made by the prestigious Californian maker Santa Cruz, it has been subtly updated to retain the type's loudness and bass response while enhancing the treble and mid tones.

Volume
The large air space in the body gives this design good volume of sound.

Mahogany neck

Dovetail joints for durability

Large body size

KEY ATTRIBUTES

- Versatile rock and pop tool
- Perfect for strummed chords
- Full, rich tone

Solid sitka spruce top

CHAPTER 1

TERRIFIC TWELVES

If you are drawn to psychedelia and especially the 1960s folk-rock sound of groups such as Crosby, Stills, Nash, and Young (right), it may be worth trying a 12-string acoustic guitar. Developed at the beginning of the 20th century, these specialist guitars have a similar silhouette to a standard acoustic, but are built more heavily to support the extra strain generated by six ultra-light "drone" strings strung alongside six conventionally tuned strings. Each of the lower four drone strings is pitched an octave above its partner string, with the upper two in unison, to produce a shimmering tone that is perfect for ballads or vintage blues styles.

GODIN 5TH AVENUE

This guitar is an archtop, a design pioneered in the jazz era of the 1920s to increase playing volume. It features a large soundchamber and a curved top that helps to project single note melodies. Revived by Godin, a Canadian maker, the style is now enjoying a real resurgence.

Body style
Made from Canadian wild cherry, the body features a molded arched top and back.

Maple neck

Pickguard "floats" above body

KEY ATTRIBUTES

- Authentic jazz and rockabilly tone
- Punchy single-note articulation
- Quality build and excellent value

"F"-holes in body

Arched top

DELTA TRICONE DELUXE

This resonator guitar by Delta is English-built, but has the authentic features of pioneering US resonators from the 1920s. Unlike conventional acoustics, resonators rely on spun metal cones inside the body, rather than the soundboard, to convert vibration into audible tone.

Construction
The Delta features nickel fret bars on an ebony fretboard. Its mahogany body has a nickel-plated coverplate.

Nut made from bone

Mahogany neck

Cutaway gives access to higher frets

Sound holes

KEY ATTRIBUTES

- Evocative metallic tone
- Superb for slide guitar
- Loud
- Breathtaking aesthetics

Metal sound plate

Metal cones within body

Mahogany body

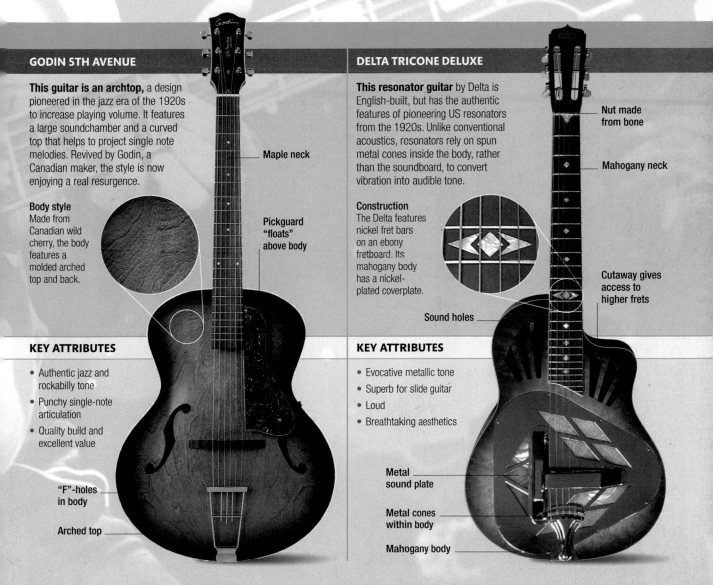

SEMI-ACOUSTIC GUITARS

As musicians began performing for larger audiences in the early 20th century, guitar manufacturers looked for ways to increase the volume produced by the instrument. The acoustic archtop guitars of the 1920s (*see pp.18–19*) went some way toward achieving this, but the advent of magnetic pickups and portable amps offered the first truly effective way to project the sound of the guitar above the noise of a large band.

Among the first full-production, semi-acoustic guitars was Gibson's ES-150 of the mid-1930s, which featured one single-coil pickup in the neck position. Later semi-acoustics would feature pickups at both neck and bridge positions for greater tonal versatility, while the volume of the space inside the guitar's body was progressively reduced over time for easier handling and a more tightly defined tone.

LANDMARK SEMI-ACOUSTIC GUITARS

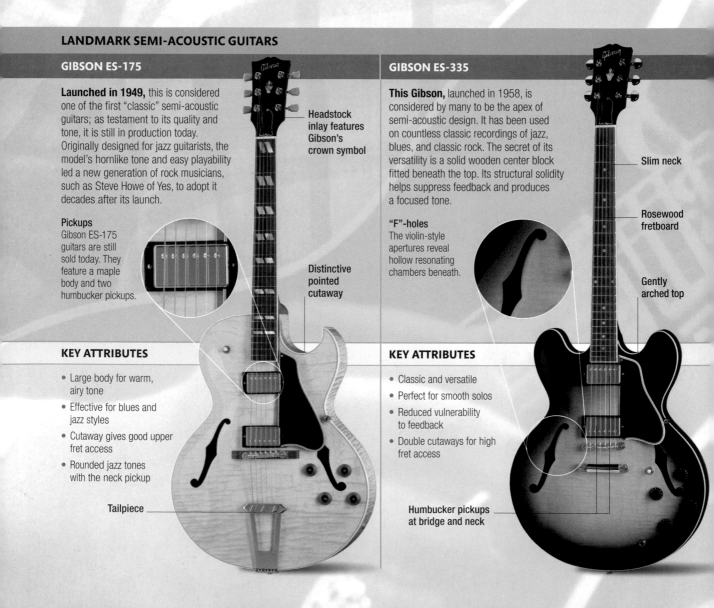

GIBSON ES-175

Launched in 1949, this is considered one of the first "classic" semi-acoustic guitars; as testament to its quality and tone, it is still in production today. Originally designed for jazz guitarists, the model's hornlike tone and easy playability led a new generation of rock musicians, such as Steve Howe of Yes, to adopt it decades after its launch.

Pickups
Gibson ES-175 guitars are still sold today. They feature a maple body and two humbucker pickups.

Headstock inlay features Gibson's crown symbol

Distinctive pointed cutaway

KEY ATTRIBUTES

- Large body for warm, airy tone
- Effective for blues and jazz styles
- Cutaway gives good upper fret access
- Rounded jazz tones with the neck pickup

Tailpiece

GIBSON ES-335

This Gibson, launched in 1958, is considered by many to be the apex of semi-acoustic design. It has been used on countless classic recordings of jazz, blues, and classic rock. The secret of its versatility is a solid wooden center block fitted beneath the top. Its structural solidity helps suppress feedback and produces a focused tone.

"F"-holes
The violin-style apertures reveal hollow resonating chambers beneath.

Slim neck

Rosewood fretboard

Gently arched top

KEY ATTRIBUTES

- Classic and versatile
- Perfect for smooth solos
- Reduced vulnerability to feedback
- Double cutaways for high fret access

Humbucker pickups at bridge and neck

PLUGGED OR UNPLUGGED?

Semi-acoustic hollow-body-type guitars, such as the Rickenbacker favored by George Harrison (*pictured right, front*) of The Beatles, are capable of being played "unplugged", but they are rarely used in this way. Like solid-bodied guitars (*see pp.22–25*), they are designed to be played amplified, and feature one or more magnetic pickups. They are not only lighter than solid-bodied guitars (making them more comfortable to hold and play), but they also produce a rounder and more woody sound. Semi-acoustics that have small cavities within a solid body are sometimes called "chambered" instruments.

FENDER THINLINE TELECASTER

The Thinline Telecaster is as close to a solid-body guitar as a semi-acoustic can get; it was a move towards a more compact design of guitar. Designed in 1968, the Thinline features relatively small acoustic chambers either side of a solid center block, which alter the wiry tone of the original Telecaster design (*see p.22*) to produce a woodier, more open voice.

**Three-way
pickup switch**
Set in the middle position, the switch combines both pickups for midrange punch.

Maple neck

Pearloid
scratchplate

KEY ATTRIBUTES

- Gritty blues-rock tone
- Woody, open voice
- Relatively lightweight
- High gloss finish

Twin, wide-range
humbucker pickups

TAYLOR T5 STANDARD

This state-of-the-art instrument by US manufacturer Taylor is a modern take on semi-acoustic design. Outwardly it resembles a slender acoustic guitar, and it is capable of producing faithful acoustic-style tones. But it can also deliver a range of electric voices, making it suitable for a wide variety of music styles including country and rock.

Pickups
The T5 combines three pickups, including a vibration-sensitive one inside the body and a stacked humbucker.

Mahogany neck

Top braced
into an arch

KEY ATTRIBUTES

- Authentic acoustic and electric tones
- Slender body
- Hugely versatile with a good choice of sounds

Modern
soundhole
design

Fully hollow
body

ELECTRIC GUITARS

The electric sound came to the public's attention in the early 1940s, partly thanks to jazz players who used semi-acoustic archtop guitars to produce a warm, blunt, amplified tone that could hold its own against the brass and percussion of big bands. But it wasn't until 1950 that solid electric guitars gained prominence with the launch of two landmark instruments by Leo Fender—a talented practical engineer. With a single cutaway and a lone pickup at the bridge, Fender's Esquire model had a zesty treble tone that suited country and early rock and roll styles. Fender also designed a more sophisticated version, with the same body shape but also with a neck pickup. Originally named the Broadcaster, it was renamed the Telecaster in 1951 and one of the most versatile and enduring designs of electric guitar was born.

LANDMARK CLASSIC ELECTRIC GUITARS

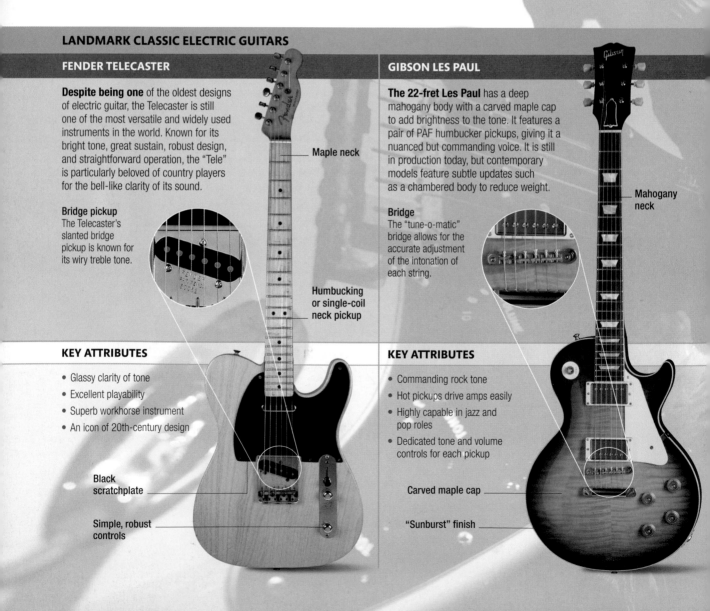

FENDER TELECASTER

Despite being one of the oldest designs of electric guitar, the Telecaster is still one of the most versatile and widely used instruments in the world. Known for its bright tone, great sustain, robust design, and straightforward operation, the "Tele" is particularly beloved of country players for the bell-like clarity of its sound.

Bridge pickup
The Telecaster's slanted bridge pickup is known for its wiry treble tone.

Maple neck

Humbucking or single-coil neck pickup

KEY ATTRIBUTES

- Glassy clarity of tone
- Excellent playability
- Superb workhorse instrument
- An icon of 20th-century design

Black scratchplate

Simple, robust controls

GIBSON LES PAUL

The 22-fret Les Paul has a deep mahogany body with a carved maple cap to add brightness to the tone. It features a pair of PAF humbucker pickups, giving it a nuanced but commanding voice. It is still in production today, but contemporary models feature subtle updates such as a chambered body to reduce weight.

Bridge
The "tune-o-matic" bridge allows for the accurate adjustment of the intonation of each string.

Mahogany neck

KEY ATTRIBUTES

- Commanding rock tone
- Hot pickups drive amps easily
- Highly capable in jazz and pop roles
- Dedicated tone and volume controls for each pickup

Carved maple cap

"Sunburst" finish

EVOLUTION OF THE CLASSICS

In the 1950s, the insights of talented players helped to shape guitar development. Gibson—a manufacturer with a long history of making archtop acoustic guitars—developed its own solid electric instrument and invited guitarist Les Paul (*see box, right*) to contribute to its design and lend his name to the guitar, which was launched in 1952. Fender's response—the Stratocaster or "Strat"—followed quickly behind. The Stratocaster had a springier, more supple voice than the Telecaster and proved hugely popular, becoming the signature instrument of many influential guitarists, including Hank Marvin and, later, Jimi Hendrix.

LES PAUL

Born Lester William Polsfuss in 1915, the American Les Paul was an accomplished jazz and country guitarist as well as an inventor. He developed his first solid-bodied electric guitar—"the log"—from a piece of solid timber (in fact part of a fence post) fitted with a bridge, neck, and pickup before collaborating with Gibson on the design of the Les Paul model.

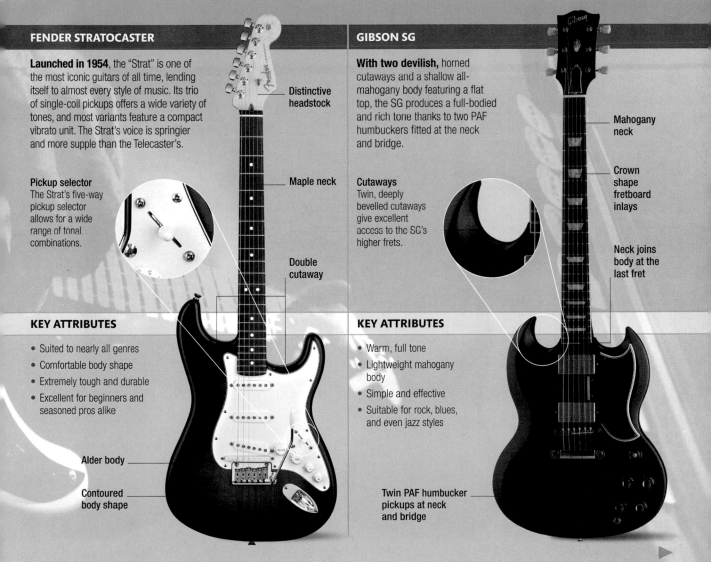

FENDER STRATOCASTER

Launched in 1954, the "Strat" is one of the most iconic guitars of all time, lending itself to almost every style of music. Its trio of single-coil pickups offers a wide variety of tones, and most variants feature a compact vibrato unit. The Strat's voice is springier and more supple than the Telecaster's.

Pickup selector
The Strat's five-way pickup selector allows for a wide range of tonal combinations.

Distinctive headstock

Maple neck

Double cutaway

KEY ATTRIBUTES

- Suited to nearly all genres
- Comfortable body shape
- Extremely tough and durable
- Excellent for beginners and seasoned pros alike

Alder body

Contoured body shape

GIBSON SG

With two devilish, horned cutaways and a shallow all-mahogany body featuring a flat top, the SG produces a full-bodied and rich tone thanks to two PAF humbuckers fitted at the neck and bridge.

Cutaways
Twin, deeply bevelled cutaways give excellent access to the SG's higher frets.

Mahogany neck

Crown shape fretboard inlays

Neck joins body at the last fret

KEY ATTRIBUTES

- Warm, full tone
- Lightweight mahogany body
- Simple and effective
- Suitable for rock, blues, and even jazz styles

Twin PAF humbucker pickups at neck and bridge

The changing needs of musicians and competition from Fender prompted Gibson to launch a greatly redesigned Les Paul model in 1961. This thinner-necked, faster-playing design failed to meet with Les Paul's approval and so was renamed the SG, or Solid Guitar, in 1963 and soon became a classic in its own right.

The iconic Telecaster, Stratocaster, Les Paul, and SG have gone on to form the major bloodlines of today's electric solid-body guitars, and many of the later developments in design and functionality were built on foundations laid down by these 60-year-old instruments. But that's not to say that their two manufacturers held a monopoly: The Beatles

achieved their jangling sound with the aid of Rickenbacker's 325, an instrument that owed little to either Fender or Gibson, and many lesser-known solid guitars from the 1950s and early 1960s command equal respect.

HOT ROD GUITARS

By the late 1970s, the energy and speed of a new generation of fast, technical players was testing the limitations of the early guitar designs. Grover Jackson, an American luthier, responded to the demand for "hot-rodded" rock guitars boasting lightning-fast playability with the Concorde model, built for Randy Rhoads. Similar guitars by other brands, such

LANDMARK MODERN ELECTRIC GUITARS

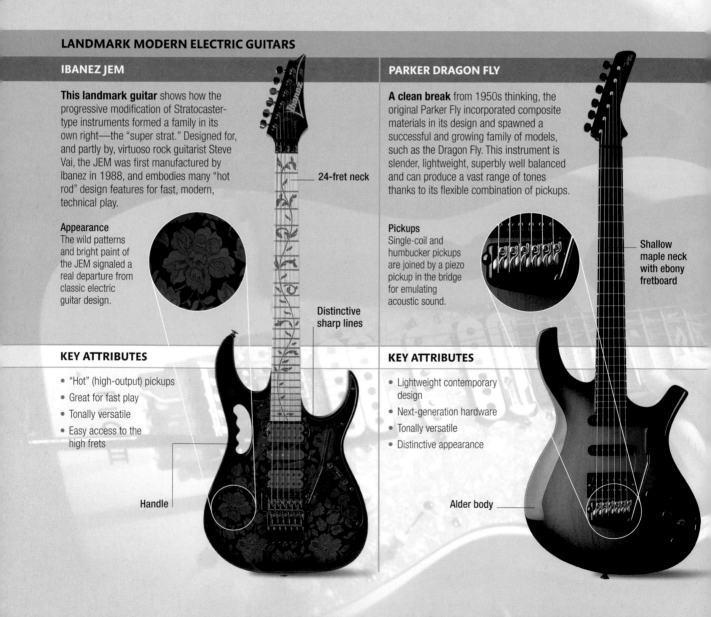

IBANEZ JEM

This landmark guitar shows how the progressive modification of Stratocaster-type instruments formed a family in its own right—the "super strat." Designed for, and partly by, virtuoso rock guitarist Steve Vai, the JEM was first manufactured by Ibanez in 1988, and embodies many "hot rod" design features for fast, modern, technical play.

Appearance
The wild patterns and bright paint of the JEM signaled a real departure from classic electric guitar design.

24-fret neck

Distinctive sharp lines

KEY ATTRIBUTES

- "Hot" (high-output) pickups
- Great for fast play
- Tonally versatile
- Easy access to the high frets

Handle

PARKER DRAGON FLY

A clean break from 1950s thinking, the original Parker Fly incorporated composite materials in its design and spawned a successful and growing family of models, such as the Dragon Fly. This instrument is slender, lightweight, superbly well balanced and can produce a vast range of tones thanks to its flexible combination of pickups.

Pickups
Single-coil and humbucker pickups are joined by a piezo pickup in the bridge for emulating acoustic sound.

Shallow maple neck with ebony fretboard

KEY ATTRIBUTES

- Lightweight contemporary design
- Next-generation hardware
- Tonally versatile
- Distinctive appearance

Alder body

as Japanese brand Ibanez, followed. These typically featured high-output, humbucking pickups, locking vibrato units (*see p.27*), and wide, shallow necks to make rapid, technical playing easier.

More recently, makers have tried to move solid-body electric guitar design beyond the basic templates laid down in the post-war years. Some make use of carbon composite materials to reduce weight and optimize tone, others focus on blending dramatic styling with innovative functionality, or incorporate digital modeling technologies that allow one guitar to produce a wide variety of authentic tones without magnetic pickups.

EXOTIC ELECTRICS

The evolution of the electric guitar has seen some weird and wonderful designs come and go: many of these were custom designs to individual specifications, but some were mainstream models from major manufacturers. Instruments like Rickenbacker's 331 model electric guitar of the early 1970s, which incorporated flashing disco lights inside the body, are memorable today mainly for their novelty. Other striking guitars, however, blended bold looks with stunning sounds to become minor classics.

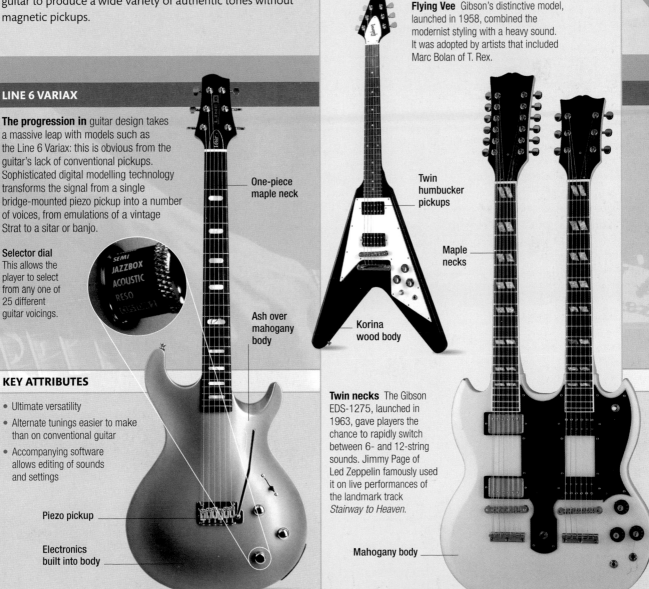

Flying Vee   Gibson's distinctive model, launched in 1958, combined the modernist styling with a heavy sound. It was adopted by artists that included Marc Bolan of T. Rex.

LINE 6 VARIAX

The progression in guitar design takes a massive leap with models such as the Line 6 Variax: this is obvious from the guitar's lack of conventional pickups. Sophisticated digital modelling technology transforms the signal from a single bridge-mounted piezo pickup into a number of voices, from emulations of a vintage Strat to a sitar or banjo.

Selector dial
This allows the player to select from any one of 25 different guitar voicings.

One-piece maple neck

Twin humbucker pickups

Maple necks

Ash over mahogany body

Korina wood body

KEY ATTRIBUTES

- Ultimate versatility
- Alternate tunings easier to make than on conventional guitar
- Accompanying software allows editing of sounds and settings

Twin necks   The Gibson EDS-1275, launched in 1963, gave players the chance to rapidly switch between 6- and 12-string sounds. Jimmy Page of Led Zeppelin famously used it on live performances of the landmark track *Stairway to Heaven*.

Piezo pickup

Electronics built into body

Mahogany body

TONE AND HARDWARE

Strings Usually made from stainless steel, strings are often nickel-plated to reduce noise.

Body The wood used in construction shapes the guitar's tone.

What an electric guitar is made of, its hardware and electronic components, and even the pick you choose to play with have a great influence on the instrument's tone. Guitar makers understand how to blend timbers, pickups, and hardware to create the voices they are seeking. Learning a little about the factors that influence tone will help you to select the right guitar for the job.

TONE WOODS

One of the biggest influences on how a guitar will sound is the wood used in its construction. Hardwoods that are strong and stable, yet resonant, are the most sought-after for use in electric guitars. This informal family of timbers is collectively known as "tone woods". Generally, when guitar makers talk about what timber a guitar is made from, they are referring to the material used for the body. It is common for the neck and fretboard to be made of different, but complementary, tone woods that meet the structural demands placed on them, but also contribute to the instrument's tone in their own way.

OTHER MATERIALS

Steel-bodied guitars, such as Trussart's Steelcaster (below), sound as distinctive as they look. Plexiglass, carbon fiber, and aluminum have also been used in guitars, but no material has yet surpassed the tone and aesthetic qualities of wood.

James Trussart Steelcaster

TONE WOOD CHARACTERISTICS

Mahogany This is a heavy, strong, and resonant hardwood. It is the tonal heart of many classic guitars such as Gibson's SG, and is associated with a warm, thick tone that is rich in woody mid-frequencies and creamy, well rounded bass.

Alder This light and hard wood has excellent acoustic qualities and is associated with a clearly defined and bell-like bottom end, with more sparkling treble than mahogany.

Ash This wood—particularly swamp ash—produces a tightly defined tone with clear treble but a hollow midrange. It is a good match with Stratocaster-style guitars, giving a funky tone.

Ebony This dark, dense, and hard-wearing wood is mainly used for fretboards. Its contribution to tone is similar to that of rosewood.

Maple Hard with a blond coloration, maple's high density makes it ideal for fretboards and one-piece necks. It produces a very bright, wiry tone, and is sometimes used to cap a mahogany body to add bite to the mahogany's warmth—as in Gibson's Les Paul Standard.

Rosewood Brazilian rosewood is an attractive dark timber once commonly used for fretboards in many electric guitar models. Its lighter, more open-grained cousin, Indian rosewood, is now more often used. Rosewood is associated with dark, warm tones.

Korina This pale-colored tone wood from Africa was used in Gibson's original Flying Vee and Explorer guitars from the 1950s. It produces a tone similar to that of mahogany, but with slightly more clarity and transparency in the midrange.

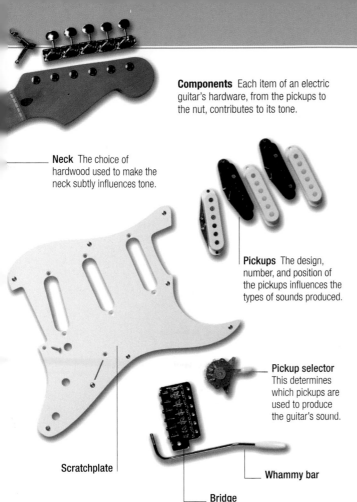

Components Each item of an electric guitar's hardware, from the pickups to the nut, contributes to its tone.

Neck The choice of hardwood used to make the neck subtly influences tone.

Pickups The design, number, and position of the pickups influences the types of sounds produced.

Pickup selector This determines which pickups are used to produce the guitar's sound.

Scratchplate

Whammy bar

Bridge

VIBRATO UNITS

Many models of electric guitar feature a vibrato unit (often called a tremolo unit or, informally, a "whammy bar") in place of a conventional bridge (*see p.16*). The design of vibrato units varies greatly, but all work by using the leverage of a metal bar, called a vibrato arm, to reduce or increase the tension of all six strings simultaneously, lowering or raising their pitch. Some, like the 1940s-era Bigsby vibrato, permit only subtle "wobbles" in pitch. By contrast, modern double-locking vibratos mount the whole bridge assembly on a see-saw pivot, allowing it to tilt so far backward and forward that upward and downward pitch bends of more than an octave are possible. Vibratos can add an extra dimension to your sound, but setting them up can be tricky and is best left to a professional technician.

Whammy bar Many vibrato units rely on two knife-edge pivot points upon which the whole bridge assembly rocks. Counter-tension is provided by springs mounted inside the body.

PICKING TONES

The pick you use to play your guitar makes a contribution to the tone produced. Most picks are made from some form of plastic, but some guitarists favor stone, wood, metal, or the polymer Tortex®, which reduces the "clicky" pick noise of other plastics. The thickness of the pick affects both its playability and the resulting tone; thick picks (over 1mm) are ideal for fast, loud picking, while thin picks (less than 1mm) give a light, bright tone. Medium picks (1mm) provide a good compromise for most players.

Choosing a pick Picks are available in a wide range of materials: it pays to experiment to find the pick that gives you the tone you want.

Tortex®

Wood

Anodized aluminum

Shaped nylon

Thick polymer

Imitation tortoiseshell

FINGERS AND THUMBS

You may see some guitarists use ringlike fingerpicks made from metal or plastic. These clip on to your fingers or thumb, and allow very precise, rapid plucking patterns to be played. They are associated with American folk styles, such as bluegrass. Fingerpicks come in a range of styles and thicknesses for different tonal effects.

Fingerpick

Thumbpick

Fingerpicking Although fingerpicks take a bit of getting used to, they can unlock a world of authentic country and folk styles.

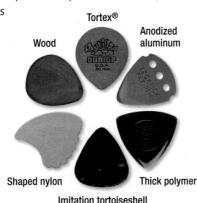

PICKUPS

The position and design of a guitar's pickups (*see p.17*) exerts a powerful influence on the instrument's tone. The neck pickup typically produces a rounded, bassy tone. By contrast, the bridge pickup produces a harder, sharper voice with a stronger treble response. If there is one, the middle pickup will offer an intermediate tone, expanding the number of possible combinations of pickups that can be selected by the player, and hence available sounds.

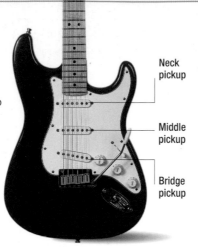

Neck pickup

Middle pickup

Bridge pickup

Pickup positions Guitar pickups may be located at the neck, bridge, and in between the two.

Single-coil pickups

Broadly speaking, these give a relatively low output, lively treble response, and detailed tone. Leo Fender equipped the Stratocaster, Telecaster, and Esquire with a slim, bright family of single-coil pickups; Tele-style tend to be glassier and harder in tone than the somewhat brighter and less powerful Strat pickups. In contrast, the Gibson-designed P-90 pickup, one of the earliest designs, has relatively high output, giving it a thicker voice, with more midrange power.

Humbucking pickups

These are quieter than single-coil pickups and usually have a "hotter" output, which means they can drive amplifiers to distort more easily. Their sound is also thicker, richer in mid- and bass frequencies, and suited to jazz and heavy rock. The cost is the loss of some detail in the tone when used on "clean" amplifier settings.

ACTIVE INTEREST

You'll hear guitarists talking about "active" pickups. These differ from conventional "passive" pickups in that they feature an integral battery-powered pre-amplifier. This yields a higher output and a fuller range of frequencies than a passive pickup can produce. The balanced tone of active pickups is too neutral for some tastes.

Zakk Wylde Ozzy Osbourne's former guitarist, Wylde—like many heavy metal exponents—uses active pickups for the clinical, high-gain tones they offer.

TONE MAP

This chart compares the tonal qualities of different guitars, plotting them on two axes—from cool to hot tones, and from thin to fat sounds. Use the chart to match your choice of guitar to the type of sound you desire.

VINTAGE TELECASTER
- **Body type:** solid
- **Body/neck:** ash/maple
- **Pickup(s):** two single-coil pickups
- **Genres:** country, blues, rock

THIN

MODERN TELECASTER
- **Body type:** solid
- **Body/neck:** ash, alder/maple
- **Pickup(s):** two single-coil pickups
- **Genres:** country, blues, rock

COOL

RICKENBACKER 325
- **Body type:** semi-hollow
- **Body/neck:** maple
- **Pickup(s):** three single-coil pickups
- **Genres:** pop, rock

VINTAGE STRATOCASTER
- **Body type:** solid
- **Body/neck:** ash, alder/maple
- **Pickup(s):** three single-coil pickups
- **Genres:** pop, rock, blues, funk

GIBSON ES-175
- **Body type:** semi-hollow
- **Body/neck:** maple
- **Pickup(s):** two humbucker pickups
- **Genres:** jazz, blues, rock

GIBSON LES PAUL
- **Body type:** solid
- **Body/neck:** maple/mahogany
- **Pickup(s):** two humbucker pickups
- **Genres:** blues, rock, metal, reggae

FAT

GIBSON SG
- **Body type:** solid
- **Body/neck:** mahogany
- **Pickup(s):** two humbucker pickups
- **Genres:** blues, rock, metal

MODERN STRATOCASTER
- **Body type:** solid
- **Body/neck:** alder/maple
- **Pickup(s):** three single-coil pickups
- **Genres:** pop, rock, blues, funk

DEAN RAZORBACK
- **Body type:** solid
- **Body/neck:** mahogany
- **Pickup(s):** two humbucker pickups
- **Genres:** metal, rock

HOT

BUYING A GUITAR

Buying a new guitar is always exciting, but before you take this step, it pays to carry out a little research. Many aspiring guitarists make a quick visit to a guitar shop and leave with an unsuitable instrument that ends up gathering dust in a corner. A little forethought will help you obtain a well-made guitar that sounds good and will grow with your abilities. This goes for both for the beginner and the more accomplished musician looking to upgrade to a premium or specialist instrument. The good news is that quality guitars are now more easily obtained at a reasonable price than ever before.

BUILT TO ORDER

For wealthy guitarists, instruments specially built or customized by luthiers are the ultimate luxury. However, some handmade guitars have more humble origins: Queen's Brian May crafted his now famous Red Special guitar (below) with his father, using the wood from an 18th-century fireplace.

Brian May's Red Special

6 KEY STEPS TO CHOOSING A FIRST GUITAR

You probably have a good idea whether you eventually wish to play an electric or an acoustic guitar, but each has its benefits to the beginner. Entry-level electric guitars are, in general, physically easier to play than acoustics of equivalent quality. However, acoustic guitars, while tougher on the fingers, will not flatter bad technique as an electric can, and starting out on one may ultimately make you a better guitarist. Below are some of the factors you need to consider when making your purchasing decisions.

MUSICAL GENRE

Buy the right guitar for the music. The types of guitar used most often in each musical genre are:

- **Rock, pop, metal:** electric
- **Acoustic rock:** steel-string acoustic
- **Blues:** semi-acoustic, electric
- **Country:** electric, archtop steel-string acoustic
- **Folk:** nylon or steel-string acoustic
- **Jazz:** archtop steel-string acoustic guitar, jazz guitar

PERFORMANCE LOCATION

An acoustic guitar can be picked up and played without having to plug in, but there are also battery-powered "microamps" that make it possible to take an electric guitar outdoors. For gigging, an electric guitar with a powerful amp is the usual choice. Acoustic guitarists aiming to play large or noisy venues might want to look at electro-acoustic models.

PRICE

Buy the best you can afford. In general, more cash will buy you a better-sounding and better-looking instrument. A well-constructed guitar made of good tone wood is a pleasure to play and learn on, whereas a cheap, nasty-sounding guitar could end up putting you off completely. Going cheap may be a false economy: good guitars tend to retain their resale value and may even appreciate over time.

BUYING NEW

New guitars come with a warranty plus the reassuring knowledge that the instrument is factory-fresh. A new model won't have the comfortable worn-in feel that used guitars often have, but neither will it have cosmetic defects or missing parts. If buying new from a shop, always ask the staff to let you try a guitar you're interested in. Take time to test it out properly and pay particular attention to how it sounds and feels: you will quickly tire of a flashy-looking model that has poor tone and playability. Don't feel obliged to buy the first instrument you try: ask the staff to help you sample different models until you find something that pleases your ears, hands, and eyes. With that in mind, it's a good idea to visit a shop during a quiet time of the day if possible. Staff will have a lot more time to be helpful on, say, a slow Tuesday morning than on a busy Saturday afternoon.

BUYING ONLINE

You can bypass the whole shop experience by shopping online. It is possible to find superb deals on new instruments on the Internet, but if you buy without direct experience of the guitar in question, you are gambling with your money. You could try out a guitar in your local shop and then buy the same model more cheaply from an online retailer, but this is rather discourteous. Better to ask if the shop will match Internet prices when you go in—often the manager can be persuaded to strike a deal, helping you to support local businesses without paying a premium to do so. You'll benefit in the long term, too—a good relationship with a local music shop can be immensely useful.

Making a selection Always try before you buy: if you're a beginner, bring a knowledgeable friend with you. Try a few samples of your chosen model if possible; there may be considerable variation between individual guitars.

OPTIONS AND EXTRAS

If you're buying an electric guitar, you'll need to decide before you buy whether you want a vibrato unit, or "whammy bar"(*see p.27*); this is part of the bridge so it can't (easily) be retro-fitted. It is worth thinking about add-ons at this point, too—you can often negotiate a discount if you package other items with your guitar purchase.

- If you're buying an electric guitar, you'll need an amplifier (*see pp.34–37*). It is worth considering a guitar/amp package.
- Picks, tuning devices, and capos (*see pp.138–39*) are inexpensive and useful: consider adding these to your package.
- A guitar stand and a hard or soft case will protect your guitar from knocks and scrapes.
- A good strap (with locking strap buttons) and professional-quality leads are useful, especially if you plan to perform live.

SIZE

Weight and dimensions are important factors. Electric guitars are heavier than acoustic guitars, and vary in weight; don't buy one that is difficult to hold for long periods. Acoustic guitars, while lighter, tend to be bigger, particularly if built in "Dreadnought" style (*see p.18*). If you are of slight build, consider a 7/8 or even 3/4 size guitar. Check the width of the neck, too, as smaller fretting hands need models with a narrower neck.

BRAND

Buying a big brand gives peace of mind—parts and technical support will be readily available. If you choose a more obscure make, ask the seller to tell you as much about its construction as they can. If you crave a big name but don't have the budget, check out Fender's lower-priced Squier brand Strat and Telecasters, and the Epiphones made by Gibson—less expensive versions of some of their classic models.

PLAYABILITY

When you get to the guitar shop, try holding your chosen instrument while seated and standing (*see p.59*). Does it feel right in your hands? Try fretting a string all the way up the fretboard—is it comfortable? The neck may be too wide or narrow for your hands, or you may prefer a guitar with deeper cutaways to access the higher frets. Try a few strums to hear what the instrument sounds like. Do you like its tone?

BUYING A USED INSTRUMENT

Buying a new instrument may not always be your best option, especially if money is an issue. Many new guitars lose a large portion of their value the moment they leave the showroom. For the same outlay, it is often possible to obtain a used instrument of a higher specification. A well-used old guitar in the classified ads may be worth buying over a new budget model if it sounds good, functions correctly, and feels comfortable to play. Ask to see and handle any used instrument and check it out thoroughly before you buy.

BODY

Check for general wear and look out for rust on the metal parts. If there are serious cosmetic flaws, ask for a discount on the price; if the flaws are structural, walk away.

PLAYABILITY

If you can play guitar a little, fret and pick notes across the whole fretboard of the guitar. If you can't play, take along a guitar-playing friend or ask the seller to demonstrate. If any of the frets buzzes badly, you'll know that you need to factor in the cost of a professional set up or undertake the work yourself.

NECK

Pick the guitar up and, looking upwards from the bridge towards the headstock, examine the length of the fretboard. If the neck is badly warped it'll be clearly visible.

SWITCHGEAR

If you are buying an electric guitar, plug it in and try it through an amp. Operate all the switches, tone, and volume controls to check they work properly without crackles, malfunctions, or unacceptable looseness.

TUNING

Rotate the machine heads and check they operate smoothly and effectively. Bring an electronic tuner with you to make sure the guitar will hold a standard tuning reasonably well.

NUT

Pay attention to the nut at the top of the neck, checking that the strings don't make a tell-tale pinging noise; this indicates that the string slots may be worn, which will cause the strings to bind during tuning.

OPTIONS FOR LEFT-HANDERS

The world we live in is designed for right-handed people: guitar shops are full of right-handed instruments and guitar tab is written for right-handers. Yet some of the most famous players of all time—from Paul McCartney and Tony Iommi to Jimi Hendrix—are or were left-handed. There are four main options available if you wish to follow in their footsteps.

• **Use a left-handed guitar** This is the mirror image of a right-handed guitar, making playing "natural" for a lefty, though guitar tab and chord diagrams are reversed. The range of left-handed guitars available off the shelf is much smaller than that of right-handed instruments, and if you desire a specific model it may need to be custom built.

• **Play a right-handed guitar upside-down** The strings remain in their original position and you play the guitar reversed, making standard notation hard to follow and placing the guitar controls and the pickguard in the "wrong" places.

Left-handed Stratocaster

• **Reverse the string order on a right-handed guitar** Not as straightforward as it may seem, this requires a little technical know-how or the services of a guitar technician. Again, the guitar controls and pickguard will be in the "wrong" places.

• **Play a regular right-handed guitar** In many ways, strumming with the right hand if you are left-handed makes a lot of sense—your left hand is more agile and better suited to complex fretting. If you can adapt to this approach, musical notation appears correctly and you can pick up almost any guitar—not just your own.

Jimi Hendrix
Guitar virtuoso Hendrix was left-handed and played a right-handed guitar upside-down.

FINDING USED BARGAINS

Despite the benefits of trying out a guitar before purchase, the lure of online auction sites, such as Ebay, may be too much to resist. Used bargains are certainly available on these sites, and the seller feedback system helps to reduce the number of scams.

Generally speaking, used guitars by established manufacturers are a safer bet than obscure budget brands when buying "blind" at online auction. If, say, a genuine Rickenbacker bought cheaply online turns out to need a little more work than the photo and seller description suggested, at least you'll know that it's worth the extra investment and will hold its resale value well.

GUITAR AMPLIFIERS

Without an amplifier, an electric guitar will produce no more than a faint acoustic jangle. The pickups (*see p.17*) of an electric guitar generate a weak, variable voltage during play, which requires an amplifier (or amp) to transform it into audible tones. Some amps are designed to suit specific applications, such as studio recording or practicing, while others can be used everywhere from the living room to large gig venues.

AMP CHOICES

Choose your amp with as much care as you select your guitar. Even the best guitar will sound terrible if teamed with a poor-quality amp. When starting out, try to buy an amp that will grow with your musicianship, rather than the cheapest on offer.

HOW AMPS WORK

The signal generated by an electric guitar passes via a lead to the amplifier input. It enters the "pre-amp" stage, where it is boosted in strength before entering the "power" stage, where the signal is boosted once again, to a level high enough to drive a speaker cone and generate sound. Pre-amps and power amps are normally built into one physical unit, but are also available as separate units.

The first amps were invented in the 1930s and used the vacuum-tubes, or valves, of radio technology; some still do, but many more utilize the solid-state circuitry developed in the 1960s. Today's digital modeling amps add a wealth of functions to the volume, tone, and gain controls of basic tube and solid-state amps (*see overleaf*).

COMBOS AND STACKS

Most amplifiers are housed in a plywood cabinet covered in vinyl or leather. Amps that mount one or more speakers in the same cabinet as the amplification gear are known as "combos." In other models, amplifier and speakers occupy separate cabinets (known respectively as the "head" and the "cab"), that are connected by a short lead. This is known as a "stack." Stacks allow the player to experiment with arrays of speakers and have an imposing presence, both sonically and visually.

Big sounds Small valve amps with an output of less than 20 watts are ideal for practice and small venues.

AMPLIFIER COMPARISONS

VALVE AMPS	SOLID-STATE AMPS	HYBRID AMPS	DIGITAL AMPS
Valve or "tube" models use the glass vacuum-tube technology of the first amps, and are the choice of purists.	The transistor, which revolutionized radio technology, is used instead of valves in the more technologically advanced solid-state amps.	A more recent development, these bring together solid-state and tube technology, using valves at the pre-amp stage and solid-state circuitry at the power stage, or vice versa.	These can be embedded in a traditional amp unit or used in software that allows a PC or smartphone to perform the functions of an amp.
Pros Fans claim a warmth and richness of tone that solid-state amps (right) cannot reproduce. Tube amps are also noticeably louder than solid-state models of the same wattage.	**Pros** Generally cheaper, more reliable and longer-lasting than valve amps. You probably won't need to touch a single piece of electronics on your amp for its entire lifetime.	**Pros** Hybrid amps combine some of the rich tone associated with valve amps with the reliability and reduced price tag associated with solid-state amps.	**Pros** Digital modeling allows the amp or software to emulate guitar effects and also reproduce the tonal characteristics of a variety of classic amps, both vintage and state-of-the-art.
Cons Usually heavier and more expensive than solid-state amps. The glass tubes can break or blow if, for example, the amp is knocked during transport.	**Cons** May lack the rich tone of valve amps and be less capable of cutting through the sound of a band.	**Cons** Only some of the tone of a valve amp is retained, but with all the risk of tube breakages and cost of replacement.	**Cons** Some guitarists find the sheer wealth of choice and scope for "fiddling" detracts from the immediacy of their playing.

BUYING AN AMP

Before setting out to buy an amplifier, make an honest appraisal of what your needs are and then choose an amp that will serve them effectively.

Power A bedroom guitarist won't need more than 20 watts of power, but if you're planning on playing sizeable live gigs, you'll need at least 40–100-watt amplification.

Format Valve, solid-state, hybrid, or digital amp? Each format has its pros and cons (*see box, opposite*); your choice may be influenced by price and also the kind of music you want to make.

Extras An amplifier can do much more than boost sound. Many amps come with built-in effects, multiple channels, and many other gizmos and gadgets. Be realistic about your requirements and don't pay for what you don't need.

Size If you're contemplating a large stack, make sure you have a suitable home for it. Cold, damp garages or basements are not suitable. Think about transporting it, too, both in terms of size and weight.

Condition You can get great deals on used amps, but always try before you buy. A mint-condition amp can have electrical faults, while a well-used vintage model can deliver great sounds. If you're unsure, get the amp checked out by a servicing engineer before you buy.

Electronics Test all switches, knobs, and any other controls on your amp. You need to be sure they do all the things they're supposed to without any crackling or clicking noises that may indicate internal damage or malfunction.

Turning up the volume The Jam's Paul Weller performs in front of a powerful Marshall stack. Marshall equipment is sought out for its distinctive distortion.

ANATOMY OF AN AMPLIFIER

Although old-fashioned valve amps offer superb tone, each model has its own distinct character, so if you want to change playing tone, you must change your amp. Digital modelling amps, such as Line 6's successful Spider series, get round this by using advanced digital processing to simulate the tones of classic amplifiers and diverse effects in one device.

Dial-an-effect
Guitar effects such as tremolo and fuzz within the amp eliminate the need for outboard effects units.

Rigid casing   Input socket   Channel indicators

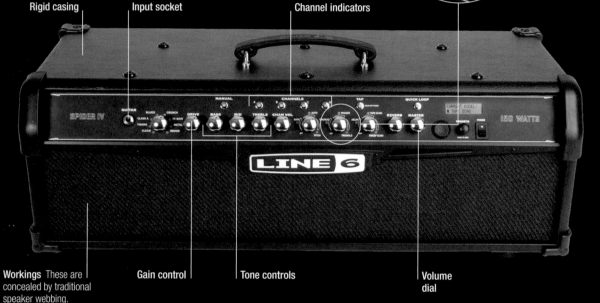

Workings These are concealed by traditional speaker webbing.

Gain control   Tone controls   Volume dial

INPUT SOCKET
The input socket is where the lead from the guitar is plugged in, and usually takes a standard ¼in (6.35mm) jack. It can also be used for a radio unit that receives from a transmitter worn by the guitarist, for cable-free performance.

PLAYING STYLES
A modeling amp allows the player to select from preset styles—anything from clean tones to full-out overdrive at the turn of a dial. The settings here are based on the sound of specific classic amp models from the best-known companies.

VOLUME DIAL
The master volume or "output" dial controls the loudness of the sound produced by the amp. Practice amps typically have a maximum output of 20 watts, while performance amps will be rated at 50 watts or higher. This amp can deliver 150 watts.

AMP-EMULATING SOFTWARE

Modeling software can now reproduce an infinite variety of guitar tones. This software can be installed on computers and, increasingly, on smartphones, allowing you to carry a raft of amplifier effects in your pocket. Programs such as Amplitube's iRig (*right*) have a friendly graphic interface that reproduces the "look" of a real amp.

Head and cab Powerful modeling amps are perfect for gigging cover bands as they can reproduce diverse guitar sounds.

Head   Head handle

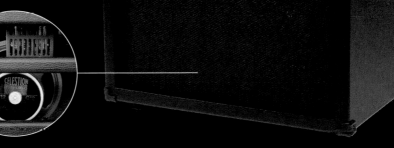

Presets Tones modeled on hundreds of the best songs and guitarists of all time can be replicated; you can also program in your own preset styles.

Cab

Speaker cloth

Loudspeaker The most common type of speaker in guitar amps is the 12in (305mm) variety, which gives a good balance of treble and bass tones; the 10in (254mm) and 14in (355mm) speakers in some amps produce brighter and bassier tones respectively.

TONE CONTROLS
Tone controls determine how much treble, bass, and midrange can be heard. Adding treble will brighten the tone; extra bass provides a fuller body to the sound; turning mid tones down gives you a grumbly metal sound; turning them up gives a purer tone.

GAIN CONTROL
The "gain," "drive," or "overdrive" dial affects how clean or distorted the amp sounds. A low gain setting produces a clean sound suitable for jazz, country, or pop; high gain produces a heavily distorted sound suitable for rock rhythm- or lead-playing.

CHANNEL CONTROLS
The channel setting allows you to alternate rapidly between different amp sounds during performance. In most models, each channel has its own dedicated tone, gain, and volume controls, allowing you to tailor and sculpt the sound you produce even more.

GUITAR EFFECTS

The unvarnished sound of a guitar played through an amp is exciting, but adding effects opens the door to new realms of expression. From the evocative reverb heard on vintage blues recordings to the supercharged mix of distortion, chorus, and delay used by many rock artists, effects have the power to radically transform the voice of the guitar. Many styles of guitar music have become so strongly associated with certain effects that it is hard to imagine that they could exist without them.

ALTERNATIVE FORMATS

The simplest type of effects unit is the classic "stomp-box" foot pedal; a range of effects is available in this format and pedals can be linked together to give a combined sound. Alternatively, multi-effects units offer tens of effects in one unit. Effects are also also built into some modern amps (*see pp.34–37*), while rack-mounted effects are useful for studios and pro touring. When you first get an effects unit, it's tempting to use it near to its maximum settings, but heavy applications like this soon wear out their welcome. The secret to using effects musically is subtle settings—unless you're aiming for all-out excess. Effects on classic recordings are frequently not as heavily applied as they seem.

Richer sounds Some players, such as Matt Bellamy of Muse, make extensive, creative use of guitar effects. Bellamy's highly modified guitars contain built-in effects circuitry.

TYPES OF GUITAR EFFECTS

Effects can be categorized according to the way in which they alter the sound coming from the guitar. They may affect frequency (pitch), tone or timbre, time (sustaining, echoing, or repeating a sound), or dynamics (subtle variations in volume within the sound). Hard to describe, they are instantly recognizable once heard.

FREQUENCY EFFECTS

CHORUS

Chorus effects split the signal from one guitar into two or more parts, then vary the pitch of one or more of these parts. The resulting guitar voices of close (but not identical) pitch are then blended together. The result is a shimmering, shifting timbre that occurs naturally in the voice of the 12-string acoustic guitar, but which can also be electronically reproduced. Electronic chorus effects appear in many genres from pop to metal, but they are particularly associated with 1990s indie rock and grunge and 1980s jazz guitar styles.

Hear the sound
• The rhythm guitar intro to *Paradise City* by Guns N' Roses.
• The strummed rhythm guitar of *Friday I'm in Love* by The Cure.
• Jazzy chord work in *A Sassy Samba* by Pat Metheny.

PITCH SHIFTERS

This family of effects, which includes octavers, harmonizers, and whammy pedals, digitally alters the pitch of the guitar's tone, either by adding a harmony above or below the true pitch of a note, or by shifting the pitch of notes upwards or downwards in real time. The classic whammy pedal is controlled using a seesaw foot pedal. Octavers can be used to produce bass lines using a conventional guitar by shifting the pitch of its signal down by a whole octave.

Hear the sound
• The whammy pedal features heavily on *The Blue* by Dave Gilmour.
• Harmonizer effects can be heard on the solo of *Owner of a Lonely Heart* by Yes.

TONE EFFECTS

WAH-WAH

The wah-wah effect is basically a foot-operated tone control. By rocking the see-saw pedal forwards and backwards, a distinctive "wah" sound—redolent of the human voice—is produced as the tone filter inside sweeps from bass to treble.

Hear the sound
- The intro of *Voodoo Chile* by Jimi Hendrix.
- The solo in *Californication* by the Red Hot Chili Peppers.

OVERDRIVE, DISTORTION, AND FUZZ

In the 1960s, rock and roll guitarists found that pushing the volume of a valve amp to its limits would cause the sound to break up, producing a "dirty" tone. These distorted sounds can now be achieved using effects units. Overdrive is a relatively subtle, expressive effect, best used for creating "crunchy" blues and classic-rock tones, while distortion offers a more heavily saturated "screaming" tone suitable for hard rock and metal genres. Fuzz, meanwhile, produces a distorted tone so saturated that it has an almost synthetic quality —useful for evoking a sixties psychedelic rock sound or a grunge-style wall of sound.

Hear the sound
- Overdrive features in the chorus of *Song 2* by Blur.
- Fuzz is used in *American Woman* by The Guess Who and in *Star Spangled Banner* by Jimi Hendrix.

RING MODULATOR

A ring modulator adds a distorted metallic quality to a guitar's tone and works in a similar way to a tremolo effect (*see right*). Unlike the tremolo, a ring modulator adds the frequencies of the volume modulation and the input signal together to produce an alien-sounding timbre. This effect created the menacing voice of the Daleks in the long-running British sci-fi series *Doctor Who*.

Hear the sound
- *Two Rivers* by Jeff Beck.
- The solo of *Paranoid* by Black Sabbath.

TIME-BASED EFFECTS

REVERB

If you stand in an empty stairwell and clap your hands together, you will hear the hard echo of the clap return to you immediately. In a cathedral, the echo is fuller and longer-lasting. This is known as reverberation. Reverb units electronically replicate this atmospheric effect and apply it to the sound of the guitar.

Hear the sound
- *Brothers in Arms* by Dire Straits.
- *Misirlou* by Dick Dale.

ECHO AND DELAY

Delay effects produce a pronounced and distinct echo, with individual notes repeating at preset intervals after the original note has been struck—from thousandths of a second to more than half a minute later. Many digital delay units can also keep a single note or phrase looping indefinitely at very long intervals. Used skilfully, digital delay pedals can be used as a live compositional tool, enabling the performer to build complex rhythmic patterns.

Hear the sound
- Echo is a feature of *Walking on the Moon* by The Police.
- Delay is used in *Black Horse and a Cherry Tree* by KT Tunstall.

PHASER

This effect gives a sweeping, jetlike quality to the tone of the guitar by modulating the phase of the signal. It is often associated with 1970s psychedelic rock because of the otherworldly character it lends to the sound.

Hear the sound
- *Keep Yourself Alive* by Queen.

FLANGER

Flanging is created when the guitar's signal is split into two identical halves, one of which is then subtly delayed by a varying period (tens of milliseconds). The effect causes shifting peaks and troughs to develop in the frequency output, creating a sweeping, whirlpool-like effect.

Hear the sound
- *Itchycoo Park* by The Small Faces.

DYNAMIC EFFECTS

COMPRESSOR

In simple terms, a compressor is an automated volume control that quashes sudden spikes in the loudness of sounds created by the guitar. Compressors help to make the sound of the guitar thicker and smoother; the trade-off is that they mask some of the finer detail in the instrument's tone.

Hear the sound
- Larry Carlton's solo on *Kid Charlemagne* by Steely Dan.
- The solo of *Comfortably Numb* by Pink Floyd.

TREMOLO

Not the same as the tremolo unit on a guitar (which is more accurately termed a vibrato), the tremolo effect makes the volume of the guitar's signal rhythmically rise and fall in what is often a gentle and sombre effect. It is particularly associated with clean rhythm guitar parts in the surf guitar and country genres, although at more extreme settings it produces an angular, strobelike effect.

Hear the sound
- *Darlin' Wait for Me* by Richard Hawley.
- The epic *How Soon Is Now?* by the Smiths.

OTHER EFFECTS

EBOW

The Ebow is a handheld effect unit that sustains notes played on an electric guitar indefinitely by manipulating magnetic field disturbances caused by the vibrations of the guitar's steel strings. It can be selectively used to sustain notes played on individual strings. The guitar firm Fernandez markets an equivalent product, which is mounted on some of the company's guitars.

Hear the sound
- *Heroes* by David Bowie.
- Used self-referentially in *E-bow the Letter* by R.E.M.

"The guitar is a small orchestra... Every string is a different color, a different voice."

ANDRÉS SEGOVIA

ESSENTIAL
THEORY

2

HOW MUSIC WORKS

Music is deeply embedded in life and culture, yet is incredibly hard to define. Its basic units are simple—sound (notes) and time (beats)—but many volumes have been written about the physics, psychology, and philosophy of what makes one sequence of sounds music, and another not music. One thing is clear: what we consider to be music has structure, dimensions (*see box, far right*), and rules. Understanding these principles of music theory will enrich your experience of playing guitar.

THE NOTES OF WESTERN MUSIC

Notes are the building blocks of music. Without them, there would be no melody, harmony, or rhythm, and it is the way notes are linked together—and note patterns varied—that generates musical diversity. Despite its phenomenal range—spanning classical, jazz, rock, and pop—all western music is made up of just 12 different notes derived from a system agreed upon in the early 1700s called Equal Temperament tuning. This is an "average" tuning used by all instruments including the guitar. Together, these 12 notes make up what is known as the "chromatic" scale, after the Greek word *chroma*, meaning color. Every scale and chord that you will play is ultimately derived from the chromatic scale, giving it a central place in music theory.

THE CHROMATIC SCALE

The 12 notes of the chromatic scale are each represented by a letter (A–G) or a letter followed by an "accidental"—a sharp (♯) or flat (♭)—that raises or lowers the pitch of the named note. All the notes of the chromatic scale are shown below. The space between any two notes is called an interval, and successive notes on the chromatic scale are separated by equal intervals, called semitones. So, the distance from A to A♯ (or B♭) is one semitone, as is the distance from B to C. After G♯ (A♭), A appears again. The distance between a low A and the next A is known as an octave.

NOTES OF THE CHROMATIC SCALE

MAP OF THE FRETBOARD

The diagram below represents the fretboard of a modern electric guitar (with 22 frets). There are six strings that are conventionally tuned to the following notes, starting from the thick, low string to the thin, high string: E, A, D, G, B, and E (*see p.58*). With this tuning, the diagram shows what note will be produced with your finger at every fret on every string. You will see that two adjacent frets on any string are separated by one semitone. A full tone (two semitones) is a distance of two frets. The diagram shows the huge versatility of the guitar. The same note at the same pitch can be played in several places on the fretboard: by contrast, on the piano, it can be played in only one location.

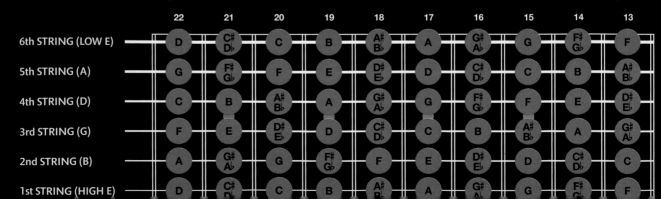

	22	21	20	19	18	17	16	15	14	13
6th STRING (LOW E)	D	C♯/D♭	C	B	A♯/B♭	A	G♯/A♭	G	F♯/G♭	F
5th STRING (A)	G	F♯/G♭	F	E	D♯/E♭	D	C♯/D♭	C	B	A♯/B♭
4th STRING (D)	C	B	A♯/B♭	A	G♯/A♭	G	F♯/G♭	F	E	D♯/E♭
3rd STRING (G)	F	E	D♯/E♭	D	C♯/D♭	C	B	A♯/B♭	A	G♯/A♭
2nd STRING (B)	A	G♯/A♭	G	F♯/G♭	F	E	D♯/E♭	D	C♯/D♭	C
1st STRING (HIGH E)	D	C♯/D♭	C	B	A♯/B♭	A	G♯/A♭	G	F♯/G♭	F

THE CHROMATIC SCALE ON THE GUITAR

The chromatic scale consists of 12 different notes. It can be played along one string at many places on the fretboard; below it is shown played on the 5th string. Notice that successive notes are separated by one fret (a semitone). In practice, guitarists rarely play the scale on one string because it involves a lot of hand movement. Instead, scales are played across several strings in one area of the fretboard (*see below*).

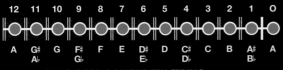

THE CHROMATIC SCALE ON THE 5TH STRING

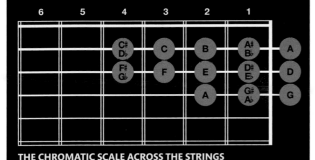

THE CHROMATIC SCALE ACROSS THE STRINGS

THE DIMENSIONS OF MUSIC

Notes, or sounds of a given pitch, are the basic units of music, but it is how they are arranged and played that gives a piece of music its character: the basic dimensions of music are described below.

Melody This is the linear progression of notes that makes up the basic framework of a song. Songs are often arranged as a series of melodic phrases to create sections known as verses and choruses.

Harmony If melody is the linear dimension of music, then harmony is the vertical dimension that results from several notes being played together either by one instrument (such as a chord on a guitar) or many (such as an orchestra or band).

Rhythm This concerns the lengths of notes and silences, the use of accents for added drama, and groupings of note patterns. Rhythms are measured against a regular beat, often grouped in two or four and also sometimes in three. Famous rhythms include the Charleston, waltz, blues swing, reggae, and bossa nova.

Timbre This is the quality and type of sound created: a guitar's timbre is different from a trumpet's or a piano's, and results from the construction of the instrument and how it is played. Different styles of guitar can produce completely different timbres, from the soft sound of a nylon-string acoustic guitar to a heavily distorted electric guitar.

CHAPTER 2

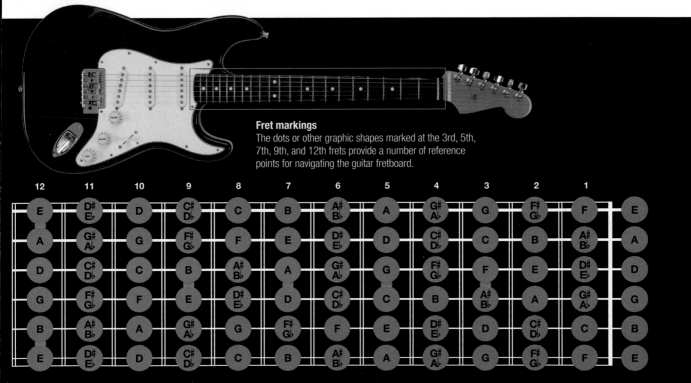

Fret markings
The dots or other graphic shapes marked at the 3rd, 5th, 7th, 9th, and 12th frets provide a number of reference points for navigating the guitar fretboard.

SCALES AND KEYS

A scale is an ordered series of notes. What gives it order is the interval between successive notes. The chromatic scale (*see pp.42–43*) contains all 12 notes separated by semitone intervals, but there are many other scales—such as the major and natural minor scales. These differ from the chromatic scale in that they use different intervals to determine which notes are included in the scale. The chromatic scale, with its regular intervals, does not have much "character" and has few real-life musical applications. Changing the intervals between notes gives scales character: the major scale has a "happy" sound, the natural minor

scale sounds melancholy. The major and natural minor scales consist of seven notes separated by a mixture of semitones (ST) and tones (T) in specific patterns. The major scale is the most important to understand, not least because the intervals in other scales are named relative to the intervals of the major scale (*see right*).

Learning to play scales is a big part of mastering any instrument and the guitar is no different. Scale practice may be repetitive, but it pays huge dividends. With good scale knowledge, you can play fluent solos and understand how chords are put together.

BUILDING THE MAJOR SCALE

The major scale contains seven different notes separated by semitone (ST) or tone (T) intervals in the following order: T, T, ST, T, T, T, ST. To find the correct sequence of notes in a major scale, choose your starting point, or root note, on the chromatic scale. In the example below, the root note (R) is C, and the resulting scale is called C major: music based on this scale is said to be in the key of C major. Use the pattern of

intervals to select the notes from the chromatic scale. One tone away from C (root note) is D; this is referred to as the major second interval (or second for short). One tone away from D is E, the major third interval (or just third). One semitone from E is F, the perfect fourth (or fourth), and so on to B (the major seventh). The scale ends one octave higher, returning to the root note of C.

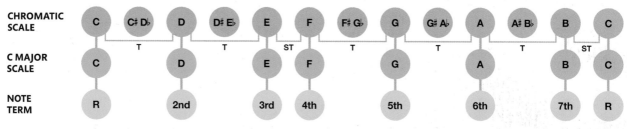

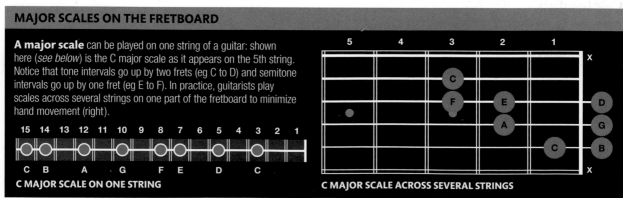

MAJOR SCALES ON THE FRETBOARD

A major scale can be played on one string of a guitar: shown here (*see below*) is the C major scale as it appears on the 5th string. Notice that tone intervals go up by two frets (eg C to D) and semitone intervals go up by one fret (eg E to F). In practice, guitarists play scales across several strings on one part of the fretboard to minimize hand movement (right).

C MAJOR SCALE ON ONE STRING

C MAJOR SCALE ACROSS SEVERAL STRINGS

SHARPS AND FLATS ON THE STAFF

The notes of the chromatic scale include not just the standard (or natural) notes, such as C, D, and E, but the accidentals—sharps (♯) and flats (♭), such as C♯, D♯, and A♭. On the staff, sharp notes are preceded by the ♯ symbol; flats by ♭. Many scales include sharp or flat notes, and using symbols before every accidental in a piece of music would lead to cluttered notation. For this reason, notation starts

with a key signature—a collection of either sharps (♯) or flats (♭) just after the treble clef. This shows the notes that are to be consistently played one semitone higher or lower than the equivalent natural notes. So, with an F♯ in the key signature, every F is the notation should be played as F♯. These key signatures provide vital information about the key of a piece of music (*see p.340*).

■ **E note** This chromatic scale begins with E and includes both ♯ and ♭ options for each accidental note.

■ **F note** The scale ends with F; if continued, the notes would rise and show as ledger line notes.

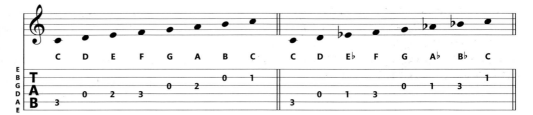

DISPLAYING MAJOR AND MINOR SCALES

Compare the notation and tab for the C major and C natural minor scales. Note the flattened third, sixth, and seventh intervals of the minor scale compared to the major.

Notice also that the C major scale contains no flats or sharps. Only the C major and A natural minor scales have no flat or sharp notes.

Scales on the staff
The musical system shown here displays the C major, then the C natural minor scales as notation and tab for comparison.

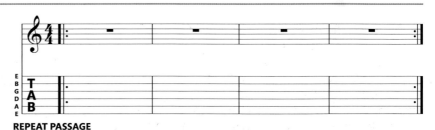

SHOWING REPEATS

Many pieces of music include repetitive notes, phrases, or chord progressions, and repetition gives much music its structure. Instead of writing the same passages over and over, notation and tab use a shorthand to indicate repeats, and repeats with alternative endings.

REPEAT PASSAGE

Repeat signs A simple repeat is indicated by two dots and two lines (*above right*). Where alternative endings are required, a bracket, a "1.," and a repeat symbol indicate the first ending. The repeat is then played, omitting the first ending and substituting the second, denoted by "2." and enclosed by a bracket (*below right*).

REPEAT PASSAGE WITH ALTERNATIVE ENDINGS

CHAPTER 2

FORMING CHORDS

Guitar music is largely based on chords and chord progressions. While there are many different chords, some with extremely exotic names, the strict definition of a chord is simple —it is three or more different notes played together. However, you will sometimes encounter reduced "chords" where one of the three notes is omitted; these two-note combinations may retain most of the chord's character. Chords are derived from scales using a principle called the "stacking of thirds." What this means is that a chord is made by taking a major scale and selecting any three alternate notes from that scale (*see below*). Deriving chords from any one scale is called "harmonizing" the scale: the resulting chords, which may be major (happy) or minor (melancholy) in character, will sound "right" when played together in a progression.

THREE-NOTE CHORDS: MAJOR AND MINOR

Major and minor chords are based on the "stacking of thirds" principle, which can best be described by example using the C major scale (*see below*).

Beginning with the first note in the scale—C—the next two alternate notes from the scale make the first chord. Stacking these three notes—C, E, and G—gives the chord of C major. These three notes are referred to as the root, the third, and the fifth notes of the chord. This first chord derived from the scale is given the Roman numeral I (*see below*).

Taking the second note of the scale—D—as the root note, the next two alternate notes from the scale make the second chord. These three notes—D, F, and A—make up the chord of D minor and are referred to as the root, the flattened or minor third (♭3rd), and the fifth notes. This second chord derived from the scale is given the Roman numeral II. Continuing through the scale in this way gives a total of seven chords, each derived from one note in the scale and assigned Roman numerals from I to VII.

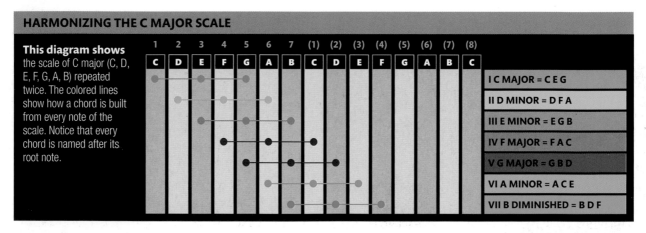

HARMONIZING THE C MAJOR SCALE

This diagram shows the scale of C major (C, D, E, F, G, A, B) repeated twice. The colored lines show how a chord is built from every note of the scale. Notice that every chord is named after its root note.

1	2	3	4	5	6	7	(1)	(2)	(3)	(4)	(5)	(6)	(7)	(8)
C	D	E	F	G	A	B	C	D	E	F	G	A	B	C

I C MAJOR = C E G
II D MINOR = D F A
III E MINOR = E G B
IV F MAJOR = F A C
V G MAJOR = G B D
VI A MINOR = A C E
VII B DIMINISHED = B D F

MAJOR AND MINOR THEORY

Some of the chords derived from the major scale are major, others minor. To understand why, consider the C major chord (C, E, G) with reference to the chromatic scale (*see p.42*): from C to E is an interval of 4 semitones; E to G is 3 semitones. Compare this with the D minor chord (D, F, A): D to F is 3 semitones and F to A is 4 semitones. This difference in interval spacing accounts for the difference in character. Minor chords have a minor third (spanning 3 semitones) while major chords have a major third (spanning 4 semitones). When harmonizing the major scale, a simple formula tells you which of the chords will be major, and which minor: I, major chord; II, minor, III, minor, IV, major; V, major, VI, minor, VII, diminished. The VII (diminished) chord creates a tense sound and is not often used in music.

CHORDS ON THE FRETBOARD

A basic chord consists of three different notes. However, many guitar chords involve sounding four, five, or even all six guitar strings. These extra notes simply duplicate the basic three notes of the chord in the same area of the fretboard. It is this doubling or even tripling of notes that creates "big" sounding chords on the guitar.

Chord notation and tab Shown here are the chords derived from the C major scale, first as three-note chords, then as "big" guitar chords. For the three-note chords, the lowest note is the root (eg C), the next is the third (eg E), and the last is the fifth (eg G).

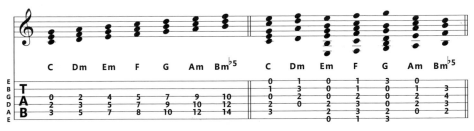

FOUR-NOTE CHORDS: 7TH CHORDS

Not all chords consist of just three notes. A very important class of chords—called 7th chords—adds another note to the basic three-note structure. These chords are common in blues and rock, and featured prominently in this book. They sound "richer" than major and or minor chords because there are more notes played. 7th chords are generated in the same way as major and minor chords—by the stacking of thirds principle. As before, the C major scale is used to illustrate the principle. Beginning with the C note, three (rather than two) alternate notes are stacked to make the chord—C, E, G, B. This chord includes not just the root (R), third, and fifth, but also the seventh scale interval. The interval between the fifth to seventh can be a major third (four semitones) or a minor third (three semitones). This gives not just major (R, 3, 5, 7), minor (R, ♭3, 5, ♭7), and diminished (R, ♭3, ♭5, ♭7) "flavors" of 7th chords, but also the dominant 7th (R, 3, 5, ♭7). These different flavors of the 7th chord have their own specific sounds (*see pp.114–15*).

CHAPTER 2

BUILDING 7TH CHORDS

This diagram shows the scale of C major (C, D, E, F, G, A, B) repeated twice. The colored lines show how 7th chords are built from every note of the scale. Notice that every chord is named after its root note.

To play C major's 7th chords as stacked thirds is very difficult on the guitar (though easy on the piano). Here, the first segment shows 7th chords played around the first few frets; the second uses barre chords (*see pp.102–03*) to ascend the fretboard.

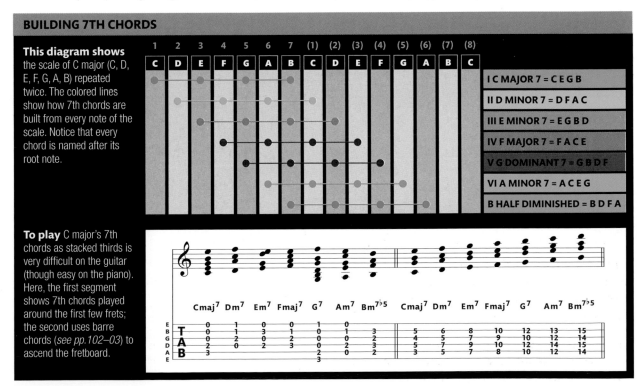

RHYTHM AND TIME

The final core aspect of music theory is rhythm. This dictates not only the duration of notes (and silences) but also their relationship to the regular beat/pulse of the music: without a basic unit of regular time in place, notes will seem to be played haphazardly. Here you will learn about note and rest terms, and how they are presented in music notation; you will see how note durations (values) relate to one another—from long to very short—and be introduced to time signatures that set the regular beat of a piece of music to a basic unit of time. Notice that only notation—not tab—is used on these pages. This is because, while tab can help you to play notes and chords, it provides no information about rhythm.

NOTE VALUES

Music notation provides information not only about a note's pitch but also its relative duration. The length of a note is indicated by a symbol—comprised of a head, often with a stem and sometimes a flag. Rests, or silences, have their own dedicated symbols. The table below shows what note and rest (silence) values can be seen in music notation. Durations can be expressed as fraction-based terms or as classical, word-based terms.

VALUES OF NOTES AND RESTS

NOTE	𝅝	𝅗𝅥	♩	♪	𝅘𝅥𝅯	𝅘𝅥𝅰	𝅘𝅥𝅱
REST	▬	▬	𝄽	𝄾	𝄿	𝅀	𝅁
FRACTIONAL TERM	whole note	half note	quarter note	eighth note	sixteenth note	thirty-second note	sixty-fourth note
CLASSICAL TERM	semibreve	minim	crotchet	quaver	semiquaver	demisemiquaver	hemidemisemiquaver

NOTE DIVISIONS

The table below shows how note durations relate to one another: a whole note (a semibreve) is the equivalent of two half notes (minims), or four quarter notes (crotchets), or eight eighth notes (quavers), and so on. Triplets (three notes grouped together) or sextuplets (six notes grouped together) squeeze in another note (or two), giving three notes in the space of two, or six notes in the space of four.

EQUIVALENT DIVISIONS

1 x WHOLE NOTE			12 x TRIPLET EIGHTH NOTES	
2 x HALF NOTES			16 x SIXTEENTH NOTES	
4 x QUARTER NOTES			24 x SEXTUPLET SIXTEENTH NOTES	
8 x EIGHTH NOTES			32 x THIRTY-SECOND NOTES	

TIME SIGNATURES

A piece of music spans a period of time. This time is broken up into short periods, called beats. The "time signature" of a piece of music appears at the beginning of the notation, after the clef and the key signature. It is a pair of stacked numbers (such as 4/4) which organizes the music's rhythm by grouping beats into bars (shown as vertical lines going through all five staff lines). The time signature appears only at the start of the music unless the rhythm changes partway through.

The upper number of the time signature states the number of beats in each bar, and the lower number states the value of that beat. So, for example, a 4/4 time signature is understood as follows: there are 4 beats to the bar and the value of each beat is a quarter note (or crotchet)—each time a beat is played it will last for one quarter note.

ALTERNATIVE RHYTHMS

4/4	Four quarter notes per measure; used in pop and rock	
3/4	Three quarter notes per measure; the waltz rhythm	
2/4	Two quarter notes per measure; used in polkas and marches	
2/2	Two half notes per measure; slow tempo for church music	
6/8	Six eighth notes per measure; used in tarantellas	
12/8	12 eighth notes per measure; triplet-based for bluesy swing	

COUNTING RHYTHMS

For variety, composers rarely use just the core note value of a time signature; for example, music in 4/4 is unlikely to contain only four quarter notes per bar. Instead, different note values are used that provide the total note length required to fit each bar correctly. The time signature tells you how to count the underlying beats in every bar; for example, in 4/4, the count for each bar is 1, 2, 3, 4. If a bar contains notes with values other than the core note value, such as in bars 2, 3, and 4 below,

these notes relate to the underlying beat. For example, bar 2 contains eight eighth notes. Relate these notes to the underlying beat for the bar—1, 2, 3, 4—but add in an extra "&" to give the rhythm of the eighth note: 1 &, 2 &, 3 &, 4 &.

4/4 counting To count the quarter note beat, use numbers (1, 2, 3, 4). Use numbers plus "&" for eighth notes (1 &, 2 &, 3 &, 4 &), and numbers with letters plus "&" for sixteenth notes (1-e-&-a, 2-e-&-a, etc).

MIXING RHYTHMS

This example shows how you can count the rhythm of a bar even when it contains notes that have different values, such as quarter, eighth, or sixteenth notes. Bar 3 also contains dotted and tied notes. The length of a dotted note is the value of the basic note plus half again. For example, a dotted quarter note equals one quarter note plus an eighth note. A tied note has a curved line (a tie) linking it to another, which indicates that you should sustain the sound for the sum of both notes. To count a bar that contains more than one note value, count the whole

bar as if it is filled with notes equal to the shortest note value in the bar. For example, the shortest notes in bars 2 and 3 below are eighth notes, so the bar should be counted: 1 &, 2 &, 3 &, 4 &; the shortest notes in bar 4 are sixteenth notes, so the bar should be counted 1-e-&-a, 2-e-&-a.

Bars with multiple note values Tap your foot or use a metronome to keep a regular beat as you clap or play this rhythm on guitar. The numbers and letters are used to help you count the rhythm.

"When you strum a guitar you have everything—rhythm, bass, lead, and melody."

DAVID GILMOUR

THE **SESSIONS**

INTRODUCING THE SESSIONS

Learning to play the guitar is hugely rewarding and great fun. The following pages will help you learn new techniques, build coordination and dexterity, and tell you more about essential music theory.

The learning program in this book is split into 10 sessions, each of which introduces new skills and essential concepts, and encourages you to put them into practice through short, specially written musical exercises. At the end of each session, you'll reach a milestone—a longer piece of music that consolidates what you have learned in the session. Features in each session explore the work of some of the world's finest and most inspirational players and what you can learn from them.

MAKING PROGRESS

This book is designed to take you from beginner to intermediate standard. If you are new to the guitar, start at Session 1 and work your way through the book, without omitting any exercises or sessions. If you have some guitar experience, it's still worth starting at Session 1 to fill any gaps in your theoretical and practical knowledge. People learn at different speeds, so it is hard to recommend how long you should spend on each session. The best advice is to play and perfect each exercise before moving on to the next. Play the exercises slowly at first, repeating difficult passages until finger-perfect. Only then increase your playing speed, perfect the piece, and move on. Once you reach the end of a session and can play the milestone piece fluently, you're ready to progress to the next session.

THE STRUCTURE

Each session is divided into 8–10 lessons which provide instruction on new skills, give you exercises to practise those skills, and set out vital theory, tips, and suggestions on how to move on, in bite-sized boxes.

Pro tips These boxes provide insights into techniques, or explain how experienced guitarists tackle problems.

Musical notation Colored bars on the notation/tab identify the steps illustrated in the photographs.

DVD icon This identifies material that you can see and hear on the DVD accompanying this book. Using the DVD alongside the book will help you progress through the sessions with more confidence.

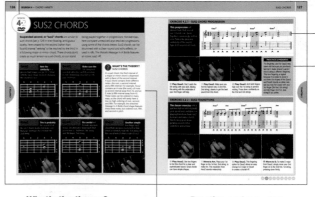

Skills These panels show you how to execute new skills, such as palm muting or string bends, or introduce new chords and scales to learn.

Exercises These panels present musical exercises for you to practice and play in order to learn and develop new skills. The exercise is presented as both standard musical notation and guitar tab (*see pp. 46–47*); photographs illustrate selected points within the exercise, such as difficult chord shapes and transitions.

What's the theory? These boxes help explain the theory underlying a new skill or technique.

Practice and progress These boxes provide ideas on how to extend the learning value of an exercise.

NAMING AND NUMBERING

In this book, strings are identified by number rather than by their tuning. So for a conventionally tuned guitar, the 1st string is the thinnest (highest in pitch) and the 6th string is the thickest (lowest in tone). The frets are numbered in ascending order away from the nut, so the 1st fret is adjacent to the nut, and the 22nd fret is closest to the body of the guitar.

HANDS AND FINGERS

This book refers to the fretting hand and the picking hand (not left and right) because some players use left-handed instruments. The fingers of the fretting hand are identified by numbers and colors as shown below. Fingers of the picking hand are identified by letters (derived from the Spanish) as shown.

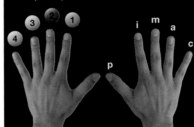

FRETS AND STRINGS

In all the fretboard diagrams shown in this book, frets are numbered from right to left (away from the nut). Strings are numbered from top to bottom (when facing the guitar). The diagram below shows the string numbers and their conventional tunings.

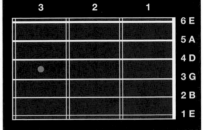

CHORD AND SCALE DIAGRAMS

Learning to play the guitar involves memorizing chords and scales. The fretboard diagrams used in this book show the finger positions needed to play scales and chords.

The fretboard is shown with the 6th string (thickest and lowest in pitch) at the top, and the 1st string (thinnest and highest in pitch) at the bottom. Frets are numbered from right to left, moving away from the nut towards the body of the guitar. Finger positions are indicated by colored dots, with the color and enclosed number indicating the finger to be used (*see above*).

PLAYING SCALES

The scale diagrams shown in this book show all the notes in a particular scale at a given position on the fretboard. The scale shown usually covers two octaves. There are countless ways to play a scale, though it's best initially to start from the lowest note on the lowest string, ascend to the highest note then descend to the lowest note.

DIAGRAM NOTATION

Use the chord and scale diagrams to guide your finger placement. Chord diagrams show the notes to be played together to sound a chord. Scale diagrams show the notes to be sounded sequentially to play a scale.

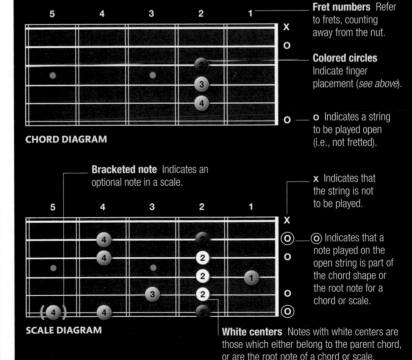

Fret numbers Refer to frets, counting away from the nut.

Colored circles Indicate finger placement (*see above*).

o Indicates a string to be played open (i.e., not fretted).

CHORD DIAGRAM

Bracketed note Indicates an optional note in a scale.

x Indicates that the string is not to be played.

⊙ Indicates that a note played on the open string is part of the chord shape or the root note for a chord or scale.

SCALE DIAGRAM

White centers Notes with white centers are those which either belong to the parent chord, or are the root note of a chord or scale.

GETTING STARTED

As a new guitarist, you have to start somewhere. You may have already experimented with your guitar, perhaps playing a few chords from a song, or learning a lead lick. All this is fine, if a little haphazard; it makes good sense to consider some fundamentals early on because these will serve you well throughout your playing career. In this session, you'll begin with some essentials: how to tune your instrument, and how to select a comfortable, repeatable playing position. You'll learn the best ways to fret and pick notes, and form simple chord shapes, so you'll soon be making a clean, powerful sound—a real confidence-booster. Get these basic techniques under your belt and you'll be well prepared for your musical journey.

SESSION

1·1 TUNING THE GUITAR

If your guitar is not in tune, nothing you play will sound good. Tuning your guitar is something you should do at the beginning of every practice session; at first it will be a chore, but it will soon become second nature. By far the most common tuning, from the sixth (thickest) string down to the first (thinnest) string, is EADGBE. It allows most chords to be fingered easily, and scales to be played with ease.

TUNING TO EADGBE

To tune your guitar, you need to tighten or loosen each string so that when played open (unfretted), it sounds a particular note. This is done by turning the tuning keys, which adjust the tension of the strings. You start with a reference point—a note of known and stable pitch—to which you can tune one of the guitar strings. This reference note can be provided by a piano, a set of pitch pipes, an electronic tuner (*see box below*), or, most simply, a tuning fork. The most commonly available tuning forks sound the note A, which can be used to tune the 5th string until it produces an identical note. Once this 5th string is tuned to A, you can use it as a reference point to tune the other strings, following the sequence below.

①

Tap the A tuning fork and place it against the body of your guitar to amplify its sound. Then sound the 5th string.

②

Find the right way to turn the tuning key so the two notes draw closer together; keep adjusting the key until they are identical.

③

Stop the 6th string at the 5th fret; tune it until it sounds an A note identical to the 5th string. When played open, it will sound E.

④

Stop the 5th string at the 5th fret; it will sound D when played. Tune the 4th string, unfretted, to this note.

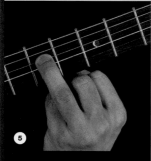

⑤

Stop the 4th string at the 5th fret; it will sound G when played. Tune the 3rd string, unfretted, to this note.

⑥

Stop the 3rd string at the 4th fret; it will sound B when played. Tune the 2nd string, unfretted, to this note.

⑦

Finally, tune the 1st string. Stop the 2nd string at the 5th fret so it sounds E, and tune the open 1st string to match it.

 PRO TIP
ELECTRONIC AIDS

Tuning by ear can be hard at first, and you may choose to invest in an electronic tuner. Simply play each string so the tuner can "hear" it via its built-in microphone or the cable of an electric guitar. The device's display will indicate how you need to adjust your tuning keys.

SESSION
1·2
DVD

PLAYING POSTURE

How you interact with your guitar is important. You should be comfortable with it whether you are seated or standing up, and be able to see both hands if needed. If you adopt a bad posture now (for example, standing with the guitar slung too low), you may develop problems that restrict your playing, such as an inability to form chords that involve wide finger stretches, or even physical ailments, such as back pain.

SITTING

Find a seated position that is comfortable and that you can replicate—keeping the guitar in one position builds familiarity. Try sitting with your right leg crossed over the left (if right-handed); this will keep your back straighter than planting both feet on the floor.

Strap well up the shoulder

Guitar held snug to the body

Guitar rests on the right leg

USING A FOOTSTOOL

You may find that using a low stool to support your left foot (for right-handed guitarists) is easier on your back and helps to stabilize and support the guitar, stopping it from sliding down your thigh. This position is favored by many classical players.

Neck of the guitar tilted upwards

Upper body straight

Knee bent at a right angle

Adjustable guitarist's footstool

STANDING

When standing, use a shoulder strap and adjust it so that you can pick all six strings comfortably without stretching. Keep your back straight and angle the guitar neck upwards so your fretting hand can easily reach the first few frets, keeping your elbow and wrist relaxed.

Shoulders should be level

Strap adjusted to raise the guitar neck

Upright posture with back straight

CHAPTER 3

1.1 **1.2** 1.3 1.4 1.5 1.6 1.7 1.8 1.9 1.10

SESSION
1•3
DVD

THE PICKING HAND

Your picking hand generates volume, determines whether a single string or a whole chord is sounded, and, critically, governs rhythm. Most rock and blues guitarists use a plectrum (pick) for greater speed, volume, and definition—commonly referred to as "attack"—while acoustic guitarists tend to use their thumb and fingers for versatility and busy chord playing. Others combine the two, using a pick and one or more fingers—this is known as "hybrid picking." Positioning and using your picking hand correctly will maximize your ability to get to the notes that you need to play. Here we introduce some of the basic picking-hand postures.

CHAPTER 3

HOLDING A PICK

Hold the pick between thumb and 1st finger, exposing 3–6mm of the tip. Don't grip too tightly, and try to keep your hand relaxed.

NOTE PICKING

Lightly rest your palm on the bridge, keeping your unused fingers loosely tucked in. Angle the pick for lighter strokes; keep it flatter for more volume.

CHORD STRUMMING

When playing passages with sustained chords it helps to lift your hand and rest one or two fingers lightly on the guitar body to stabilize the hand's movements.

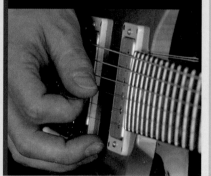

HYBRID PICKING

When using both a plectrum and fingers to pick the strings (hybrid picking), try letting your hand "float" so that it doesn't rest on the guitar body or bridge.

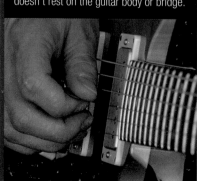

FINGERPICKING

Keep your hand floating, without resting on the body or bridge. Long nails are an advantage on steel strings and (almost) mandatory on nylon-strung guitars.

✳ PRO TIP
PICKING TECHNIQUE

Hold the pick between your thumb and first finger only. It is tempting to add your second finger to enhance grip, but it's a bad habit. You may drop the pick quite a bit when starting out, but do persist.

Experiment with where you pick along the strings: toward the neck will give you warm-sounding notes, toward the bridge you'll generate a brighter tone.

When strumming, generate the up-and-down movement with your wrist and elbow, not your thumb and finger. For louder and more vigorous strumming, add more elbow motion.

THE FRETTING HAND

Your fretting hand needs to be particularly agile. Whether it's making chord shapes, fretting for single-note solos, or performing other techniques, it certainly has its work cut out. Learning good fretting-hand technique is essential to get the most out of your playing. Hold your fingers slightly curved away from the fretboard, but as close as possible to a right-angle at the point of contact. They must work with your thumb to put just the right amount of pressure on the strings to produce a clean sound. Some of the basic techniques and fretting-hand postures are outlined below.

THUMB POSITION

Don't encircle the neck with your fretting hand—brace your thumb against the back to act as a support and pivot when fretting with your fingers.

SINGLE NOTES

Fret the strings with the tips—not the pads—of your fingers. Position your fingers just behind—not on—the fret bar for crisp-sounding notes.

FRETTING CHORDS

Keep fingertip contact near the fret bar to avoid "buzzing." Don't let the pad of a finger touch and mute an adjacent string that needs to sound.

ONE FINGER PER FRET

Put all four of your fingers to work on consecutive frets to build up strength and fluency. Don't get into the habit of playing everything with just your 1st finger.

BIG STRETCHES

When tackling wide fretting-hand stretches, keep your thumb in the middle of the neck to maintain stability, and be careful not to mute strings accidentally.

 **PRO TIP**
FINGER CARE

In common with all new guitarists, you will probably find that your fingertips hurt for the first few weeks of playing. Don't overdo your practice until they naturally harden up, and take it easy with big fretting stretches to avoid joint pain.

Use a low string gauge (see pp.294–95). A set of .09s or 0.10s on an electric guitar and 0.11s or 0.12s on an acoustic is ideal.

Keep your fingernails short so that your fingertips can hit the strings cleanly.

Use all four fingers evenly; in particular, don't avoid working your fourth (little) finger—you will need it!

SESSION 1·5 DVD

DOWN PICKING

Now that you know how to hold a pick and fret notes, it's time to start playing. You can pick strings with one of two movements: down (denoted by a symbol under the tablature; *see opposite page*) or up (a V symbol). You never up pick continuously; up picking is used with down picking in what is called "alternate picking" (*see pp.66–67*). Here we'll concentrate on down picking open and fretted strings.

DOWN-PICKING TECHNIQUE

Down-pick from the wrist rather than by flexing the fingers; after sounding the string, lift the pick up and away, avoiding contact with the strings. Try varying your "attack" with the pick and notice the differences in volume and "sustain"—how long the note lasts.

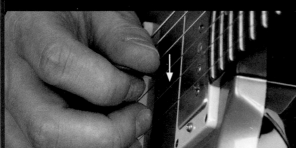

PRO TIP
SUPPRESSING NOISE

Good guitarists not only play good notes, but actively reduce unwanted noise from the natural vibration of unplayed strings and from the player's hand accidentally brushing against strings. Unwanted noise can become significant when playing loudly or with a distorted amp sound. It is good practice at all levels of playing to mute unplayed strings by damping their vibration. You can mute strings with your picking or fretting hand to achieve pro-levels of sound control.

To mute with your picking hand, let your thumb or other fingers rest lightly against the unplayed strings as you pick.

To mute with your fretting hand, let the finger pad of a fretting finger rest against the string or strings above. As you practice, you'll incorporate these techniques subconsciously into your playing.

EXERCISE 1.5.1 – PICKING AN OPEN STRING WITH DOWN STROKES

Hone your down stroke technique in this exercise, in which you play just one note—E—on the open 1st string. This will help you feel comfortable and confident picking single notes of varying lengths. This exercise has a simple 4/4 time signature, with four beats in each bar. Concentrate on achieving steady, even notes as you count the beats. The next two exercises (*see opposite page*) will use exactly the same rhythm.

Play the E note. Rest your palm lightly on the bridge; down-pick the 1st string.

Control the pick. Stop the stroke just after you have picked the string.

Regain position. Bring the pick up without accidentally brushing the 1st string.

CHAPTER 3

EXERCISE 1.5.2 – PICKING TWO OPEN STRINGS WITH DOWN-STROKES

Crossing strings—moving the picking action from one string to another—is the skill you'll develop in this exercise. It sounds simple, but you'll need to practice to cross strings fluently, without conspicuous gaps between the notes.

■ **Play the B note.** For bar 1, down-pick the 2nd string for four steady beats.

■ **Control the pick.** Play the last B of the bar, then pause with the pick instead of bringing it up.

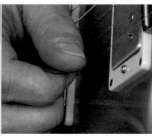

■ **Play the E note.** Pick down on the 1st string and let the E ring out for two beats.

PRACTICE & PROGRESS

The 4/4 timing used in all the exercises on these pages is by far the most common timing in music. Try tapping the four beats of the bars out with your foot, or use a metronome, to measure out the 1-beat notes (bars 1 and 3), 2-beat notes (bar 2), and 4-beat semi-breve (bar 4). For more information on timing and note values, see pp.50–51.

EXERCISE 1.5.3 – A SIMPLE MELODY ON 1ST AND 2ND STRINGS

Combine your down picking skills with some simple fretting. In this exercise you will fret different notes on the 2nd string, then add more variety with the open 1st string.

■ **Play the C note.** Use your 1st finger to fret the 2nd string at the 1st fret. Ensure that you press down with your fingertip just behind the fretwire to sound a clear, ringing note without any buzzing.

■ **Play D.** Use your 3rd finger to fret the same string at the 3rd fret to sound D. Keeping your 1st finger in place makes no difference to the note; you then lift them both off to play B on the open string.

PRACTICE & PROGRESS

You can use a metronome or drum machine not only to keep in time, but to speed up your playing while keeping consistent timing. Set the bpm (beats per minute) to a tempo that you can play comfortably without making mistakes—try 80 bpm at first. Once you have mastered the exercise, gradually increase the bpm. Your coordination will improve with practice.

CHAPTER 3

① **Punk-inspired**, chord-driven songwriting is the trademark of Green Day's energetic frontman Billie Joe Armstrong.

INSPIRATIONAL GUITAR SONGWRITERS

Writing songs is something every guitar-player should aspire to. It's with songs that guitarists demonstrate their creativity and musicality—with the potential to appeal to worldwide audiences. Chords, riffs, high-string melodies—all these and more feature in the musical vocabularies of global songwriting icons.

❶ BILLIE JOE ARMSTRONG

The frontman for US trio Green Day excels at vibrant, punk-pop-oriented songs that feature memorable riffs and rhythmic chords.

ESSENTIAL TRACKS *Basket Case* ◆ *Minority* ◆ *Good Riddance (Time of Your Life)* ◆ *Boulevard of Broken Dreams* ◆ *American Idiot*

SIMILAR ARTISTS Rivers Cuomo (Weezer) ◆ Tom de Longe (Blink 182) ◆ Noodles (The Offspring)

❷ KURT COBAIN

The definitive grunge-rocker and frontman for Nirvana was no soloist, but penned resonant riffs and unforgettable, driving chord progressions.

ESSENTIAL TRACKS *Smells Like Teen Spirit* ◆ *Come As You Are* ◆ *Lithium* ◆ *Heart-Shaped Box* ◆ *In Bloom*

SIMILAR ARTISTS Jerry Cantrell (Alice in Chains) ◆ Billy Corgan (Smashing Pumpkins) ◆ Dave Grohl (Foo Fighters) ◆ PJ Harvey

❸ NOEL GALLAGHER

Oasis' guitarist and singer has written some of the best pop songs ever; his solid chords and laid-back soloing hugely influenced young 90s guitar fans.

ESSENTIAL TRACKS *Cigarettes and Alcohol* ◆ *Don't Look Back in Anger* ◆ *Wonderwall* ◆ *Live Forever* ◆ *Morning Glory*

SIMILAR ARTISTS Mark Collins (The Charlatans) ◆ Gaz Coombes (Supergrass) ◆ Paul Weller

❹ KEITH RICHARDS

With legendary riffing and five-string playing, the Rolling Stones' "Keef" is indisputably one of the best guitarists and guitar-songwriters of all time.

ESSENTIAL TRACKS *Honky Tonk Women* ◆ *Jumping Jack Flash* ◆ *Street Fighting Man* ◆ *Sympathy For The Devil* ◆ *(I Can't Get No) Satisfaction*

SIMILAR ARTISTS Chuck Berry ◆ Marc Bolan ◆ Bo Diddley ◆ John Lennon ◆ Ronnie Wood

SESSION
1·6
DVD

ALTERNATE PICKING

When up- and down-picking strokes are used together, the result is alternate picking—an essential technique for all pick players. Alternate picking is more economical than down picking alone, because both the up and down movements of the pick can sound notes, so you can play faster. Here you will develop your picking versatility and learn about inside and outside picking.

Alternate picking involves a down stroke followed by an up stroke (or vice versa). When crossing strings, there are two main options: "inside" and "outside" picking (*see right*). Most people find outside picking easier, but you should practice—and become equally fluent with—both techniques.

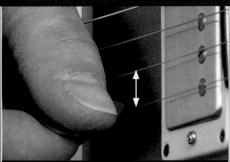

For inside picking, up pick the lower (thicker) string and down pick the higher (thinner) string. You should make contact with the "inner" sides of the strings.

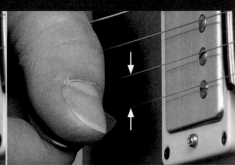

For outside picking, down pick the lower (thicker) string and up pick the higher (thinner) string. You will make contact with the "outer" sides of the strings.

EXERCISE 1.6.1 – ALTERNATE PICKING ON THE 1ST AND 2ND STRINGS

This simple foray into alternate picking starts with four steady down picks, then from bar 2 moves into alternate picking for the shorter notes. Outside and inside picking are used in bar 3.

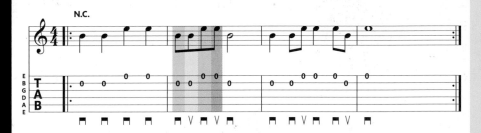

■ **Down pick B.** Sound the first B note of bar 2 with a down pick on the 2nd string.

■ **Up pick B.** Control the pick, then up pick the 2nd string to sound the second B.

■ **Down pick E.** Bring the pick up and over the 2nd string and down pick on the 1st string.

■ **Up pick E.** Play an up pick on the 1st string; remember to pivot from the wrist.

CHAPTER 3

EXERCISE 1.6.2 – ALTERNATE PICKING AND FRETTING ON THE 1ST STRING

Try alternate picking in combination with fretted notes on the 1st string in this exercise. You'll find it requires a little more coordination between left and right hands.

■ **Fret the F note.** Place your 1st finger on the 1st string. Use enough pressure to sound the note cleanly.

Play the F note. Perform an up pick on the 1st string to sound the F.

■ **Fret G.** Place your 3rd finger on the 3rd fret. There's no need to remove your 1st finger.

Play the G note. Use a down pick on the 1st string to sound the G.

EXERCISE 1.6.3 – A SIMPLE MELODY ON 1ST AND 2ND STRINGS

Combine the picking and fretting skills you have developed in this exercise. Take your time and learn it in one-bar segments. When you're fluent with each bar, perform all four bars together.

■ **Fret the D note.** This note occurs in bars 1 and 3, where it is performed with up picks.

Pick the D note. Control the pick to avoid the 1st string then up pick the 2nd string.

■ **Play E.** In bar 2, down pick the open 1st string as you move your fretting fingers between strings.

Be consistent. Pick confidently, aiming for consistent volume on up and down picks.

CHAPTER 3

THREE-STRING CHORDS

A basic chord consists of three different notes—the root, third, and fifth notes of a scale (*see pp.48–49*). The root gives the chord its foundation and its name; the third dictates the chord's happy (major) or sad (minor) sound; and the fifth gives the chord "stability." You can play a chord using just three strings to sound the root, third, and fifth or you can play more strings to double up some of the notes for a "fuller" chord sound (*see pp.90–95*). For simplicity, you can omit the fifth or the third (*see pp. 70–71*) and still get a recognizable chord sound. To begin, here are two major chords that are played with just one fretted string.

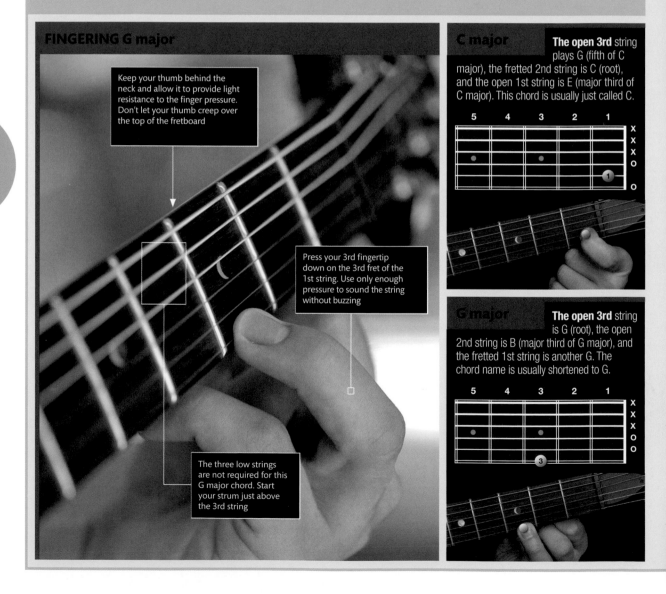

FINGERING G major

Keep your thumb behind the neck and allow it to provide light resistance to the finger pressure. Don't let your thumb creep over the top of the fretboard

Press your 3rd fingertip down on the 3rd fret of the 1st string. Use only enough pressure to sound the string without buzzing

The three low strings are not required for this G major chord. Start your strum just above the 3rd string

C major

The open 3rd string plays G (fifth of C major), the fretted 2nd string is C (root), and the open 1st string is E (major third of C major). This chord is usually just called C.

G major

The open 3rd string is G (root), the open 2nd string is B (major third of G major), and the fretted 1st string is another G. The chord name is usually shortened to G.

STRUMMING CHORDS

Playing a guitar chord requires you to sound the strings almost simultaneously with your pick or finger. You can strum the strings down or up; in either case, you should strike the strings with a firm, even stroke, using your wrist—rather than arm—to provide the motion. Down strokes have a strum and recovery phase.

STRUM DOWN

RECOVER POSITION

 WHAT'S THE THEORY?
FIRST STEPS WITH CHORDS

Don't be disheartened by chord jargon such as "roots" and "intervals" at this stage. Many guitarists learn chords by name and "shape"—the position of your fretting fingers—alone.

It's easy to "sing" the notes of the C major scale in your head—do, re, mi, fa, sol, la, ti, do. The C major chord picks out the first (root), third, and fifth notes: **do**, re, **mi**, fa, **sol**, la, ti, do—**C**DE**F**G**ABC.

When you move onto the "full" versions of these chords in Session 2 you will be using more strings, but you won't be adding more notes. The extra strings in the full version repeat the same three notes. So the full C major chord uses CEG from the first three strings as fretted here, but adds another C with the fourth string and another E with the fifth string.

CHAPTER 3

EXERCISE 1.7.1 – SWITCHING BETWEEN C AND G

In this exercise, you will be using down strums across the top three strings to sound C and G chords. Concentrate on making the motion light and quick.

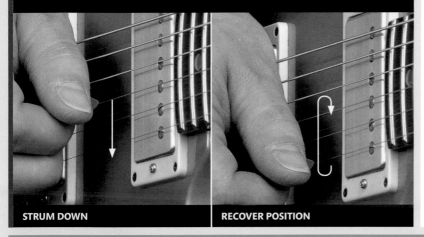

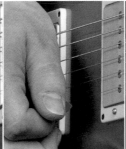

■ **Finger the C chord.** Use your 1st finger to fret the 2nd string precisely and avoid muting the strings on either side.

Play the C chord. Position the pick on the 3rd string; use one quick down strum to sound all three of the high strings.

Recover position. After the strum for the first C chord, pivot your hand up from the wrist to perform the next strum.

■ **Move from C to G.** Lift your 1st finger in the same moment that you plant your 3rd finger on the 3rd fret, 1st string.

Fret and play G. Be careful not to mute the 2nd string; this will rob the chord of its major third.

SESSION
1·8 POWER CHORDS
DVD

In some musical situations, even three-note chords are simply too much. For example, when playing rock using distortion (*see pp.38–39*), they can seem muddy. In such cases, you can discard the third interval and play only the root and fifth interval on two strings; these chords (which are not technically chords because they contain just two, not three, different notes) are known either as fifth chords (*e.g.* E5—the root E and the fifth interval—B) or, more simply, power chords. Using a third string to "double" the root note—*i.e.* playing it twice—adds fullness to the sound, as you'll hear in the chords below and the exercises on the opposite page.

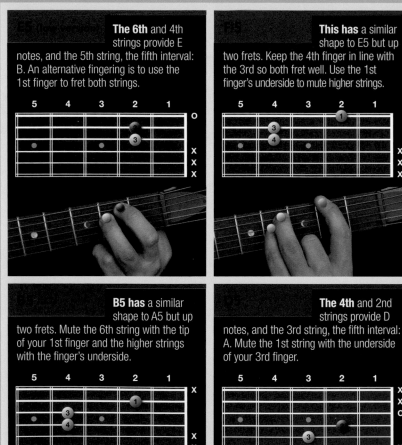

E5
The 6th and 4th strings provide E notes, and the 5th string, the fifth interval: B. An alternative fingering is to use the 1st finger to fret both strings.

F5
This has a similar shape to E5 but up two frets. Keep the 4th finger in line with the 3rd so both fret well. Use the 1st finger's underside to mute higher strings.

A5
The 5th and 3rd strings provide A notes, and the 4th string, the fifth interval: E. An alternative fingering is to use the 1st finger to fret both strings.

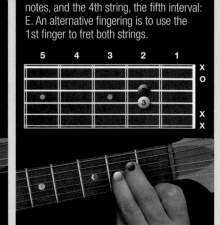

B5
B5 has a similar shape to A5 but up two frets. Mute the 6th string with the tip of your 1st finger and the higher strings with the finger's underside.

D5
The 4th and 2nd strings provide D notes, and the 3rd string, the fifth interval: A. Mute the 1st string with the underside of your 3rd finger.

E5 (higher)
This higher version of E5 has a similar shape to D5 but up two frets. It demands a big stretch and may need some practice to perform fluently.

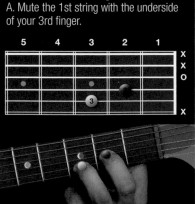

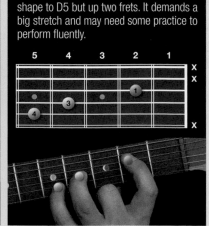

EXERCISE 1.8.1 – ROCK POWER CHORDS

This exercise puts together three simple power chords: A5, D5, and E5 (low version). Use precise down strums across the three strings. Have fun—power chords are easy to play. See how fast you can strum them, punk-rock style.

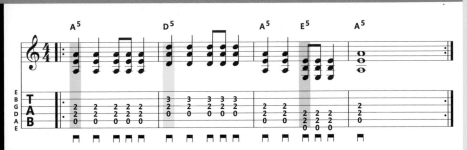

■ **Fret A5.** Mute the 2nd string with the pad of your 3rd finger. To play the chord, down strum from the 5th to the 3rd string.

■ **Fret D5.** Use the same fingers as for A5 but move them down one string and bring the 3rd finger up one fret.

■ **Fret E5.** Use the same fingers as for A5 but on the 2nd and 3rd strings. Aim to make the chord change swiftly.

PRACTICE & PROGRESS

Power chords are excellent confidence builders because they are fairly easy to play almost anywhere on the neck. Try playing them distorted through an amp or pedal, when their "hollow" quality provides a quick route to a great, edgy, rock sound.

EXERCISE 1.8.2 – POWER CHORD CHALLENGE

This exercise alternates picking one note from a power chord with strumming the whole chord. This is followed by a tricky run of power chords that will challenge your fretting hand.

■ **Fret the B5 shape.** You may need to build strength in your 4th (little) finger before you can sound the note cleanly.

■ **Move to E5.** Keep your pick strokes precise as the rhythm picks up in bar 2. Avoid striking the higher strings.

■ **Jump to A5.** Use the fingering shown above, or alternatively use your 1st finger to fret both strings together.

■ **Sound F#5.** Get all three fingers firmly in place before down strumming for this thick-sounding power chord.

CHAPTER 3

PALM MUTING

Some sound effects are exclusive to the guitar—and palm muting is one of them. Think of the opening riff to Led Zeppelin's *Whole Lotta Love* and you'll know exactly what it sounds like.

Palm muting involves resting the palm of your picking hand across the guitar's bridge to mute the strings, then picking or strumming. It's good to learn the technique early to get your picking hand used to forming the "karate-chop" position. A key rock and heavy metal effect, palm muting can produce strong,

percussive rhythms that add menace to distorted low-string riffs. But it can also be used to control volume, even on an acoustic guitar, so the guitar doesn't overshadow the vocals.

This session introduces the palm muting technique and uses it with simple power chords. For more palm muting inspiration, check out *Enter Sandman* by Metallica, Zakk Wylde playing *Crazy Train* with Ozzy Osbourne, or Al Di Meola's *Race With Devil On Spanish Highway*.

PALM POSITION AND THE MUTED SOUND

Positioning the picking hand
To get the desired muted sound, you need to position your palm correctly. Let it rest on the strings just where they leave the bridge: too far back and you won't mute the strings; too far forward and you'll mute too much, losing note definition. Practice keeping the pressure constant across your palm: uneven pressure will result in some strings sounding bright, while others are muted.

Picking the muted strings
Once your palm is in place, lower your pick, strike the string(s), and listen to the quality of the sound. Try to achieve an even, controlled sound and be prepared to move your palm forward or backward several times (a millimeter or two either way can make a big difference) before achieving the desired bass-heavy/treble-light percussive sound.

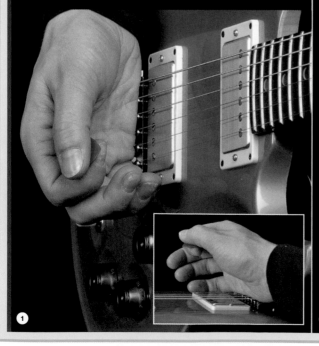

1

2

EXERCISE 1.9.1 – PALM-MUTED POWER CHORDS

This exercise features four of the power chords introduced on pp.70–71. Try it with some amp distortion (see pp.34–37) for greater effect. Note the "PM" and dotted line on the notation that indicates palm muting and its duration.

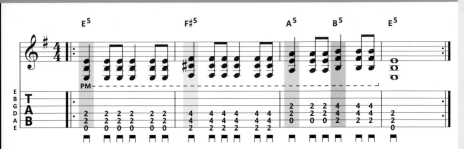

■ **Play the E5 chord.** Use palm-muting and down-strums, sounding only the lowest (thickest) three strings.

■ **Play F#5.** Shift to F#5 using your 1st, 3rd, and 4th fingers. The military-style rhythm used is the same as in bar 1.

■ **Change to A5.** Play the chord with a muted down-strum. Make sure you don't pick the higher strings by accident.

■ **Switch to B5.** Take the A5's 2nd and 3rd fingers off and quickly place B5's 1st, 3rd, and 4th fingers down.

EXERCISE 1.9.2 – PALM-MUTED POWER CHORDS AND SINGLE NOTES

As great as it sounds, palm muting isn't just for distorted power chords. Any string, anywhere along the fretboard, is suited to muting. There is more on this in later sessions, but for now, here is an exercise that mixes power chords with higher-string single notes. Although down and up strokes can be muted, this exercise requires only down strokes, to make it easier to achieve muting consistency.

Mute the strings. Be sure to mute consistently across all six strings: allow the fleshy part of your palm to do all the work.

■ **Play the E5 power chord.** Strum the lowest (thickest) three strings only. Aim for the distinctive palm-muted "chugging" sound.

■ **Play the individual notes.** These notes on the 2nd string are challenging to play muted as your hand is at a stretch.

 1.1 1.2 1.3 1.4 1.5 1.6 1.7 1.8 1.9 1.10

CHAPTER 3

SESSION
1·10
DVD

MILESTONE PIECE

This piece of music pulls together skills you have learned in Session 1, featuring down picking, alternate picking, three-string chords and power chords, and palm muting. The 16-bar piece comprises eight 2-bar phrases arranged in a "call and response." The first of the two bars (the call) consists of chord-playing, either low palm-muted power chords (such as the E5 in bar 1) or higher unmuted chords (such as the C in bar 9). The second of the two bars (the response) then answers with a different chord followed by a four-note lead line.

CHAPTER 3

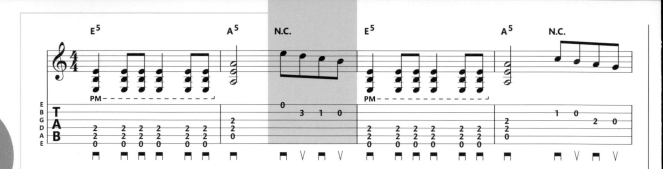

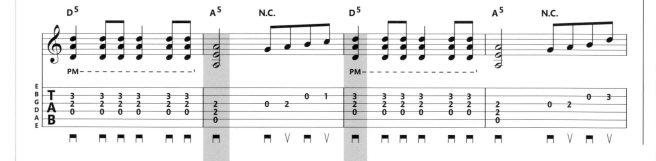

Use alternate picking to play the notes on the two high strings that make up part of the "call" in bar 2.

Fret the A5 power chord with great accuracy to allow it to sustain here: inaccurate fingering will not let it ring out.

Perform the D5 chord with palm muting and a military-style rhythm. The chord occurs in bars 5, 7, and 15.

Be careful not to mute the open 3rd or 1st strings with your 1st finger when playing the C chord in bars 9 and 11.

As you move the C chord's 1st finger, simultaneously put your 3rd finger on the 3rd fret, 1st string for the high G note.

PRACTICE & PROGRESS

This is your first long piece, and if you're learning to read music as well as play, it's going to look daunting. Remember, if you follow the tablature below the staff, you can't go wrong. Try learning it in 4-bar chunks, repeating them until you feel confident and are maintaining consistency, then link them together.

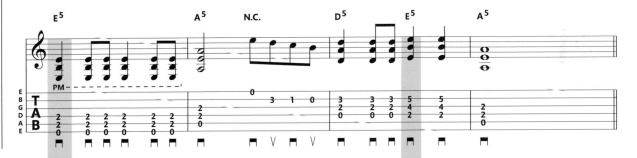

Play the low version of power chord E5 with palm-muted down strums when it occurs in bars 1, 3, and 13.

Practice this fingering stretch for a high E5, which occurs twice in bar 15. It is the toughest chord in the piece.

THE ESSENTIALS

In this session, you will explore alternate picking in more depth,
to improve your hand skills and coordination when crossing between
strings. Regardless of your stylistic preferences, this is an essential
aspect of guitar fluency. You'll then take a break from doing picking
exercises to explore hammer-ons and pull-offs; these are expressive,
fluid ways to produce notes. If you ever wondered how guitarists like
Jimi Hendrix and Eddie Van Halen developed their effortless sound,
these fretting-hand techniques are a must. To complement these new
lead guitar moves, there are some rock-based riff ideas and new
rhythm techniques. To round the session off, you'll be introduced
to full, big-sounding chords using four or more strings.

SESSION
2·1
DVD

PICKING DEVELOPMENT

A faster, more accurate picking hand that moves between strings with ease is something that all beginner guitarists aspire to. Unfortunately there are no real shortcuts: this skill demands time and dedicated practice, and it's a question of repeating picking exercises until you're happy with the level of precision you've reached.

This lesson begins with exercises that hone and extend your string-crossing technique, using outside and inside picking, which you learned earlier (*see p.66*). You will pick not only neighboring strings, as before,

but also strings farther apart. Use a metronome for these exercises, as there's little point in getting faster if your picking is uneven.

There's something new to learn too: double picking. This involves alternate picking the same note twice (or more) so it sounds machine-like. It works well on both low-string riffs and lead lines, creating a precise and exciting sound.

To sample double picking, listen to the Red Hot Chili Peppers' *Parallel Universe*, Led Zeppelin's *Wanton Song*, or Paul Gilbert's version of *I Feel Love*.

EXERCISE 2.1.1 – OUTSIDE AND INSIDE PICKING ON TWO STRINGS

This exercise will improve your string-crossing technique, as it uses first outside picking (bar 1), and then inside picking (bar 2). Practice this slowly at first to develop precision, then start to build up your speed.

OUTSIDE PICKING

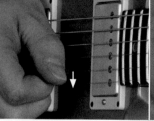

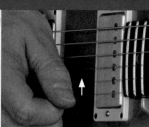

■ **Play the D note.** With your 3rd finger on the 3rd fret of the 2nd string, down pick for a D. Keep the lower strings quiet by muting them with your picking hand's palm. Aim to maintain consistency in the volume of all the notes played in this bar.

■ **Play the F note.** Following the D, bring your pick to a position just below the 1st string. Place your 1st finger on the 1st fret on the 1st string and up-pick to sound F. These two strokes together—the D then the F— use outside picking.

INSIDE PICKING

■ **Play the G note.** Down pick the 1st string, fretted at the 3rd fret with your 3rd finger, to sound G. After the down stroke, lift the pick up and over the 1st string, ready to perform an up pick on the 2nd string.

■ **Play the C note.** With your 1st finger on the 1st fret of the 2nd string, up pick for C. These two strokes together— the G then the C—use inside picking. Try to achieve the same playing speed when inside and outside picking.

EXERCISE 2.1.2 – OUTSIDE AND INSIDE PICKING CROSSING THREE STRINGS

This exercise will test your string-crossing skills further; it involves switching between outside and inside picking more often, and jumping strings so that you pick non-adjacent strings.

OUTSIDE PICKING

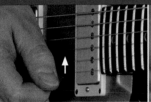

■ **Play the G note.** Fret the 1st string at the 3rd fret with your 3rd finger, then up pick the 1st string to sound G.

■ **Play the A note.** Lift the pick away and up to just above the 3rd string and, with your 2nd finger fretting the string at the 2nd fret, down pick to sound A.

INSIDE PICKING

■ **Play the F note.** Fret the 1st string at the 1st fret with your 1st finger, then down pick to sound F.

■ **Play the A note.** Lift the pick away and up to just below the 3rd string and, with your 2nd finger fretting the string at the 2nd fret, up pick to sound A.

EXERCISE 2.1.3 – DOUBLE PICKING

Each note in this exercise is picked twice to produce the doubling effect. There are two picking patterns under the tab; once you have mastered the first (which begins with a down-stroke) try the other pattern to increase your picking flexibility.

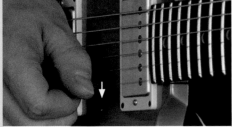
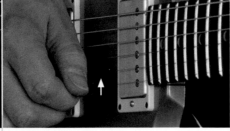

Play the down stroke. Down pick the 1st string, keeping your stroke controlled, your hand movement minimal, and your pick close to the string.

Play the up stroke. As soon as the down pick is complete, pick upward. Make sure your up pick doesn't drag, slowing your timing down.

PRACTICE & PROGRESS

Try accenting your picking to energize note sequences. When double picking down-up, try more attack on the down stroke so that it's louder than the up stroke. This will add interest to the sound. Practice this accented picking slowly at first, before increasing your speed.

HAMMER-ONS/PULL-OFFS

You don't need to pick twice to produce two notes. Hammer-ons and pull-offs are fretting-hand techniques that are used to play another note (or two) after picking a note. In a hammer-on, you sound a string (fretted or open) normally and then sharply snap a fretting-hand finger down onto a higher fret. The result is a new note. A pull-off is the reverse; you sound a fretted string, then pull your finger off the fret to sound a lower, fretted or open note. In both cases, since you don't re-pick to achieve the new note, the result is a smoother—though less bright—sound,

and note sequences can often be played faster than when using picking alone. The fundamentals of these two techniques are shown here, with exercises that explore their potential overleaf.

If you need inspiration you don't have to look too far. Check out Jimmy Page's solo in Led Zeppelin's *Stairway To Heaven*, Eric Clapton's intro riff and lead to *Layla*, Keith Richards' chord riff to the Rolling Stones' *Start Me Up*, and John Frusciante's fast chordal sequences during the intro and verses of the Red Hot Chili Peppers' *Snow*.

HAMMER-ON: F TO G ON THE 1ST STRING

Play the F note on the 1st string
Place your 1st finger on the 1st fret, 1st string. Sound the note with a down stroke. Keep your other fingers—especially the 3rd—close to the fretboard.

Hammer-on with your 3rd finger
Hit the string on the 3rd fret, 1st string to sound the G note. Use the tip of your finger and aim between the two fretwires for best results. Be sure to hit the string accurately, or it will not ring.

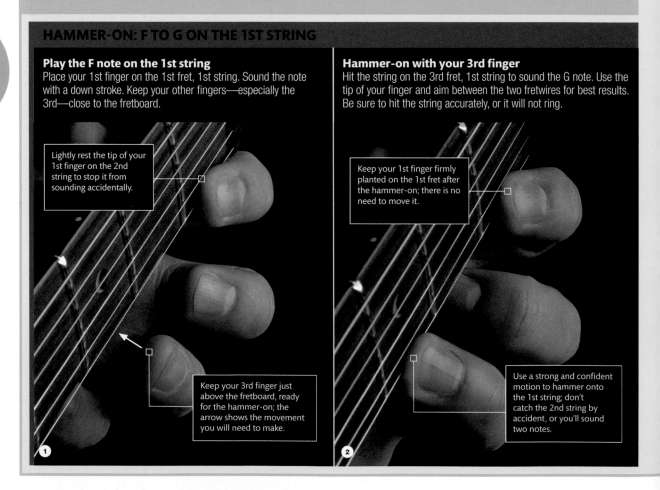

Lightly rest the tip of your 1st finger on the 2nd string to stop it from sounding accidentally.

Keep your 1st finger firmly planted on the 1st fret after the hammer-on; there is no need to move it.

Keep your 3rd finger just above the fretboard, ready for the hammer-on; the arrow shows the movement you will need to make.

Use a strong and confident motion to hammer onto the 1st string; don't catch the 2nd string by accident, or you'll sound two notes.

① ②

PULL-OFF: G TO F ON THE 1ST STRING

Position your fingers
Place your 1st and 3rd fingers on the 1st and 3rd frets of the 1st string, respectively. Sound the G note with a down pick. Remove the tip of your 3rd finger from the string with a strong sideways flick to make the string vibrate and sound the F note.

Sound the F note
As you pull off strongly, you'll sound the 1st finger's F note. Be careful not to make your pull-off plucking action too wide; performing a pull-off on the 2nd string (or lower) could result in sounding the higher strings accidentally.

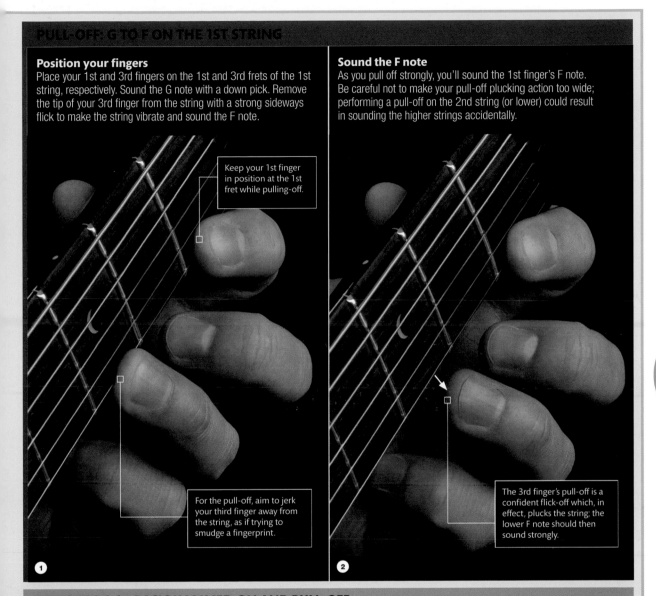

Keep your 1st finger in position at the 1st fret while pulling-off.

For the pull-off, aim to jerk your third finger away from the string, as if trying to smudge a fingerprint.

The 3rd finger's pull-off is a confident flick-off which, in effect, plucks the string; the lower F note should then sound strongly.

① ②

CHAPTER 3

EXERCISE 2.2.1 – BASIC HAMMER-ON AND PULL-OFF

This short exercise on the 1st string develops your basic hammer-on and pull-off techniques using F to G hammer-ons and G to F pull-offs. Note the eyebrow-shaped notation linking notes; called "slurs," they represent both hammer-ons and pull-offs.

Practice hammer-on and pull-off techniques in more depth with the exercises below, which use the top two strings. Listen for the differences in the sound produced by these fretting hand techniques as opposed to picked notes. Pull-offs are essentially hammer-ons in reverse, but the two have different characteristics. Pull-offs can generate string vibrations, so the resulting note can be louder than the first, picked, note; while hammer-ons rely on the original vibration, so the second note can be quieter than the first. Although these techniques are explored here on an electric guitar, which makes them easier to perform, they can also be used on the acoustic guitar, to embellish open chords.

EXERCISE 2.2.2 – HAMMER-ONS

Develop strong hammer-ons with this exercise, both from open strings and fretted notes. You will make one, then two, hammer-ons from a single down pick.

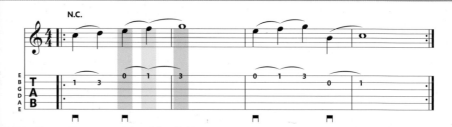

■ **Play the open 1st string.** Play the E and have your 1st finger ready to perform a hammer-on.

■ **Hammer-on** by placing your 1st finger onto the 1st fret while the original note still sounds.

■ **Do a second** hammer-on by placing your 3rd finger onto the 3rd fret so the note changes to G.

PRACTICE & PROGRESS

Hammer-ons demand strength in your hand, and 4th-finger hammer-ons tend to be the hardest to achieve. Experiment with the distance from finger to fretboard and the degree of projection that produce the best results for you.

EXERCISE 2.2.3 – PICKING AND HAMMER-ON COMPARISONS

Hammer-ons should not sound timid in comparison to picked notes. In this exercise, you'll play four picked notes, followed by three hammer-ons from a single down stroke.

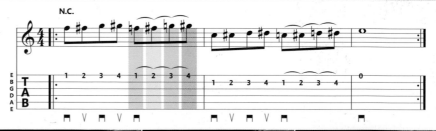

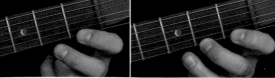

■ **Fret F.** Sound the note with a down pick; have your 2nd finger ready for a hammer-on.

■ **Hammer-on to the 2nd fret.** Bring your 2nd finger down and the note will change to F♯.

■ **Hammer-on to the 3rd fret for G.** Keep your 1st and 2nd fingers on the lower frets.

■ **Hammer-on to the 4th fret for G♯.** Keep your other fingers on their frets.

EXERCISE 2.2.4 – PULL-OFFS

Practice pulling-off on the top two strings with this exercise. Keep your timing steady and don't move your finger excessively when pulling-off so that you avoid sounding neighboring strings by accident.

■ **Play a G note.** Fret the 1st string at the 3rd and 1st frets, respectively, then perform a down stroke for G.

■ **Pull off your 3rd finger.** Pluck the string as you do so. With the 1st finger already in place, an F note will sound.

■ **Pull off your 1st finger.** Flick the finger towards the floor; this pull-off will sound the open first string—an E note.

PRACTICE & PROGRESS

Pull-offs can be trickier to master than hammer-ons for two reasons: first, you must prepare a finger for the second note almost at the same time as sounding the first; second, there's the action itself—you must flick your finger to the side without catching the higher, thinner string(s). Practice slowly at first; over time your precision and speed will improve.

EXERCISE 2.2.5 – PICKING AND PULL-OFF COMPARISONS

Test your pulling-off technique in this exercise by picking a string, then using pull-offs to sound another three notes. Concentrate on keeping your timing consistent throughout.

■ **Fret with four fingers.** Evenly space your four fingers on the 1st, 2nd, 3rd, and 4th frets of the 1st string. Sound the G♯ note.

■ **Pull off your 4th finger.** Flick your finger away from the 4th fret. Use enough exertion to sound G with the 3rd fretting finger.

■ **Pull off your 3rd finger.** Your 2nd fretting finger will sound the F♯ note. Keep your 1st finger in position.

■ **Perform the last pull-off.** Your 1st fretting finger will sound the F note, completing the sequence of pull-offs.

① **Wearing his signature Fender guitar** (nicknamed "Soul Power") high, and in a rare static pose, Tom Morello launches into a groove riff.

② ③ ④

GREAT RIFF PLAYERS

Think of a great rock song—say, AC/DC's *Back in Black*. It's almost certainly that insistent riff that pops into your head first, which is then gradually overlaid by the lead lines and vocals. Great riff masters like the four featured here have an instinctive talent for combining notes and rhythms into riffs that hook you in and stay in your head all day.

❶ TOM MORELLO

Influenced as much by hip-hop music as classic rock players, Rage Against the Machine's Tom Morello is a modern riff icon.

ESSENTIAL TRACKS *Killing In The Name* ◆ *Bombtrack* ◆ *Bullet In The Head*

SIMILAR ARTISTS John 5 (Marilyn Manson) ◆ Matt Bellamy (Muse) ◆ The Edge (U2) ◆ Jonny Greenwood (Radiohead) ◆ Jimmy Page (Led Zeppelin)

❷ FRANCIS ROSSI

The singer and guitarist for UK band Status Quo uses just a handful of chords to create an endless supply of outstanding, bluesy rock-and-roll riffs.

ESSENTIAL TRACKS *Carolina* ◆ *Down Down* ◆ *Rocking All Over The World* ◆ *Whatever You Want*

SIMILAR ARTISTS Billy Joe Armstrong (Green Day) ◆ Chuck Berry ◆ Billy Gibbons (ZZ Top) ◆ Malcolm Young (AC/DC; see below)

❸ JAMES HETFIELD

In the world of metal, Metallica's James Hetfield is one the finest riff players, concocting some of the fastest, meanest hooks in the genre.

ESSENTIAL TRACKS *Battery* ◆ *Enter Sandman* ◆ *Master of Puppets* ◆ *Sad But True*

SIMILAR ARTISTS Scott Ian (Anthrax) ◆ Dimebag Darrell (Pantera) ◆ Tony Iommi (Black Sabbath) ◆ Kerry King (Slayer) ◆ Dave Mustaine (Megadeth)

❹ MALCOLM YOUNG

Australia's finest rock band, AC/DC features guitarist brothers, with Angus Young's mean solos driven along by Malcolm's chugging, train-like riffing.

ESSENTIAL TRACKS *Back In Black* ◆ *For Those About To Rock (We Salute You)* ◆ *Hells Bells* ◆ *Whole Lotta Rosie* ◆ *Highway To Hell*

SIMILAR ARTISTS Jimmy Page (Led Zeppelin) ◆ Billy Gibbons (ZZ Top) ◆ Joe Perry (Aerosmith)

SESSION
2·3
DVD

LOW-STRING RIFFS

CHAPTER 3

Riffs are an essential aspect of all styles of guitar playing, especially in blues, rock, and metal. They are the short, repeated melodic phrases—the memorable "hooks" in guitar music—and they appear in song introductions, verses, and choruses. The riff "sells" the song to listeners, grabbing their attention and making them want more. The vast majority of riffs are played on the lower, thicker strings using overdrive or distortion effects and with the guitar's bridge pickup selected for a bright and cutting sound. They can contain a variety of notes: power chords, major and minor chords, or single notes derived from scales like the minor pentatonic (*see pp.148–149*) and the blues scale (*see pp.158–159*). The simplest consist of just two notes, but there are also many complex riffs. For famous low-string riffs, check out Led Zeppelin's *Heartbreaker*, Van Halen's *Mean Streets*, Metallica's *Sad But True*, Aerosmith's *Walk This Way*, T-Rex's *20th Century Boy*, and Michael Jackson's *Beat It*.

In this session, you will explore the low strings and learn about riffs and how they will improve your playing. You will continue using the power chords explored in Session 1 (*see pp.70–71*), as well as playing low single notes.

EXERCISE 2.3.1 – SINGLE-STRING RIFF WITH DOWN STROKES

This simple riff is played on just the 6th string. Use down strokes throughout to give the riff a driving consistency. The last four notes form a rather satisfying descending sequence, as you lift your fingers one by one from the frets.

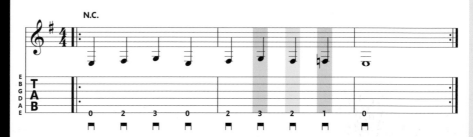

■ **Fret G with your 3rd finger,** but also line up your 2nd and 1st fingers behind it as shown, in readiness for the two notes that follow. Sound the G with a down stroke.

■ **Lift your 3rd finger.** Remove the finger fretting for the G note that you have just played, leaving the string fretted at the 2nd fret. Sound this note—F♯—with a down stroke.

■ **Lift your 2nd finger.** Remove the finger fretting for the F♯ that you have just played, leaving the string fretted at the 1st fret. Sound this note—F—with a down stroke.

EXERCISE 2.3.2 – POWER CHORD RIFF

Four power chords—E5, F5, C5, and A5—are brought together to create the powerful low-string riff in this exercise. Use down strokes across each chord's three strings to ensure the results sound consistent.

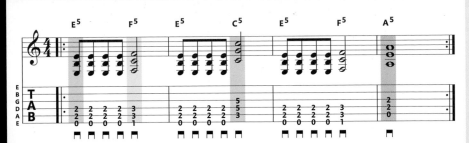

■ **Play E5.** Place your 2nd and 3rd fingers at the 2nd frets of the 5th and 4th strings respectively to fret the power chord E5.

■ **Play F5.** Fret the second power chord—F5—using your 1st, 3rd, and 4th fingers; avoid fretting or sounding the upper strings.

■ **Fret the C5 power chord.** Use the same fingers as for F5, but moved down one string and down 2 frets.

■ **Play the A5 power chord.** Note that the fingering is very similar to E5. Let the chord ring out for the whole four beats.

EXERCISE 2.3.3 – PALM-MUTED RIFF

This exercise showcases a "call and response" riff. The palm-muted notes of bars 1 and 3 are the "call;" the big, unrestrained power chords of bars 2 and 4 provide the "response."

■ **Pick the E note.** Begin the call section of the first bar with two palm-muted E notes picked with down strokes.

■ **Pick the C note.** Place your 3rd finger at the 3rd fret, 5th string. Play the note twice with palm-muted down strokes.

■ **Pick the B note.** Place your 2nd finger at the 2nd fret, 5th string. Play the note twice with palm-muted down strokes.

■ **Pick the G note.** Place your 3rd finger at the 3rd fret, 6th string. Play the note twice with palm-muted down strokes.

■ **Reach the G♯ note.** Bar 3 ends with a stretch for your 4th finger. Play the note twice with palm-muted down strokes.

SESSION 2·4 DVD

RIFFS AND FILLS

A riff is a low-string melodic phrase that creates a song's instrumental "hook;" a fill contrasts to the riff, often "filling" when the vocalist isn't singing. It's like a tiny guitar solo cutting through the band's sound to briefly grab the listener's attention. Moving between riffs and fills is very common in smaller bands containing three or four instruments, and combining riffs and fills is a playing approach used by countless rock and blues guitarists. Hear it from Jimi Hendrix in *Little Wing*, Eric Clapton in *Bad Love*, Eddie Van Halen in *I'm The One*, and Nuno Bettencourt in Extreme's *Decadence Dance*. All use riffs and fills in the same way: to fit in with the band and then to soar above it.

EXERCISE 2.4.1 – ROCK-STYLE RIFF AND FILL

In this simple riff-and-fill exercise, you play a one-bar E5 power chord riff, a one-bar lead fill, and then two bars of riffing to finish. The piece also introduces triplets (*see box*), which are used for rhythmic variation.

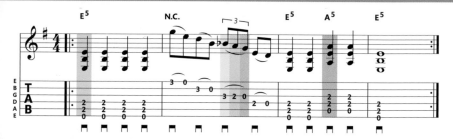

■ **Play the E5 power chord.** Use the fingering shape shown combined with strong down strums. Don't pick above the 4th string.

■ **Play the B♭ note.** This occurs in the lead fill in bar 2. Have your 2nd finger fretted behind the B♭ note's 3rd finger ready for the pull-off.

■ **Play the A note.** This follows the B♭ note. To sound it, pull off the 3rd finger, 3rd fret to leave the 2nd finger, 2nd fret on the 3rd string.

■ **Play the G note.** This follows the A note. To sound it, pull off from the 2nd finger, 2nd fret to the open 3rd string.

■ **Play the A5 power chord.** This occurs twice in bar 3. Fret with your 2nd and 3rd fingers and strum with down strokes.

? WHAT'S THE THEORY?
TRIPLETS

A triplet squeezes three notes into a beat instead of two. You can recognize a triplet in notation by the number "3" between square brackets above the group of notes. In the exercise featured on this page, there is a triplet at beat 3 of bar 2. It may help to tap your foot to the four main beats of the bar, and say "1-2-3" (or "straw-ber-ry") to each beat. Keeping the beat, try switching between "1-2" and "1-2-3."

Chuck Berry was famous for the inspired two-note chords—or double stops—of his song intros and guitar solos. A master of triplet hammer-ons and pull-offs, his intro to *Johnny B. Goode* is considered a defining example of rock and roll guitar.

GETTING THE SOUND

Chuck Berry – rock and roll

Chuck Berry's guitar style, appearance, and famous "duck walk" are the essence of rock and roll. Influenced by blues guitarists such as T-Bone Walker and Muddy Waters, from the 1950s onwards he incorporated bluesy soloing, boogie-woogie piano riffs, and country-style licks in an appealing sound. In particular, his double picking and string-bending (*see pp.162–63*) are rock guitar essentials. From the Beach Boys to Keith Richards, Angus Young to Slash, you can hear Chuck's influence everywhere. Chuck always favored Gibson semi guitars like the ES-330, ES-350, and ES-355. His double-string bends and bluesy licks were fueled by Fender Twin amps; these powerful valve amplifiers, turned up loud, provided the thick and cutting overdriven sound.

ESSENTIAL TRACKS	SIMILAR ARTISTS
Johnny B. Goode	Charlie Christian
Roll Over Beethoven	T-Bone Walker
School Days	Carl Wilson
Maybellene	Bo Diddley
Back In The USA	Carl Perkins
You Never Can Tell	Brian Setzer

SESSION

2·5   BASIC MAJOR CHORDS

Major chords, with their full, upbeat sound, are widely used in popular music. Major chords are made up of three different notes: the root after which they are named, the major third, and the perfect fifth. You played three-string chords in Session 1; now it's time to tackle some bigger shapes. Although more than three strings are sounded in these chords, there are still only three different notes; this is because some notes are repeated (doubled or tripled) to produce a bigger sound. The fingerings below are the most common for the selected chords shown but there are many ways to make the same chord (see p.94).

E
Place your fingers as shown. Don't mute the 6th string with your 2nd finger or the top two strings with the underside of your 1st finger.

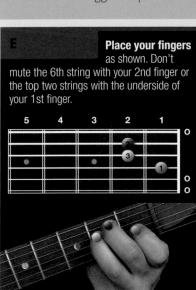

G
This is the big version of the G chord on p.68. Reach over to the low strings with your 1st and 2nd fingers without muting any open strings.

A
Place your 4th, 3rd, and 2nd fingers on the 2nd fret and play all strings except the 6th. Don't mute the 1st string with the underside of your 4th finger.

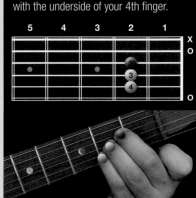

C
This is the big version of the C chord on p.68. Only the 6th (thickest) string is unplayed. Don't mute the 1st string with your 1st finger.

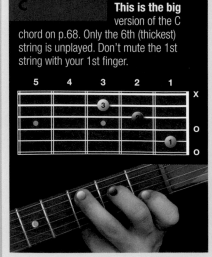

D
The shape of this chord is a triangle formed with your 1st, 3rd, and 2nd fingers. Use the very tip of the 3rd finger so the 1st string's note isn't muted.

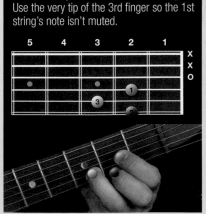

F
This is the only chord here that doesn't feature any open strings. Notice that your 1st finger frets both the 1st and 2nd strings.

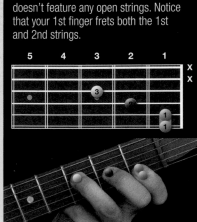

PERFORMING CHORDS WELL

Chords can take time to master. It's better to spend time getting one chord sounding great than three or four sounding just about functional. Perfecting your chords is a matter of applying just the right amount of pressure on the frets and using the correct fingers at just the right angle to either mute—or not mute—other strings. If your chord doesn't ring out, play each string in turn, listening out for string-buzzing or muted sounds, and correct the offending finger. Below are some tips for playing two chords well; apply the same scrutiny to all the chords you learn and you'll lay down strong foundations.

PERFECTING THE A CHORD

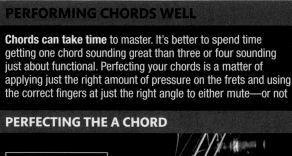

Move your 2nd finger as far forward as possible to avoid the fretwire and produce a clean note. Make sure your fingernail avoids the 5th string.

Keep your fingers at right angles to the fretboard—don't let them flatten.

Arch your 4th finger well to avoid muting the 1st string accidentally.

PERFECTING THE F CHORD

Place your 1st finger across the 1st and 2nd strings at the 1st fret. Use even finger-pad pressure so both notes sound clearly.

Don't let your thumb creep over the top of the fretboard.

Fret the F note well with your 3rd finger, and use the tip of the finger to mute the 5th string slightly.

EXERCISE 2.5.1 – FULL SIX-STRING STRUMMING PATTERNS

This exercise focuses on basic up- and down-strumming patterns using just E major. The piece includes "ghost" strums, which are performed silently, with no string contact. Many guitarists use them to keep time when a chord is sustaining or silenced. Ghost strums are indicated under the tab by bracketed pick strokes.

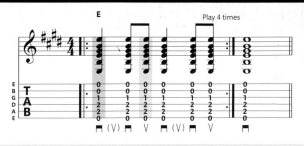

■ **Down strum E major.** Begin your movement a short distance above the 6th string so you generate sufficient momentum.

■ **Up strum E major.** Start a short distance below the 1st string. Strum up from the 1st to the 6th string.

Getting each chord to sound great is your first goal, but you'll soon want to start linking chords together into progressions of two or more chords. Moving seamlessly from one chord to another is a fundamental skill for any guitarist, and one that needs practice. Don't rush: work at a tempo that lets you play a progression perfectly before increasing speed, and always try to think ahead—plan the path of your fingers and think of the best sequence in which to place them in position. It may help to visualize your hand lifting off one chord and moving on to another before you play. With practice, you will be able to make smooth transitions without having to look where your fingers go. The following exercises use simple down or up-down strumming so you can concentrate on chord transitions.

EXERCISE 2.5.2 – CHORD DOWN STRUMS WITH E, A, AND D

This exercise develops your ability to change chords sharply and confidently using a simple down-strumming pattern. It involves three major chords only—E, A, and D. In the first three bars you use down strums, letting the last note of the bar sustain for two beats. During this sustain, think ahead to the next chord and then aim to change to that chord as quickly as you can.

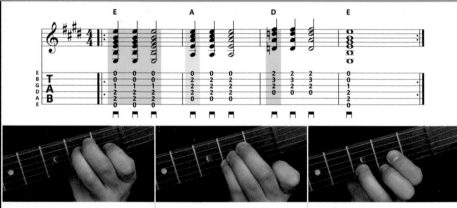

■ **Play the E chord.** Use the shape shown; the last longer note lets you plan the change to A.

■ **Change to A major.** From the E shape move your 2nd and 3rd fingers before placing the 4th.

■ **Change to D major.** Place your 1st and 3rd fingers down before your 2nd.

EXERCISE 2.5.3 – CHORD DOWN STRUMS WITH C, G, AND F

This exercise will give you a little more chord variety and help you develop fluency in moving between the chords of C, G, and F. As above, use the third down strum to plan ahead for the chord change. Use the tips suggested in the captions to stagger your fingering movements.

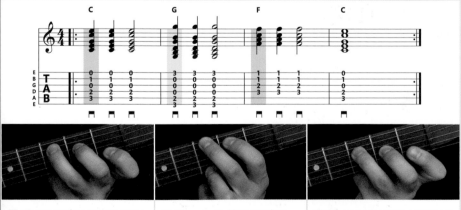

■ **Play C major.** Use the shape above and strum from the 5th string so you don't sound the 6th.

■ **Move to G.** Move your first two fingers to the 5th and 6th strings; place the 3rd finger last.

■ **Move to F.** Lay your 1st finger across the top two strings; the 2nd and 3rd fingers follow.

EXERCISE 2.5.4 – CHORD DOWN AND UP STRUMS WITH F, G, AND C

This exercise uses the same chords as the last, but mixes up the transitions. The strumming requirements are a little more involved, with two up strums required among the down strums.

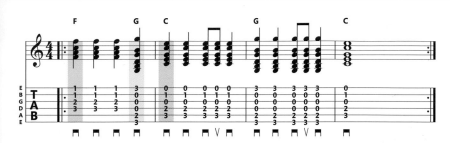

■ **Play the F chord.** Perform three down strums, ensuring that the top two strings fretted with the 1st finger sound clearly. At the end of this bar, think about the change to G.

■ **Change to G.** Fret the low strings before the 1st string when moving from F—you will have effectively prioritized the majority of the chord's shape for the down strum.

■ **Play the C chord.** Place your 3rd finger on the 5th string and then follow with the 2nd and 1st fingers. This makes for a smooth and easy transition from G.

EXERCISE 2.5.5 – CHORD DOWN AND UP STRUMS WITH E, A, C, AND D

Adding a fourth chord and busier down and up strumming makes this exercise even more challenging. Practice any difficult chord transition in isolation until it's good enough to put back into the exercise.

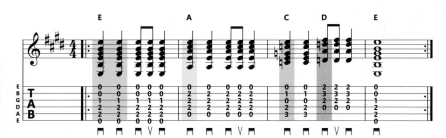

■ **Play the E chord.** Play the first two beats of bar 1 with down strokes and be ready to perform a down and up strum at beat 3.

■ **Change to A.** Move your 2nd and 3rd fingers down a string; only then place your 4th finger on the 5th string.

■ **Change to C.** Make the transition from A by placing your 3rd finger on the 5th string and then follow with the 2nd and 1st fingers.

■ **Change to D.** Move your 3rd finger to the 2nd string and your 1st finger to the 3rd string. Place your 2nd finger last.

CHAPTER 3

SESSION
2·6
DVD

BASIC MINOR CHORDS

Minor chords are commonly used in all styles of guitar—from folk and pop to blues and heavy metal—for their sad and moody quality. Like major chords, minor chords are formed with only three different notes; the root (or home note), which gives the chord its name, the perfect fifth (so-called because this interval is the same—or perfect—for both minor and major chords), and the minor third. The minor third is what makes a chord minor; in contrast, the presence of a major third makes a chord major. As with major chords, some notes may be repeated (doubled or tripled) on different strings to produce a bigger sound.

In this session you will be introduced to three minor chords: Em, Am, and Dm (the small "m" after the note name denoting "minor"). There are many, many more minor chords to learn but these three are particularly guitar-friendly and provide a great starting point.

WHAT'S THE THEORY?
ALTERNATIVE CHORD FINGERINGS

If you watch enough guitarists on TV or online, you will soon notice variations in how they fret simple chords. The shapes they form remain the same, but the choice of fingering varies.

The reasons for these variations are many—some players don't like using their fourth finger as it's too weak to get a clean sound. Others like to use their thumb to fret the low strings (a style frowned upon by most guitar teachers) and some like to use as few fingers as possible to sound a chord. Some use particular fingerings to make chord changes easier or quicker. Keep this in mind when you work with the chord fingerings shown in this book: you may decide to change them to suit your own playing style.

There are no "right" or "wrong" fingerings: the fingering that may be easiest when playing a chord in isolation might not be the best choice when playing that chord in context, within a progression.

CHAPTER 3

Em

Place your 2nd and 3rd fingers at the 2nd fret on the 5th and 4th strings, respectively. Make sure the remaining four open strings sound clearly.

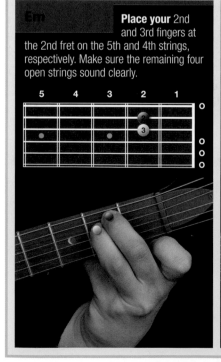

Am

Place your 2nd and 3rd fingers at the 2nd fret on the 4th and 3rd strings, respectively. Your 1st finger is placed on the 1st fret, 2nd string.

Dm

This chord uses only the top four strings, so don't sound the 6th or 5th strings. Place your 1st, 2nd, and 3rd fingers as shown.

EXERCISE 2.6.1 – DOWN AND UP STRUMS WITH Am, Dm, AND Em

You will get used to the characteristic melancholy sounds of minor chords in this exercise, which features Am, Dm, and Em. The down and up strumming in each bar is quite busy, adding to the challenge.

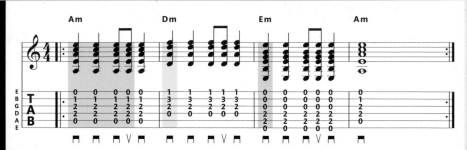

■ **Play Am.** Place your 1st, 2nd, and 3rd fingers on the frets as shown. Sound the chord with down strums, except at beat 3 in bar 1 where a quicker down/up strum is needed.

■ **Change to Dm.** From the Am position, move your 2nd then your 3rd finger. Once they are in place, finish with the 1st finger at the 1st fret.

■ **Make the transition to Em.** Take your 1st finger off the fretboard, then move your 2nd and 3rd fingers over to the 4th and 5th strings respectively.

EXERCISE 2.6.2 – DOWN STRUMS WITH Am, Dm, AND Em

This exercise may only require simple down strums but the chord changes are much more frequent and will develop your transition skills. Learn this slowly, bar by bar, until you feel confident playing the chords all together.

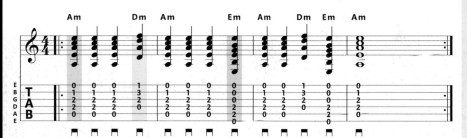

■ **Play the Am chord.** First place your 2nd and 3rd fingers on the 2nd fret, then position your 1st finger on the 1st fret. You will fret Am at four different times in this exercise.

■ **Play the Dm chord.** Position your 2nd and 3rd fingers before fretting the 1st string with your 1st finger. This chord occurs twice in this exercise.

■ **Play the Em chord.** Place your 2nd and 3rd fingers simultaneously on the 5th and 4th strings to make the Em shape. This chord is strummed on two occasions in this exercise.

CHAPTER 3

2.1 2.2 2.3 2.4 2.5 2.6 2.7

SESSION
2·7
DVD

MILESTONE PIECE

Many of the techniques explored in Session 2 feature in this 16-bar piece—alternate picking, hammer-ons and pull-offs, and low-string riffs, as well as the riff-and-fill approach favored by rock and blues guitarists. The first half consists of two four-bar phrases. In each phrase, there is a descending low riff followed by down and up strumming using three chords: Em, D, and G. The second half features a "call and response" riff and fill, with two chord strums followed by single-note pull-offs and hammer-ons. To close, there is a return to the opening low riff.

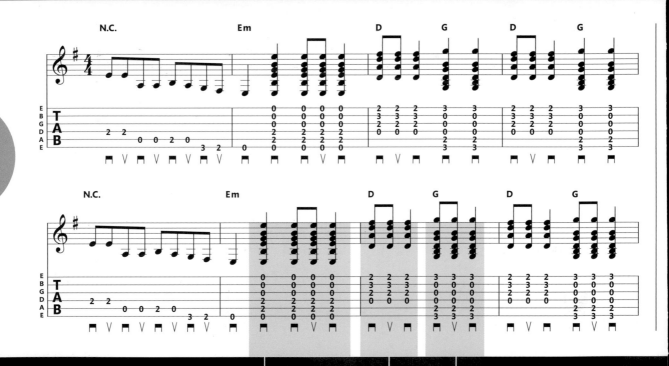

Make the Em shape after the opening low-string riff; the last note of the riff is E, making the transition to Em simple.

Make the transition from Em to D by fretting with your 1st and 3rd fingers first, followed by the 2nd finger.

Move to G, placing your 2nd and 1st fingers before the 3rd finger, as the 1st string will be the last one sounded.

Play the C chord to begin the middle section of the piece starting at bar 9. Place your 3rd and 2nd fingers before the 1st.

Make the Am chord shape by placing your 2nd and 3rd fingers first, followed by your 1st finger.

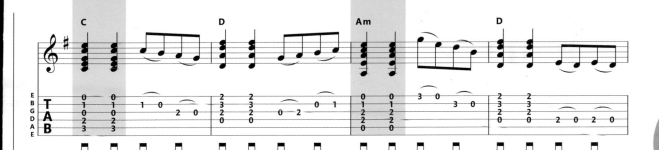

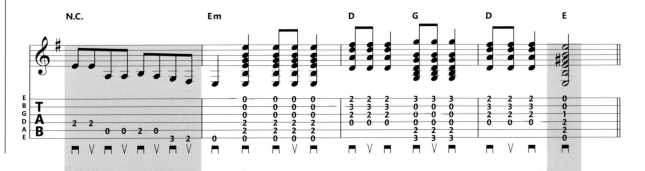

CHAPTER 3

Use alternate picking to play the descending sequence on the three lowest strings.

The E chord brings a surprise ending—the song's expected final minor chord is swapped for a major (*see box right*).

 PRO TIP
SURPRISE ENDINGS

When you experiment with chord sequences, try a musical trick that dates back to the 17th century—finishing a minor piece with a major chord. Hear it on the Beatles' version of *A Taste of Honey* and Lionel Ritchie's *Hello*.

NAVIGATING THE FRETBOARD

In this session you will learn the relationship between chords and their related scales. You'll begin to see the fretboard as a series of linked fingering positions, and you'll become more comfortable fretting notes and chords anywhere—not just on the first few frets. The process for learning chords and scales all over the fretboard involves adopting the CAGED system. At its heart are just five simple chord shapes for your fretting fingers that can be moved all over the fretboard. To make the chords moveable, you will learn about barre chord technique. Finally, you will look at 7th chords—new chords enhanced with an additional note to add color to your playing.

SESSION 3·1 DVD
CHORDS AND SCALES

A chord is a series of notes picked from a scale (*see pp.44–45*). You have already seen that a major chord consists of the root note of a major scale, the third interval, and the fifth. So, taking the scale of C major (C, D, E, F, G, A, B), it is easy to see that the chord C major is made up of C, E, and G. Each chord, therefore, has a "parent" scale from which it is derived. Knowing these scales and where to find them on the fretboard is a basic skill. It's vital for soloing over a chord, because the notes in its parent scale will sound harmonious, but other scales can clash.

Shown here are chords that you learned in Session 2. Learn the parent scale and fingerings for each until you are note-perfect. The chord shape is highlighted in white (and as circled open strings) on the diagrams below; bracketed notes are optional.

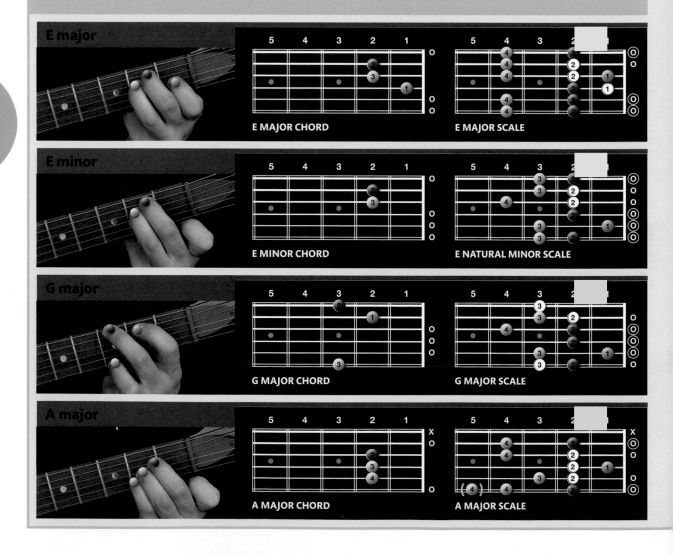

E major
E MAJOR CHORD   E MAJOR SCALE

E minor
E MINOR CHORD   E NATURAL MINOR SCALE

G major
G MAJOR CHORD   G MAJOR SCALE

A major
A MAJOR CHORD   A MAJOR SCALE

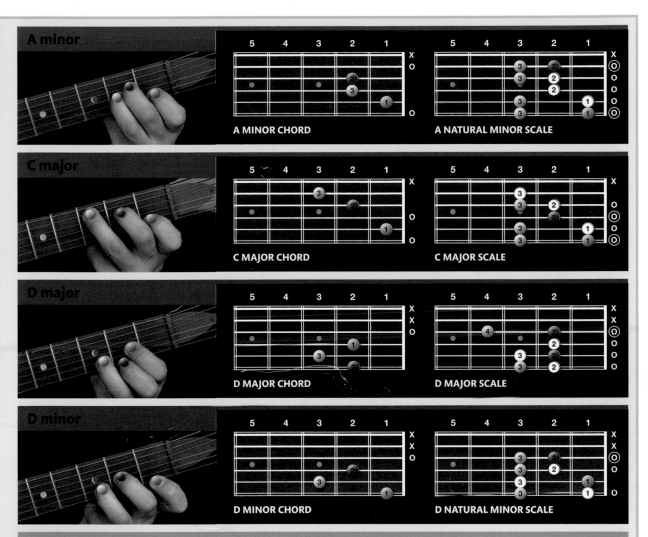

A minor

A MINOR CHORD

A NATURAL MINOR SCALE

C major

C MAJOR CHORD

C MAJOR SCALE

D major

D MAJOR CHORD

D MAJOR SCALE

D minor

D MINOR CHORD

D NATURAL MINOR SCALE

CHAPTER 3

EXERCISE 3.1.1 – PRACTICING CHORDS AND SCALES TOGETHER

Strum and sustain the full chord (here, D) then ascend and descend through its complete scale shape (here, D major). To finish, strum the chord again. Practicing all the eight chord/scale relationships here like this will greatly improve how you see the fretboard now and in the future.

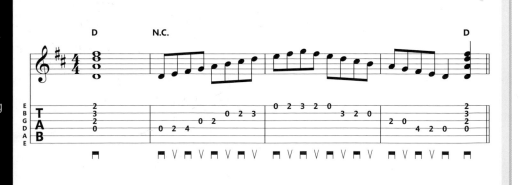

BARRE CHORDS

Major and minor chords have some fretted and some open strings, as you have already learned. Now it's time to tackle barre chords ("barre" is French for "bar"), which are formed by using your first finger as a bar to hold down strings at one fret—effectively making a new nut further up the neck. You'll use the other three fingers to form the chord shapes.

Most barre chords are based on the familiar chord shapes you've already met; using the barre, these shapes can be moved up and down the fretboard.

The chords keep their original quality—major remains major, and minor stays minor—but they change in pitch and name. Barre technique allows you to play any chord using one shape, or any chord using several different shapes (good for increasing your options). It also allows you to play chords and scales anywhere on the fretboard through a system called CAGED, which you'll meet overleaf. Barre chords are hard on the fretting hand at first, so begin with these simple exercises.

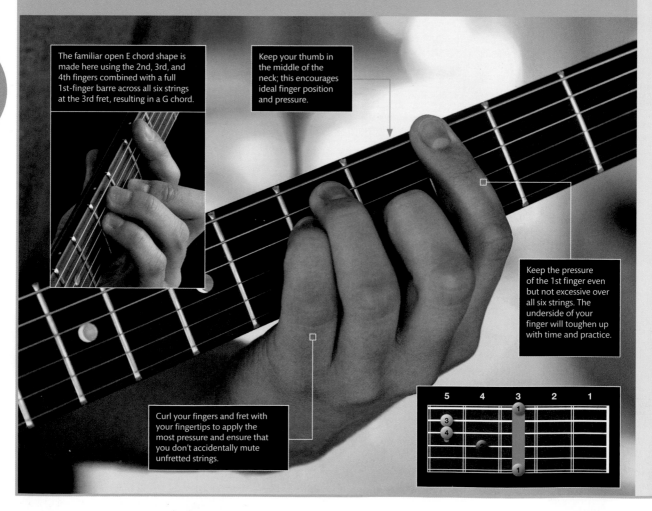

The familiar open E chord shape is made here using the 2nd, 3rd, and 4th fingers combined with a full 1st-finger barre across all six strings at the 3rd fret, resulting in a G chord.

Keep your thumb in the middle of the neck; this encourages ideal finger position and pressure.

Keep the pressure of the 1st finger even but not excessive over all six strings. The underside of your finger will toughen up with time and practice.

Curl your fingers and fret with your fingertips to apply the most pressure and ensure that you don't accidentally mute unfretted strings.

EXERCISE 3.2.1 – STRENGTHENING THE 1ST FINGER

Get used to forming a barre with your 1st finger by doing this exercise. As you extend the barre, strum precisely and listen out for poorly sounded notes.

■ **Barre two strings.** Place your 1st finger at the 3rd fret and use it to exert equal pressure on the 1st and 2nd strings.

■ **Barre three strings.** Move your finger up so the 1st, 2nd, and 3rd strings are fretted. Listen for muted notes.

■ **Barre four strings.** Unclear notes are likely so apply more pressure (thumb or finger) or move the finger slightly.

■ **Barre five strings.** A small move to fret the 5th string may not be enough; try relaxing and reapplying pressure.

■ **Barre all six strings.** You'll need to practice, but once all strings sound clearly, try this exercise in reverse.

EXERCISE 3.2.2 – THE E-SHAPED BARRE CHORD UP THE FRETBOARD

This demonstrates the power and versatility of the E-shaped barre chord to play three chords: G, C, and D. Navigating the large fretboard shift at the ending, from D to G, will test your skills.

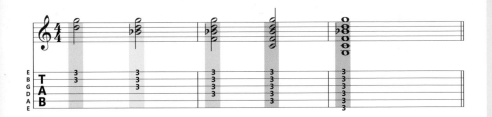

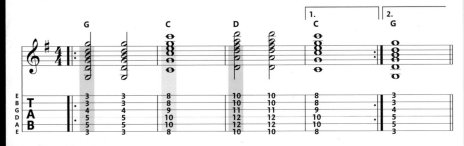

■ **Play G.** This is a six-string barre. Keep the pressure of your 1st finger even so the notes sound clearly with no string-buzzing.

■ **Play C.** Form the E shape at the 8th fret to finger C major. Listen to how thick it sounds when played well.

■ **Play D.** Form the E shape at the 10th fret to finger D major. Notice that it sounds bigger than the standard open D.

PRACTICE & PROGRESS

Mastering barre technique isn't easy, and can even be painful. If practice is proving really uncomfortable, try changing your strings to a lighter set starting with a first-string measurement of .010–.012 (acoustic), or .009–.010 (electric). If you're still having difficulties, you could try lowering your guitar's "action:" the distance from the fretboard to the strings (see p.302).

3.1 3.2 3.3 3.4 3.5 3.6 3.7 3.8 3.9 3.10

CHAPTER 3

SESSION
3•3
DVD

THE CAGED SYSTEM

In Sessions 1 and 2 you learned how to play five simple open major chords—C, A, G, E, and D—found at the first few frets. Knowing these familiar shapes gives you the key to playing chords and scales up the fretboard, all the way to the "dusty" end (near the guitar body). The system you need to find your way around every part of the fretboard is called CAGED, and it gets its name from these five basic chords.

Once understood and learned, the CAGED system opens up countless options for playing and soloing, and it is the basis for more advanced playing.

To use the CAGED system you need to be able to form barre chords (*see pp.102–03*) and understand a little about the chord and scale shapes you are about to learn. These patterns are part of how a guitar "works," at least in standard EADGBE tuning.

(see pp.102–03)

CHAPTER 3

ONE CHORD ALL OVER THE FRETBOARD

To begin, think of a full C major chord. The notes that make up this chord—C, E, and G—occur many times up the fretboard. To form a C major chord, you could play C, E, and G notes from any combination of positions. Plotting all the C, E, and G notes playable produces the pattern shown right.

Look closely at the pattern of notes above, and you'll notice something really interesting: it is the open chord shapes (CAGED) put end-to-end from left to right. This means that you can play a C chord in different positions on the fretboard using the basic chord shapes of the C, A, G, E, and D chords, as shown here (*right*).

Notice how the five basic chord shapes overlap in the same repeating order—C-A-G-E-D—and how they share notes. Making a first-finger barre at the overlap positions enables a chord shape's original open-string (unfretted) notes to sound correctly.

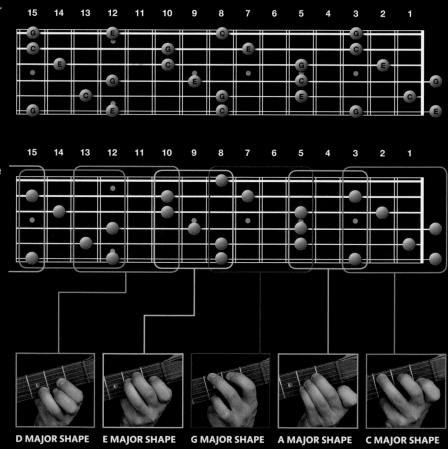

D MAJOR SHAPE **E MAJOR SHAPE** **G MAJOR SHAPE** **A MAJOR SHAPE** **C MAJOR SHAPE**

THE FIVE CAGED SHAPES

For clarity, let's look at the five chord shapes for C using the CAGED system. Use your first finger to make each shape into a barre chord, placing it on the fretboard as shown right. This gives us the barre chord shapes of C, A, G, E, and D.

Using these five shapes to play any chord you want is quite simple. Just remember that the lowest note played by any CAGED shape gives you the name of the chord. For example, consider the E shape: its lowest note always falls on the 6th string. So, if you make this shape with the barre on the 8th fret, you create a C chord, because the sixth string, 8th fret, is a C note (*see the fretboard navigator diagram on pp.42–43*). Get used to this thought process for finding chords along the fretboard.

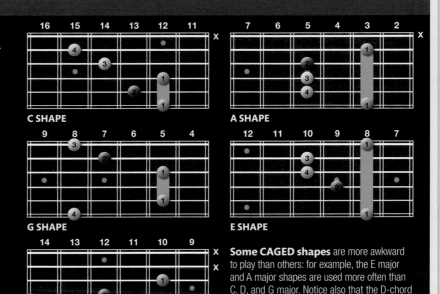

C SHAPE

A SHAPE

G SHAPE

E SHAPE

D SHAPE

Some CAGED shapes are more awkward to play than others: for example, the E major and A major shapes are used more often than C, D, and G major. Notice also that the D-chord shape is not really a barre chord because it has no barre; however, it is still classed as a moveable chord shape.

ONE SHAPE TO PLAY ANY CHORD

You can also move any of the five CAGED shapes up the fretboard to create all 12 major chords. You have already used the E shape to generate three chords (*see p.103*); here's the A shape and the results of moving it up the fretboard, fret by fret. This means you can now play a song by moving just one shape up and down the fretboard: many punk and garage rock bands have excelled at this.

Moving the A major shape (*below*) up the neck one fret at a time gives you all the major chords. The lowest note of the A shape (on the 5th string) gives you the chord's name.

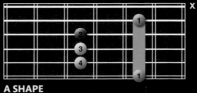

A SHAPE

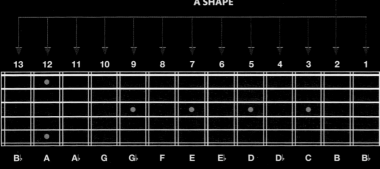

The CAGED system also works with minor chords and all the other chord types —such as 7th, sus4, and sus2—that you'll learn later in this book.

E SHAPE

E MINOR SHAPE

Just as the E major chord shape can be played all the way up the fretboard to give every major chord, so can the E minor shape.

PLAYING CAGED CHORDS

Now you've seen the theory behind the CAGED system, put it into practice in the key of D with five versions of D major and three of D minor. Some of these are tough, but they'll really help build your dexterity. You can then translate this drill to the chords of E, A, G, and C. To give your fretting fingers a break, try experimenting with the "reduced chords," using fewer fingers, shown on the opposite page.

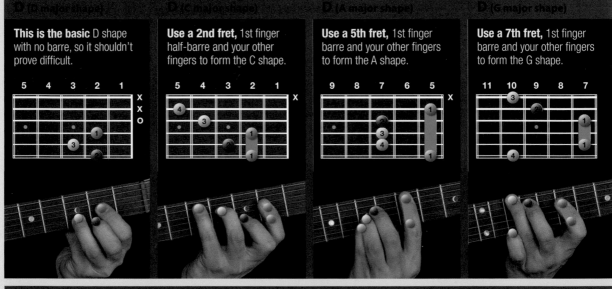

D (D major shape)

This is the basic D shape with no barre, so it shouldn't prove difficult.

D (C major shape)

Use a 2nd fret, 1st finger half-barre and your other fingers to form the C shape.

D (A major shape)

Use a 5th fret, 1st finger barre and your other fingers to form the A shape.

D (G major shape)

Use a 7th fret, 1st finger barre and your other fingers to form the G shape.

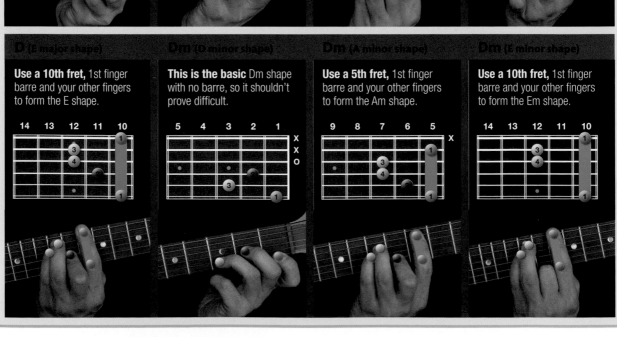

D (E major shape)

Use a 10th fret, 1st finger barre and your other fingers to form the E shape.

Dm (D minor shape)

This is the basic Dm shape with no barre, so it shouldn't prove difficult.

Dm (A minor shape)

Use a 5th fret, 1st finger barre and your other fingers to form the Am shape.

Dm (E minor shape)

Use a 10th fret, 1st finger barre and your other fingers to form the Em shape.

EXERCISE 3.4.1 – PLAYING REDUCED CHORD SHAPES

The full CAGED chord shapes (such as those shown on the opposite page) include barres and long stretches, which can be awkward and uncomfortable to play, especially when starting out. Many guitarists avoid this by playing reduced chords—omitting notes repeated in a chord (*see pp.68–69*). The chords formed are often more manageable three-string groupings: big enough to represent the chord's sound but small enough to fret easily. Many musicians use reduced chords—from jazz artists like Wes Montgomery to rockers like Keith Richards. Try it out on the D chords you have just learned. You'll find you can move around the fretboard quicker, opening up more melodic possibilities, if you avoid playing every chord's full shape.

D MAJOR CHORDS ON THE 1ST, 2ND, AND 3RD STRINGS

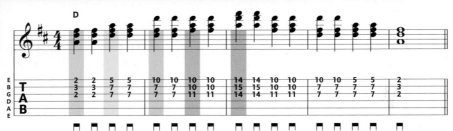

■ **Play the D chord.** Use the standard fingering but play only the 1st, 2nd, and 3rd strings to reduce the chord.

■ **Play D, 1st finger at the 5th fret.** You don't need to make a barre for this mini version of the A major CAGED shape.

■ **Play D, 1st finger at the 7th fret.** Make a half-barre for this mini version of the G major CAGED shape.

■ **Play D, 1st finger at the 10th fret.** Make a two-string barre for this mini version of the E major CAGED shape.

■ **Play D, 1st finger at the 14th fret.** Make a three-string barre for this mini version of the D major CAGED shape.

D MAJOR CHORDS ON THE 2ND, 3RD, AND 4TH STRINGS

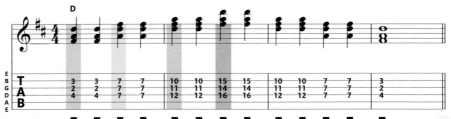

■ **Play D, 1st finger at the 2nd fret.** Use a mini version of the C major shape. Be sure not to sound the 1st string.

■ **Play D, 1st finger at the 7th fret.** Use a mini version of the A major shape. Be sure not to sound the 1st string.

■ **Play D, 1st finger at the 10th fret.** Use a mini version of the E major shape. Be sure not to sound the 1st string.

■ **Play D, 1st finger at the 14th fret.** Use a mini version of the C major shape. Be sure not to sound the 1st string.

PRACTICE & PROGRESS

Small three-string chords have strong melodic possibilities because you can easily switch between them for variety. In addition, it leaves you with "spare" fretting fingers—try using them at other frets to add new notes.

CHAPTER 3

① **Pete Townshend** is a theatrical chord player who emphasizes his chords by extending his strumming action into an eye-catching, windmilling arm movement.

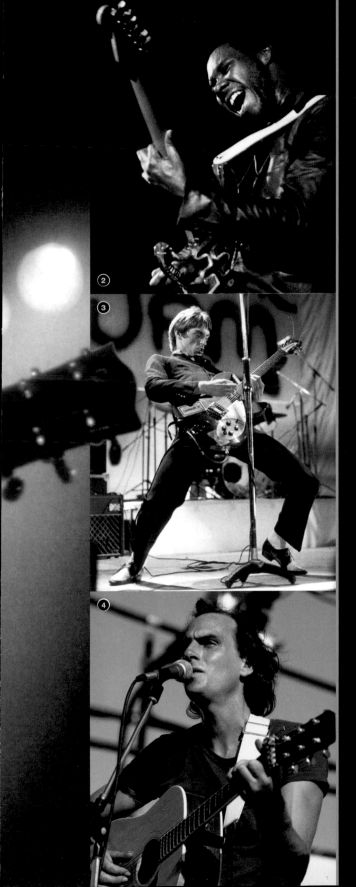

GREAT CHORD PLAYERS

Countless great guitar songs feature an evocative chord progression—a phrase made up of several chords—that helps its audience appeal. Many songwriters start with chords—from simple power chords to elaborate jazz chords—and build their arrangements on top. Here are four guitarists considered to be amongst the world's greatest chord players.

❶ PETE TOWNSHEND

Power chords, or two-note chords (*see pp.70–71*) played with unique conviction are a trademark of the Who's legendary guitarist and songwriter.

ESSENTIAL TRACKS *I Can't Explain* ◆ *Substitute* ◆ *Pinball Wizard* ◆ *My Generation* ◆ *Behind Blue Eyes*

SIMILAR ARTISTS George Harrison ◆ Paul McCartney ◆ Paul Weller ◆ Johnny Marr

❷ NILE RODGERS

American guitarist and producer Nile Rodgers is best known as Chic's guitarist and cowriter. During the 70s, Rodgers' choppy strumming of clean, clipped Stratocaster chord rhythms defined modern funk.

ESSENTIAL TRACKS *Good Times* ◆ *Le Freak* ◆ *I Want Your Love* ◆ *We Are Family* (with Sister Sledge) ◆ *Let's Dance* (with David Bowie)

SIMILAR ARTISTS Jimmy Nolen (James Brown) ◆ David Williams (Michael Jackson) ◆ Al McKay (Earth, Wind and Fire) ◆ Leo Nocentelli (The Meters)

❸ PAUL WELLER

Weller fronted UK band The Jam before his successful solo career. From energetic barre chord strumming to reflective sus chord arpeggio picking, he knows how to augment a song's vocal melody on guitar.

ESSENTIAL TRACKS *Going Underground* ◆ *That's Entertainment* ◆ *Wild Wood* ◆ *The Changingman*

SIMILAR ARTISTS The Small Faces ◆ The Kinks ◆ Noel Gallagher ◆ The Strokes

❹ JAMES TAYLOR

Californian singer-songwriter James Taylor came to prominence in the 1970s. His fretting hand is adept in the use of 7th, add9, sus2, and slash chords.

ESSENTIAL TRACKS *Fire and Rain* ◆ *You've Got A Friend* ◆ *Sweet Baby James* ◆ *Copperline*

SIMILAR ARTISTS Paul Simon ◆ Joni Mitchell ◆ John Denver ◆ Neil Young

SESSION 3·5 DVD

CAGED SCALES

It's time to link the chords to their related scales, using the major and minor chords all the way up the fretboard with the CAGED system. Here, you'll practise with the D-orientated chords that you learned on pp.106–107, playing their "parent" major or natural minor scales all the way up the fretboard.

The beauty of the CAGED system is that the scales you play are in the same fretboard area as where you play the chords. You will notice that the chord shapes you learned initially at the first few frets hold true further up the fretboard, albeit using different fingers.

Compare the C major chord and scale on p.101 with the D major (C major shape) chord and scale below. For clarity, each chord shape is highlighted within the scale shape with white circles (and circled open strings where applicable).

Practice these scales regularly to improve your coordination and develop your ear; shifts between chord rhythms and single note soloing will soon become second nature. But be realistic: learning scales is like learning new words, and you wouldn't expect to learn a dictionary in one sitting.

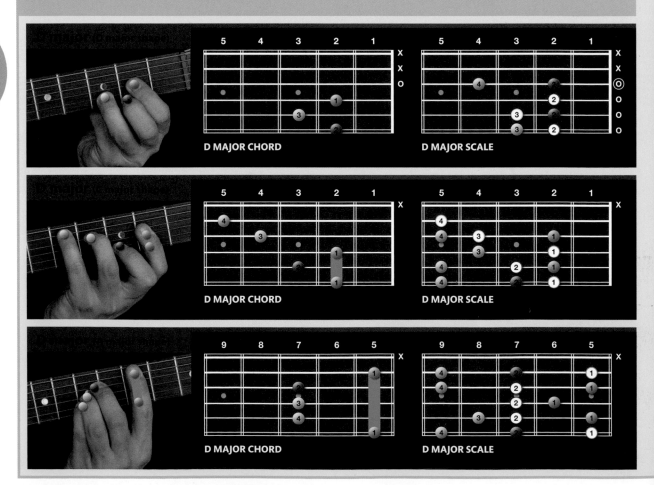

D MAJOR CHORD D MAJOR SCALE

D MAJOR CHORD D MAJOR SCALE

D MAJOR CHORD D MAJOR SCALE

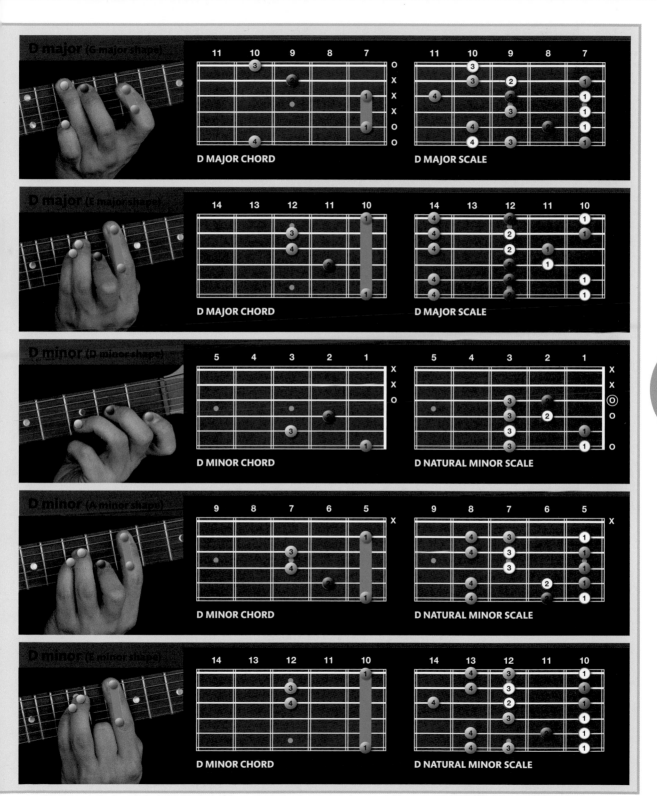

D major (G major shape)

D MAJOR CHORD

D MAJOR SCALE

D major (E major shape)

D MAJOR CHORD

D MAJOR SCALE

D minor (D minor shape)

D MINOR CHORD

D NATURAL MINOR SCALE

D minor (A minor shape)

D MINOR CHORD

D NATURAL MINOR SCALE

D minor (E minor shape)

D MINOR CHORD

D NATURAL MINOR SCALE

CHAPTER 3

SESSION
3·6 SCALE FLUENCY
DVD

Develop your fretboard knowledge with the exercises here, which link CAGED system chords and scales. You will work on three exercises based in D major—the first two use the D shape, the last uses the C and A shapes. Take your time and learn them carefully. Once mastered, apply the chord and scale approach to the other four shapes (C, A, G, and E) so you're fluent all over the fretboard.

These exercises will help you to explore ways to link chord shapes to scale shapes. When playing songs, you will rarely need to play a chord and then a full scale, so experiment with shortened scales to explore the musical possibilities. You can do this by leaving out some notes from the scale and/or arranging the notes in a different order. It takes time to learn, but this practice will ultimately help you to become a much more proficient guitarist.

PRO TIP
FLEXIBLE FRETTING FINGERS

The more you play, the more you need to be flexible with the fingering choices you make with your fretting hand. In everyday playing, you may not be able to use the finger ordering you initially learned to finger scale or chord shapes all the time. Sooner or later, you will learn a musical passage that requires new fingering options for you to play it at its best.

Take your time (days or even weeks) to consider how best to play a musical passage. Once you have decided, practice slowly and repeatedly until you can play the passage at the required speed.

If you find an exercise difficult, decide which fingers are best to fret with, and then commit to that decision and practice repeatedly. A consistent approach is a fast route to excellence.

EXERCISE 3.6.1 – CHORD AND ONE-OCTAVE SCALE COMBINATION

Play the chord twice and then play the scale from D to D (over one octave). Once you've learned to do this, play this exercise using D major's four other chord and scale shapes (C, A, G, and E), shown on pp.110–12.

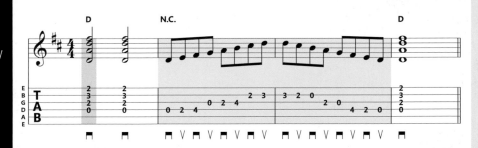

■ **Play the D major chord.** This D major chord uses the D major shape and features open strings.

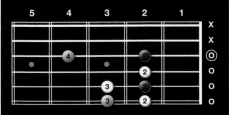

■ **Play the D major scale.** Begin with the low D on the open 4th string. Notes in the chord are shown as white circles and circled open strings.

PRACTICE & PROGRESS

After you have applied the picking directions suggested in this exercise, feel free to explore other options. You may like to try out the hammer-on and pull-off techniques that you learned on pp.80–81. Pick each new string and then use the note-ascending technique (hammer-on) or note-descending technique (pull-off) as required.

CHAPTER 3

EXERCISE 3.6.2 – CHORD AND SCALE DESCENT

Here you will play the chord twice, then descend from the scale's highest note to the lowest D. Then tackle the other four chord and scale shapes (C, A, G, and E) in the same way. Experiment by skipping some scale notes.

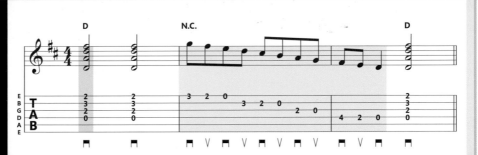

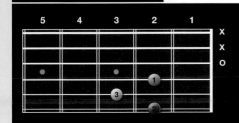

■ **Play the D major chord.** This D major chord uses the D major shape and features an open 4th string.

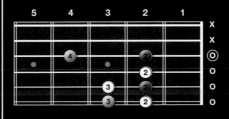

■ **Play the D major scale.** Play all 11 notes from the scale's shape. Notes in the chord are shown as white circles and circled open strings.

PRACTICE & PROGRESS

To create a fresh sound for this exercise's scale passage, try changing the rhythm. As shown above, all the notes in the scale (except the final D) last for the same length of time. Consider playing each group of two notes as long-short ("baaaa-di, baaaa-di") instead of medium-medium ("baa-baa, baa-baa").

CHAPTER 3

EXERCISE 3.6.3 – SCALE AND CHORD: MOVING BETWEEN SHAPES

In this exercise you will play the D major scale and chord in two fretboard positions, using C major and A major shapes. Despite the change in shape and position, notice that the notes in the two scale passages sound the same.

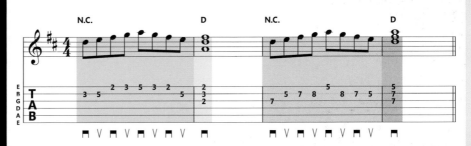

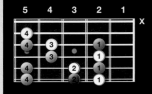

■ **Play the D major scale** (C shape). Play notes found on the 2nd and 1st strings derived from the C-shape scale.

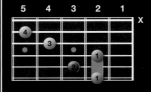

■ **Play the D major chord.** Use the C shape: make sure you fret well with your 1st and 4th fingers.

■ **Play the D major scale** (A shape). Play notes found on the 3rd, 2nd, and 1st strings derived from the A-shape scale.

■ **Play the D major chord.** Use the A shape—keep the 2nd, 3rd, and 4th fingers tightly together.

SESSION
3·7 7TH CHORDS

It's time to add a new type of chord to your vocabulary. The 7th chord resembles the major and minor chords you have already met, but adds a new note—the seventh interval away from the root note. This is used to add color to both major and minor chords. Three commonly used types of 7th chords, all with a distinct "flavor" (*see box, opposite page*), are introduced here. These are often used in place of simpler major or minor chords to lend a jazz, blues, or other moody sound.

MAJOR 7TH (maj7) CHORDS

Don't mute the 2nd string with the bottom of your 2nd finger. The major 7th interval is D#: 1st fret, 4th string.

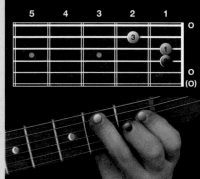

Avoid muting the 1st string with the underside of your 3rd finger. The major 7th interval is G#: 1st fret, 3rd string.

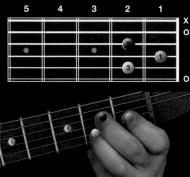

Dmaj7

Put your 1st finger across the 1st, 2nd, and 3rd strings at the 2nd fret. The major 7th interval is C#: 2nd fret, 2nd string.

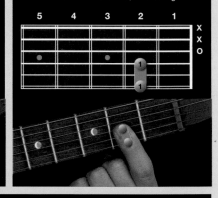

DOMINANT 7TH (7) CHORDS

This is easier to play than E major as only two fingers are used. The minor 7th interval is D: open 4th string.

This is similar to the Amaj7 shape, but with the 1st finger removed. The minor 7th interval is G: open 3rd string.

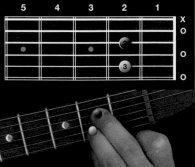

Avoid muting the 2nd string with the tip of your 3rd finger. The minor 7th interval is C: 1st fret, 2nd string.

MINOR 7TH (m7) CHORDS

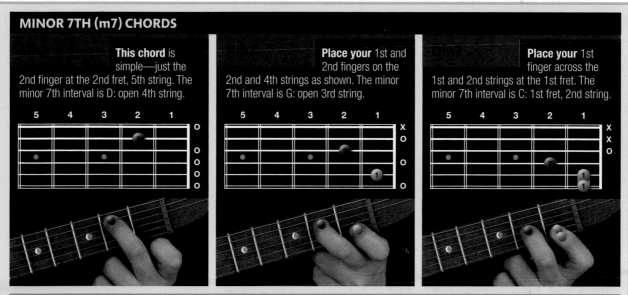

This chord is simple—just the 2nd finger at the 2nd fret, 5th string. The minor 7th interval is D: open 4th string.

Place your 1st and 2nd fingers on the 2nd and 4th strings as shown. The minor 7th interval is G: open 3rd string.

Place your 1st finger across the 1st and 2nd strings at the 1st fret. The minor 7th interval is C: 1st fret, 2nd string.

EXERCISE 3.7.1 – MAJOR, DOMINANT, AND MINOR 7TH CHORDS

This exercise allows to hear the color and melodic movement provided by the 7th variations of just three major chords—A, D, and E.

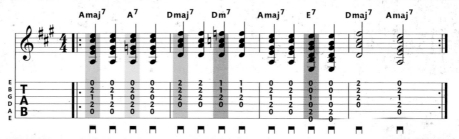

■ **Play Amaj7.** Use your 1st, 2nd, and 3rd fingers. Strum from the 5th string.

■ **Change to A7.** Take your 1st finger off the 1st fret, 3rd string.

■ **Change to Dmaj7.** Keep even pressure on the 1st, 2nd, and 3rd strings.

■ **Change to Dm7.** From Dmaj7, slide your 1st finger to the 1st fret.

■ **Play E7.** This dominant 7th occurs only in bar 3.

◗ WHAT'S THE THEORY?
INTERVALS AND 7TH NOTES

The seventh interval gives 7th chords great character, making them appealing, especially for blues, jazz, and country styles where they feature very prominently.

As with regular chords, 7th chords may be major or minor: as ever, their character depends on whether the third interval of the chord is major, or minor (flattened). So, major 7th (maj7) chords consist of the following intervals: root/major third/perfect fifth/ major seventh, and have a slightly jazzy feel. Minor 7th (m7) chords have four notes too, but use the minor third and minor seventh instead, giving them a sad jazz or bluesy texture.

There is another permutation of the 7th chord, which is identical to the major 7th, but in which only the seventh note (not the third) is flattened into a minor. This twangy chord is called a dominant 7th—or just simply 7—and is a staple of blues and jazz music. Despite the seemingly complex theory, many of these chords are easy to play and immensely satisfying.

CHAPTER 3

MOVEABLE 7TH CHORDS

Here you'll bring together the CAGED system with the 7th chords you've just learned, to play three G-based 7th and three C-based 7th chords at different points on the fretboard. The G chords are derived from the CAGED E shape and the C chords from the A shape (*see pp.104–105*). Once you can play the chords, try linking them together in simple progressions (for example Gmaj7–Cmaj7, G7–Cm7, or C7–Cm7–G7).

G-BASED 7TH CHORDS (BASED ON THE CAGED E SHAPE)

Gmaj7 — **Stretch your** 1st finger and tuck in your 2nd for this tricky shape.

G7 — **Your 1st finger** full barre provides notes on the 6th, 4th, 2nd, and 1st strings.

Gm7 — **Your 1st finger** barre needs to fret five strings clearly, applying even pressure.

C-BASED 7TH CHORDS (BASED ON THE CAGED A SHAPE)

Cmaj7 — **The 1st finger** barre provides high and low notes. Place the 4th finger well.

C7 — **The 1st finger** provides three notes on the 5th, 3rd, and 1st strings.

Cm7 — **This chord** is similar to C7 but is made minor by the 2nd finger.

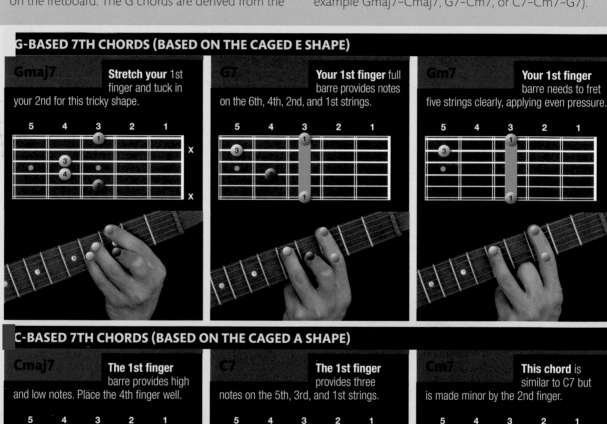

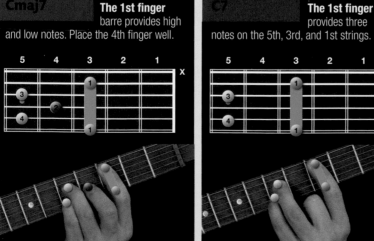

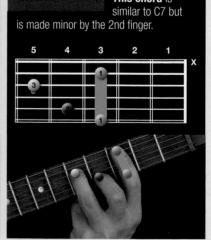

Johnny Marr – indie rock

Johnny Marr is considered one of the best song-oriented guitarists England has ever produced. His six-string skills are considerable but always serve the song: you'll be hard-pressed to find him playing grandiose rock solos. He came to fame in the Manchester four-piece, The Smiths, fronted by Morrissey during the early 1980s. Marr's use of quickly strummed chords, evocative electric sounds, and multilayered guitar arrangements made him an icon. Favoring a thumb pick, his chords and fingerpicking approaches suggest folk influences (he's a fan of Bert Jansch) as well as 60s bands like The Kinks and The Beatles. Over the years, he's favored a variety of equipment including Rickenbacker 330, Gibson ES335, and Gibson Les Paul guitars, and Fender and Marshall amplifiers.

ESSENTIAL TRACKS	SIMILAR ARTISTS
This Charming Man	Mick Jones (The Clash)
Panic	James Honeyman-Scott (The Pretenders)
The Boy With A Thorn In His Side	
How Soon Is Now?	Graham Coxon (Blur)
William, It Was Really Nothing	John Frusciante (Red Hot Chili Peppers)
Sheila Take A Bow	

After leaving The Smiths, Marr's guitar skills were used by The Pretenders, Bryan Ferry, Paul McCartney, The The, and his band with New Order's Bernard Sumner, Electronic.

SESSION
3·9
DVD

CHORD PROGRESSIONS

Guitar music is based on chords and most songwriters start with a chord progression before constructing the melody. The progressions you hear in pop and rock music are usually fairly simple—typically made up of just a few chords. So how do you select the right chords for a satisfying progression? The simple answer is to choose only from the seven chords created when you harmonize a scale (see pp.48-49). Of these chords, some are used far more often than others: for example, progressions moving through chords I–IV–V–I are a rock and roll staple, and the II–V–I progression features in many jazz tunes.

Here, you will play three exercises to explore the qualities of three popular chord progressions. Each progression is in two sections: the first half (two bars) consists of major or minor chords; the second half (also two bars) uses 7th chord variations instead. Listen out for the distinctive sound given by the 7th chords.

 WHAT'S THE THEORY?
ROCK STRUCTURE

When you harmonize a major scale (see p.48), the resulting seven chords are given the Roman numerals I, II, III, IV, V, VI, and VII. Of these, only chords I, IV, and V are major chords, which makes the I–IV–V progression so strong in rock and pop music. Many rock progressions begin with the I chord (the "home" chord of the song) and finish—or "resolve"—with the same chord. You don't need to look far to find this song structure—it is amazingly common. Try Elvis Presley's *All Shook Up* (in B♭: B♭, E♭, F); Bryan Ferry's *Let's Stick Together* (in A: A, D, and E); Stevie Ray Vaughan's *Pride and Joy* (in E♭: E♭, A♭, B♭); and Dire Straits' *Walk Of Life* (in E: E, A, and B).

EXERCISE 3.9.1 – I–IV–V–I PROGRESSION IN D MAJOR

In this exercise, you play the I–IV–V progression—a very common blues progression also often heard in rock, pop, and country. It features D (I), G (IV), and A (V) chords in major and 7th varieties.

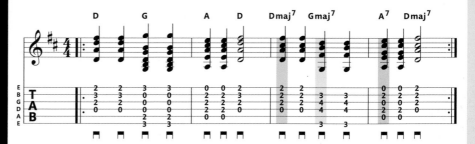

■ **Play Dmaj7.** Make sure you apply even pressure with your 1st finger when playing the Dmaj7—the first 7th chord.

■ **Play Gmaj7.** Make sure that the notes fretted by your 1st and 2nd fingers sound clearly, without string buzzes.

■ **Play A7.** Place your 2nd finger first, then your 3rd to fret the A7. Finish the exercise with the resolving Dmaj7.

PRACTICE & PROGRESS

When you harmonize a scale to include 7th intervals (see p.49) the I and IV chords become major 7 (maj7) chords and the V becomes a dominant 7th (7) chord. But blues music often defies standard music theory, and major blues progressions often swap the major 7ths for dominant 7ths. Try playing the 7th chords here as D7, G7, and A7 and hear the difference.

CHORD VARIETY

There are many more chords available than just major, minor, and 7ths, and countless guitarists use them in their playing. In the following session you will be introduced to some of these new chords, such as sus2, sus4, and slash chords, and learn how to use them to add spice to your performance. Despite their exotic names, none are very difficult to put into practice and, in time, you'll probably favor them over the standard major and minor chords. You will also be shown how to use a popular guitarist's tool: the capo. This is a fretboard clamp that effectively reduces the length of the strings and so changes the pitch of strings played unfretted—helpful when accompanying singers or creating new chords alongside another guitarist.

SUS4 CHORDS

Sus4, or suspended fourth, chords depart from the usual triad pattern of major and minor chords (*see box*) and suit all playing styles, from folk and clean pop to rock overdrive. They can be linked together over long passages, but are more often used to create a restless, open sound, which is "resolved" by following up with the major or minor chord that has the same root note (for example, Dsus4 resolving to D major). Four common sus4 chords are introduced here.

 WHAT'S THE THEORY?
SUSPENDED CHORDS

Unlike a major chord, which is made up of a root, a third, and a fifth (*see p.90*), sus4 chords have no third. This is "suspended" and replaced by a fourth. For example, an Asus4 contains an A note (the root), a D note (a fourth interval from A), and an E note (a fifth away from A). As it is does not have the third interval, it is neither major nor minor.

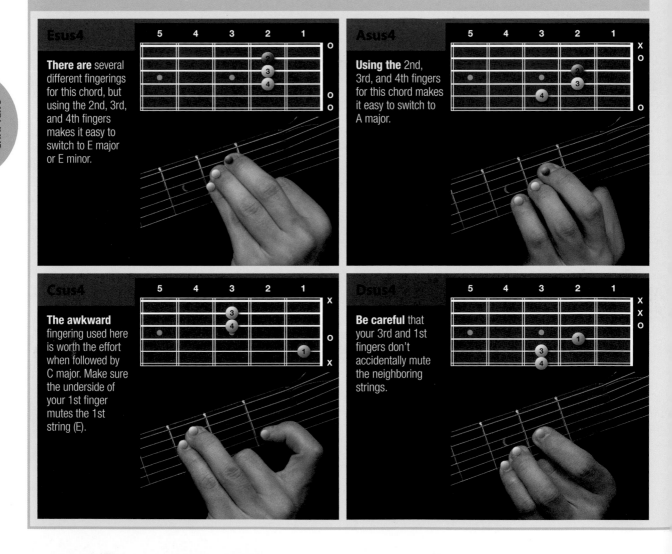

Esus4
There are several different fingerings for this chord, but using the 2nd, 3rd, and 4th fingers makes it easy to switch to E major or E minor.

Asus4
Using the 2nd, 3rd, and 4th fingers for this chord makes it easy to switch to A major.

Csus4
The awkward fingering used here is worth the effort when followed by C major. Make sure the underside of your 1st finger mutes the 1st string (E).

Dsus4
Be careful that your 3rd and 1st fingers don't accidentally mute the neighboring strings.

EXERCISE 4.1.1 – SUS4 CHORDS AND RESOLVING CHORDS

This demonstrates how sus4 chords are used to enhance the resolving majors. Notice how the fourth interval (D in Asus4, A in Esus4) resolves to the major third interval (C# in A major, G# in E major): this is classic sus4 usage.

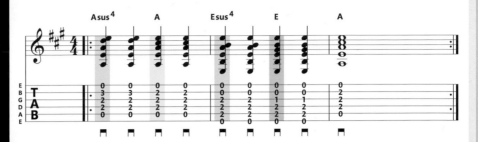

■ **Play Asus4.** Fret with your 4th, 3rd, and 2nd fingers. This fingering makes the transition to the following A chord easy.

■ **Move to A.** When moving from Asus4, be careful that your 4th finger doesn't rest against and mute the 1st string.

■ **Play Esus4.** This fingering of Esus4 is not only comfortable, but allows a simple finger change to resolve to E.

■ **Play E.** Don't lose the big six-string sound by letting the underside of your 1st finger mute neighboring strings.

EXERCISE 4.1.2 – SUS4 TRANSITIONS

Practice moving between sus4, major, and minor chords. Notice the new rhythm: the first chord in bars 1 and 3 is held for a little longer, then a shorter chord is played with an up strum.

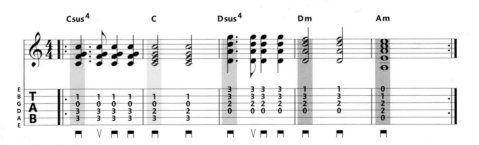

■ **Play Csus4.** Use your 4th finger to fret the fourth interval (C major's F note) to achieve the unique Csus4 sound.

■ **Move to C.** Take your 4th finger off the 3rd fret. Have your 2nd finger ready on the 2nd fret to sound C.

■ **Play Dsus4.** Use precise fingering to achieve a clear sound: this may be a squeeze for your 4th, 3rd, and 2nd fingers.

■ **Move to Dm.** Change from the 3rd fret to the 1st fret on the 1st string to play Dm—a pleasing but sad sound.

■ **Finish with Am.** Notice how the piece sounds "finished" despite A minor not having occurred earlier in the exercise.

SESSION 4·2 DVD

SUS2 CHORDS

Suspended second, or "sus2" chords are similar to sus4 chords (*see p.124*) in their floating, ambiguous quality, here created by the second (rather than fourth) interval "seeking" to be resolved by the third in a following major or minor chord. These chords don't create as much tension as sus4 chords, so can stand being played together in progressions; the exercises here compare unresolved and resolved progressions using some of the chords below. Sus2 chords can be strummed with a clean sound and echo effects, or used in riffs; The Police's *Message In A Bottle* features an iconic sus2 riff.

Esus2

Note the similarity to a power chord shape (*see pp.70–71*) but with the open strings involved, changing the sound to Esus2.

Gsus2

Make sure the 1st string isn't sounded, either by carefully avoiding it while strumming or by muting with your 3rd finger.

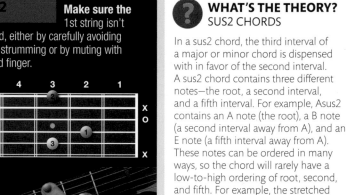

WHAT'S THE THEORY?
SUS2 CHORDS

In a sus2 chord, the third interval of a major or minor chord is dispensed with in favor of the second interval. A sus2 chord contains three different notes—the root, a second interval, and a fifth interval. For example, Asus2 contains an A note (the root), a B note (a second interval away from A), and an E note (a fifth interval away from A). These notes can be ordered in many ways, so the chord will rarely have a low-to-high ordering of root, second, and fifth. For example, the stretched *Message In A Bottle* chord shape features these three notes, but ordered root, fifth, and second in pitch.

Asus2

This is probably the easiest of all the sus2 chords to play, but make sure that your 3rd finger doesn't mute the 2nd string.

Csus2

Be careful not to mute any open strings. An alternative fingering to that shown here is: 3rd finger, 5th string; and 4th finger, 2nd string.

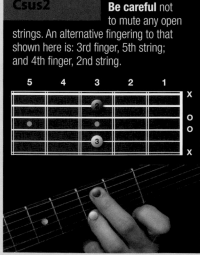

Dsus2

Another simple two-finger sus2 chord that can move easily to D or Dm. Don't accidentally mute the 1st string: it's the crucial note (E) that creates Dsus2.

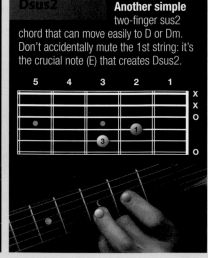

EXERCISE 4.2.1 – SUS2 CHORD PROGRESSION

This progression will demonstrate that several sus2 chords can stand together convincingly on their own. Notice the pleasing ambiguity of the sound, typical of suspended chords.

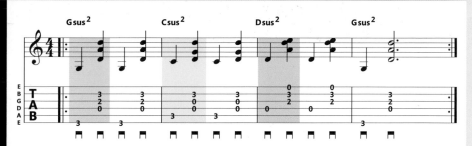

■ **Play Gsus2.** Don't catch the 5th string with your pick. Muting this string with the underside of your 2nd finger will help.

■ **Play Csus2.** Make sure you fret the highest note, D (3rd fret, 2nd string), cleanly to get the best sound from this chord.

■ **Play Dsus2.** Arch both fingers high over the 1st string to prevent muting. Press down confidently on the 2nd and 3rd strings.

PRACTICE & PROGRESS

The fingering used for Csus2 may seem odd because you previously learned C major (Csus2's parent chord) using a different fingering. This new fingering is logical because it is easier to move to and from the shapes of the Gsus2 and Dsus2 chords on either side, but you may fret Csus2 with your 3rd finger (3rd fret, 5th string) and 4th finger (3rd fret, 2nd string) if you prefer.

EXERCISE 4.2.2 – SUS2 TRANSITIONS

This busier exercise with a quicker rhythm will help build your speed and confidence in playing transitions from sus2 to major and minor chords. Aim to keep your down picking consistent for even tone and volume.

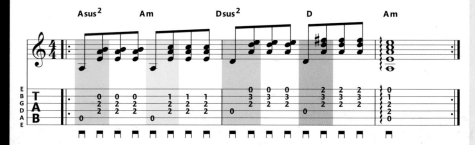

■ **Play Asus2.** Use two fingers to fret this chord for a clear and sophisticated sound. Great chords can have simple shapes.

■ **Move to Am.** Place your 1st finger on the 1st fret, 2nd string, to make Am. This resolution from Asus2 sounds melancholy.

■ **Play Dsus2.** This fingering option for Dsus2 allows an easy change to D major or Dsus4 to create a chordal riff.

■ **Move to D.** To make D major from Dsus2, simply move your 2nd finger on to the 2nd fret, 1st string, pressing down firmly.

CHAPTER 3

ADD9 CHORDS

Add9 chords add the ninth interval note to a major or minor chord, making it bigger and warmer-sounding. They can have the "floaty" effect of a sus2 chord, but as enhanced majors or minors, they're not so ambiguous. These chords are often played with a clean sound, but light overdrive can sound good too. Avoid the temptation to use these chords too often—the effect can be overly emotive. The exercises on the opposite page use the four add9 chords shown below.

 WHAT'S THE THEORY?
ADD9 CHORDS

An add9 chord adds the ninth interval to the root, third, and fifth of a major or minor chord. So an add9 chord contains four different notes: the root, the third, the fifth, and the ninth. For example, the major chord Aadd9 contains: A (the root); C♯ (a major third away from A); E (a fifth away from A), and B (a ninth away from A).

Emadd9

Make sure that your 3rd finger doesn't accidentally mute the 3rd string; Emadd9 should be a big-sounding, six-string chord, full of drama.

Gadd9

Fret the low G on the 6th string really well, while at the same time muting the 5th string with the underside of the same (3rd) finger.

Aadd9

This is a quick two-finger version of the Aadd9 chord. You will need to make a mini-barre with your 1st finger, arching it over the 1st string to play the high E on the open 1st string. If this is too difficult, don't play the 1st string at all.

Cadd9

You need three fingers for this version of Cadd9; the 1st string is left open. Use precise fingertip fretting so that the notes sound well and no strings are muted.

EXERCISE 4.3.1 – ADD9 CHORD PROGRESSION

Try this simple progression of just three add9 chords. Keep your down strums quick and precise and not staggered. Listen for the characteristic open sound of these chords.

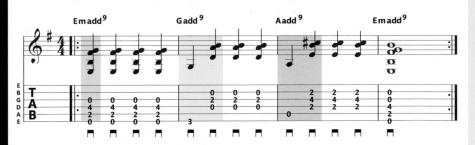

Emadd⁹   Gadd⁹   Aadd⁹   Emadd⁹

■ **Play Emadd9.** Stretch your 1st and 3rd fingers wide to play this chord, which has great moody appeal.

■ **Play Gadd9.** Sound the low G first (3rd finger) then strum down from the 4th string to play this chord.

■ **Move to Aadd9.** Practise the 1st-finger mini-barre of this chord before incorporating it into this exercise.

PRACTICE & PROGRESS

While there are countless chords to explore, much of their appeal lies in how they are articulated. Every time you learn a new chord, consider how you may like to play it: down and/or up strummed, fingerpicked, and with quick or slow rhythms. This flexibility is part of what defines a player's musical individuality.

EXERCISE 4.3.2 – ADDING TEXTURE WITH ADD9 CHORDS

Hear how a few colorful chords enhance a simple C major to G major progression. The first three are C-based, with a descending top note creating melodic movement. Gadd9 is used to finish—note the lush quality it adds.

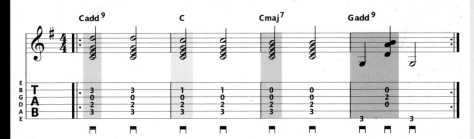

Cadd⁹   C   Cmaj⁷   Gadd⁹

■ **Play Cadd9.** Use the very tips of your fingers for the notes here; don't accidentally "lean into" the open 3rd string.

■ **Jump to C.** There's minimal movement required here from Cadd9: just place the 1st finger on the 2nd string, 1st fret, for the C.

■ **Move to Cmaj7.** This is an easy change—simply lift your 1st finger off the 2nd string to move from C major to Cmaj7.

■ **Play Gadd9.** The change to Gadd9 isn't hard, but make sure that your 2nd finger isn't straining to reach the note.

SESSION
4·4 DVD

SLASH CHORDS

A slash chord isn't one that's played aggressively—it's one that has a slash line in its name. In a slash chord, a note other than the root note assumes the bass (lowest) position. It is written with a slash line separating the chord (for example, C) from the required bass note (for example, E). The resulting

chord, written C/E, is pronounced "C slash E." Slash chords sound quite sophisticated, so limit your use of distortion in favor of clean tones that allow all the notes to be clearly heard. There are five great slash chords to learn here, explored in the exercises on the opposite page.

C/E

Make the same chord shape as C major, but include the open 6th string. This provides an E bass note for C/E: C major in first inversion (*see box, right*).

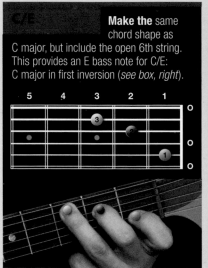

C/G

From C major, move your 3rd finger to the 3rd fret, 6th string. This is the G bass note for C/G: C major in second inversion.

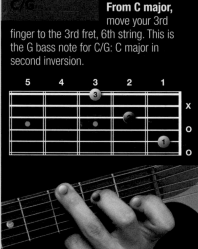

? WHAT'S THE THEORY?
TYPES OF SLASH CHORD

The slash chords here are made using the theory of "chord inversion:" the third, fifth, or seventh interval of the chord takes the bass position instead of the root. If the third interval is in the bass (e.g. C/E), it's called a "first inversion;" if the fifth (e.g. C/G) it's a "second inversion;" and if the seventh (e.g. C7/B♭) it's a "third inversion."

You can also make a slash chord by adding a bass note that is not in the chord itself (such as E/A or C/F♯). This slash naming is really useful in styles like jazz or fusion: "C/F♯" is much easier to grasp than the alternative name of "F♯7♭5♭9 (no 3rd)."

G/B

Try this fingering option—it has all the notes of the G major chord, but with B as the lowest note instead of G: this is G major in first inversion.

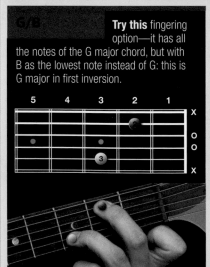

Gm/B♭

Begin with G minor and change the bass note from B to B♭; note how this inversion makes a much more melancholy sound than G/B because it is minor.

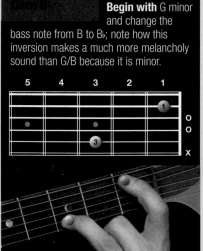

D/F♯

The D/F♯ chord is D major with a low F♯ note in the bass: D major in first inversion. This chord can also be fretted with the 2nd and 3rd fingers.

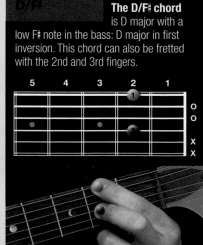

EXERCISE 4.4.1 – ATMOSPHERIC PROGRESSION WITH SLASH CHORDS

Switching between a minor chord and a first inversion chord can produce an atmospheric sound. You'll hear this clearly in this Em–C/E–Em transition.

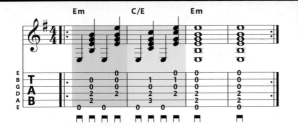

■ **Play Em.** Fret precisely to play this chord, so that the open strings are not muted.

■ **Switch to C/E.** Watch that your 3rd fingertip doesn't accidentally mute the 6th string.

EXERCISE 4.4.2 – BASS PROGRESSION

In this exercise you pick the bass note of each chord, then play its higher notes. Notice how the use of chord inversions allows for a very smooth descending bass line; this can't be achieved with straight major or minor chord shapes.

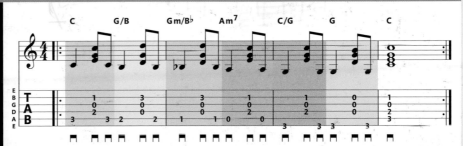

■ **Play C.** Down pick the low C then strum the upper part of the chord, omitting the 1st string.

■ **Play G/B.** Place your 3rd finger after the 2nd to form this shape. Avoid muting the 4th string.

■ **Move to Gm/B♭.** After playing G/B, reach back with your 1st finger for the 1st fret, 5th string.

■ **Play Am7.** This is a root position chord of Am7 and uses just two fingers.

■ **Change to C/G.** Add your 3rd finger at the 3rd fret, 6th string to the Am7 shape for this chord.

■ **Play G.** Fret this minimal version of the G chord—you need only one finger.

PRACTICE & PROGRESS

Once you have mastered an exercise, it's worth taking some time to explore the creative possibilities it opens up before moving on to new skills. Try these differing approaches to exercise 4.4.2.

To deepen your appreciation of the music, try repeating the neighbouring chords of C and G/B or C/G and G. Listen to what the high and low notes are doing.

Try a different rhythm: try triplet groupings ("straw-ber-ry" as on p.88) on each beat, performing each chord as bass note, then chord, then bass note again before changing to the next.

Omit the highest note of the chords. This will make the results sound warmer as there is an emphasis on lower notes.

CHAPTER 3

SESSION
4·5
DVD

ARPEGGIATING CHORDS

So far, you have looked at ways of strumming chords, but there is another widely used technique for sounding chords. It's called "arpeggiating" (from the Italian *arpeggio*, meaning "broken chord") and it involves picking the notes individually while the chord shape is fretted. You don't have to stick to picking the strings in regular order up or down: you can pick alternately or jump around. Arpeggiating extends a chord's appeal by providing melodic contours not possible with strumming. However, it does require dexterity and practice. Arpeggios can be played open, or with the strings lightly muted with your palm (*see right, and also Session 1.9*) to vary the tonal texture. These three exercises feature arpeggio picking with some familiar chord shapes.

OPEN AND MUTED ARPEGGIOS

Open arpeggio picking
Rest your 4th finger lightly on the guitar body as a pivot point and let your hand "float" above the strings to avoid muting them.

Muted arpeggio picking
Rest your palm edge lightly at the point where the strings leave the bridge, to mute the arpeggio for a dampened, more percussive effect.

CHAPTER 3

EXERCISE 4.5.1 – ARPEGGIO WITH ALTERNATE PICKING

Use this exercise to get comfortable with strict alternate picking (*see pp.66–67*). Down pick the first note, up pick the second, and so on. Alternate picking provides good note definition and consistent timing for arpeggios.

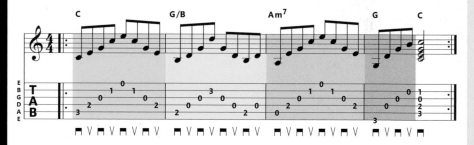

■ **Fret C.** Hold the C chord down and then alternate between picking down and up as you move across the strings.

■ **Move to G/B.** Place your 2nd finger first: this is the first note picked. Your 3rd finger can "catch up" as you move to higher strings.

■ **Fret Am7.** Pick the open 5th string first so you have enough time to get your 2nd, then 1st, finger in place for what follows.

■ **Fret G.** Down pick the 6th string first, then omit the 5th string and up pick the 4th. This is known as "string skipping."

EXERCISE 4.5.2 – PALM-MUTED ARPEGGIOS

Practise your palm muted down picking with this exercise. Although palm muted alternate picking works well (and is the better option for quick arpeggiating), using down strokes only can provide a more consistent tone.

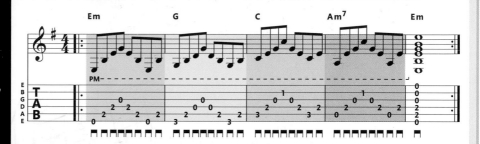

■ **Fret Em.** Using only the 3rd, 4th, 5th, and 6th strings, focus on evenly timed and tight-sounding down picking.

■ **Fret G.** From Em, move your 3rd finger to the 3rd fret to make G. Move quickly: the G note is the first to be picked for the G chord.

■ **Fret C.** Concentrate on getting your 3rd and 2nd fingers down first, as these strings are picked before the 1st finger's C note.

■ **Fret Am7.** Lift your 3rd finger from the fretboard: that's all you need to do to change from C major to Am7.

EXERCISE 4.5.3 – MORE ADVANCED ARPEGGIATING

Increase your proficiency with this exercise, which involves arpeggiating nonadjacent strings. Tackle each bar separately at first, slowly honing your alternate picking until all the notes sound crisp and free from timing hesitations.

■ **Fret D.** Fret the whole chord and then practice string skipping (jumping over one or more strings) with alternate picking.

■ **Fret Cadd9.** Notice how this chord has a couple of skips within a basic up-and-down arpeggio. Keep your timing consistent.

■ **Fret G5.** Note the very big string skip here (6th to 2nd string); practice very slowly and carefully until it feels comfortable.

PRACTICE & PROGRESS

Fast arpeggiating sounds great, but at this stage, don't be tempted to sacrifice accuracy and clarity for speed. Trying to get too quick too soon will increase your body tension and make mistakes more likely. Pick slowly, observe your technique, relax your body, and get it consistently right. Only then think about increasing your speed.

CHAPTER 3

SESSION
4·6 CHORD NOODLING
DVD

Noodling, or playing around with chord shapes without any particular goal in mind, can be really fruitful. Choose a chord and play around with it; try taking a finger off one fret or moving it onto another one. Like the sound? Then make a mental note. If not, just move on.

Below are three chords which result from making a full E major chord shape, then adding or shifting just one finger. The exercise opposite puts them together but also tries out some different fingering options—remember, there are many ways to fret one chord (see p.94). The first two bars feature small, three-string versions of the chords, the latter two bars bigger, four-string versions. There's variety in the execution, too; the early small chords require alternate picked arpeggiating, the later chords need some palm muted down picking. There's a lot going on here, considering that it all evolved from a humble E major. Next time you're noodling, see how you can adapt your favorite chords.

WHAT'S THE THEORY?
ALTERED TUNINGS

Changing one finger in a familiar chord shape is just one way to increase your musical vocabulary. Another is to alter the tuning of one string. Countless guitarists favor the "drop D" option: tuning the sixth string down a tone from E to D. With drop D, power chord shapes that used to take three fingers now take one; F5, for example, is now played by fretting across the three lowest strings (3rd fret) with your first finger. Try D major—adding the low D makes for a bigger sound. If you listen to rock or metal, you'll soon notice that drop D is a popular tuning choice for guitarists in these genres.

Another option is to drop the tuning of the first string from E to D. Chords like C, Am, and E now sound more intriguing and ripe for songwriting—just ask Mike Rutherford (Genesis). Or do as Chris Martin (Coldplay) has in the past and detune more, dropping the first string from E to C♯. An E major shape played with this tuning produces a very fresh-sounding E chord.

E6   **Fret the** E major shape, then place your spare 4th finger at the 2nd fret, 2nd string. It's this finger that provides the sixth note (C♯).

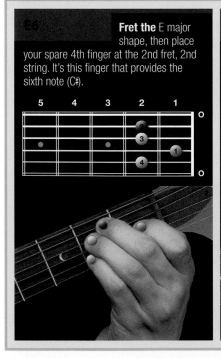

Eadd♭6   **Make this** moody chord from E6, by moving one fret lower on the 5th string to the low C, which is the minor sixth (♭6) note of the chord.

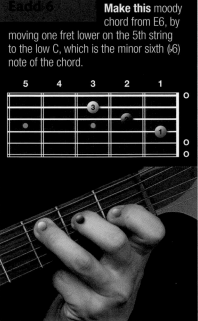

E5add11   **Make this** exotic chord by taking your 1st finger off an E major chord and putting the 4th finger at the 3rd fret, 3rd string instead.

CHAPTER 3

EXERCISE 4.6.1 – E CHORD VARIATIONS

This exercise has a constant eighth-note rhythm, allowing you to focus on variations of the E chord. You will "splinter" chord shapes—playing three-string versions in the first two bars, then bigger four-string versions—using both arpeggios and palm-muting.

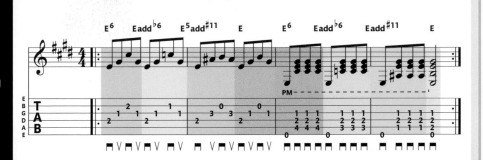

■ **Play E6** (version 1). This three-string chord is arpeggiated and requires accurate fretting from the 1st, 2nd, and 3rd fingers. Do not play any open strings.

■ **Move to Eadd♭6** (version 1). To change from E6, take your 3rd finger off the fretboard then use your 1st finger to fret across the 3rd and 2nd strings at the 1st fret.

■ **Jump to E5add♯11.** Remove your 1st finger and place your 3rd finger at the 3rd fret, 3rd string. Make sure this finger doesn't mute the open 2nd string.

■ **Change to E** (version 1). Take your 3rd finger off and place your 1st finger at the 1st fret, 3rd string. This is a small E major chord that does not use many of the strings.

■ **Play E6** (version 2). Use palm muting from this point in the exercise. You may find the 4th finger stretch awkward at first in this shape.

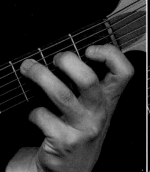

■ **Move to Eadd♭6** (version 2). This four-string version of Eadd♭6 is played with palm muting. Down pick the low C note on the 5th string, before you strum the remainder of the chord.

■ **Play Eadd♯11.** Although palm-muted picking can disguise poor fretting, aim to get an effective 1st finger mini-barre across the 1st fret so the 5th and 3rd strings sound clearly.

■ **Finish on E** (version 2). Down strum the lowest four strings to finish the piece with an E chord—which was the starting point for your exploration of chord noodling.

CHAPTER 3

4.1 4.2 4.3 4.4 4.5 **4.6** 4.7 4.8 4.9

SESSION
4•7
DVD

TWO-FINGER CHORDS

Some chords have simple names but are awkward to play, and vice versa. It's the "tough to name, easy to play" type of chords that are briefly considered here. In particular, we'll look at four- and five-string shapes that are formed using only two fingers, with at least two strings left open. Making chords in this way may seem like a simple option, but don't underestimate the ability of open strings to transform otherwise mundane chord shapes into extraordinary sounds. Check out players like Andy Summers (*see opposite*), Bryan Adams, Paul Simon, and Johnny Marr for open-string chord inspiration.

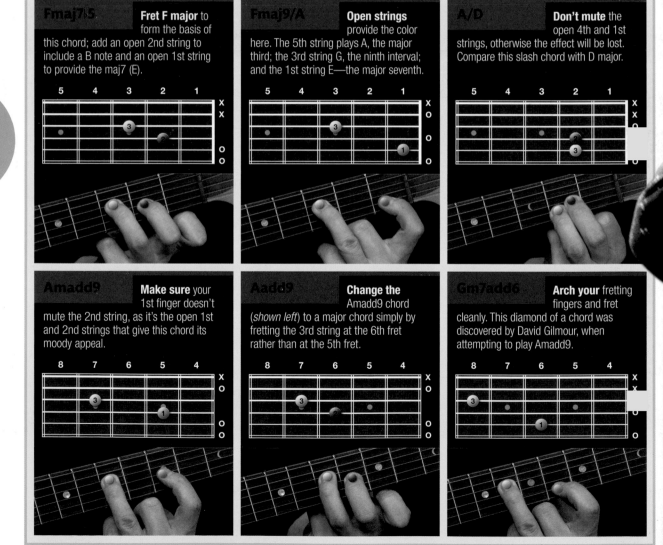

Fmaj7♭5 — **Fret F major** to form the basis of this chord; add an open 2nd string to include a B note and an open 1st string to provide the maj7 (E).

Fmaj9/A — **Open strings** provide the color here. The 5th string plays A, the major third; the 3rd string G, the ninth interval; and the 1st string E—the major seventh.

A/D — **Don't mute** the open 4th and 1st strings, otherwise the effect will be lost. Compare this slash chord with D major.

Amadd9 — **Make sure** your 1st finger doesn't mute the 2nd string, as it's the open 1st and 2nd strings that give this chord its moody appeal.

Aadd9 — **Change the** Amadd9 chord (*shown left*) to a major chord simply by fretting the 3rd string at the 6th fret rather than at the 5th fret.

Gm7add6 — **Arch your** fretting fingers and fret cleanly. This diamond of a chord was discovered by David Gilmour, when attempting to play Amadd9.

CHAPTER 3

GETTING THE SOUND

Andy Summers – pop-rock

Only a handful of pop trios have achieved iconic status. One of these is without a doubt The Police, a band that found worldwide fame during the 1970s and 80s. Fronted by Sting on vocals and bass, many of their songs feature inventive guitar-playing courtesy of Andy Summers. Although he used other guitars (and guitar synthesizers), it was his clean- to driven-toned Telecaster that fueled the band's reggae-rock-tinged hits. With rarely a solo taken, Andy Summers's pop-rock legacy was primarily built on arpeggiated riffs, clipped reggae rhythms, and chords such as sus2 and add9.

ESSENTIAL TRACKS	SIMILAR ARTISTS
Roxanne	The Edge (U2)
Walking On The Moon	Bruce Watson (Big Country)
Message In A Bottle	Charlie Burchill (Simple Minds)
Can't Stand Losing You	Eric Johnson
Don't Stand So Close To Me	Nick McCabe (The Verve)
Every Breath You Take	

Much of Andy Summers's playing in The Police was precise and minimalist without overuse of distortion. This approach meant his riffs and chords created the songs' main hooks, filling in the gaps in Sting's bass line, setting the scene before the vocals entered.

USING A CAPO

Part of the guitar's popularity comes from its great versatility. It is easy to enhance or extend playing options with various tools and gadgets, and one of the best and least expensive of these is the capo. This is essentially a mechanical finger which is attached to the fretboard, changing the pitch of open strings—just like a semi-permanent barre (see pp.102–103). The capo comes into its own when you accompany a singer using CAGED chord shapes; if the chords are too low for the singer's voice, just move the capo up the fretboard until the vocalist is comfortable. The capo can also be used to make the guitar sound different; move it up to the higher frets for mandolin-like sounds. Experiment with this below, then try the "two-guitar trick" on the opposite page—this is a great way to create a big sound with just two guitars and a capo.

FIXING A CAPO

Capo models range from cheap elasticated to those with a metal frame and, usually, a hinged side, as shown here. Place the capo's rubber strip at the fret of your choice, then swing the hinged arm around the back of the neck. Once positioned, lock it in place with its latch and you're ready to play.

EXERCISE 4.8.1 – THE MANDOLIN SOUND

Get a mandolin-like sound with a capo at the 7th fret. The bracketed chord names below the notation (right) refer to parent CAGED shapes; fret numbers in the tab take the 7th fret as the new nut and call it fret 0; the 8th fret is now fret 1, and so on.

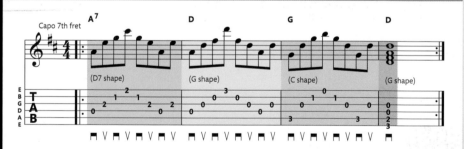

Capo 7th fret

A⁷   D   G   D

(D7 shape)   (G shape)   (C shape)   (G shape)

■ **Play A7.** With the capo fixed at the 7th fret, make the basic D7 shape to get A7. Finger accurately —the frets are tightly packed here.

■ **Play D.** The 7th fret capo converts the G major chord shape into D major. The chord requires just one finger.

■ **Play G.** Spot the CAGED shape —the C major shape is converted to G with the 7th fret capo. Watch out for poorly fretted notes.

■ **Move to D.** Play this fuller version of D major to finish—the 7th fret capo changes the G major shape to D major.

EXERCISE 4.8.2 – TWO GUITARS, ONE CAPO

GUITAR 1: NO CAPO

Get together with a guitar buddy, or record yourself playing for this exercise, because it has two parts played simultaneously. Each guitar plays the same chords: the first (right) using standard fretting; the second (below) using a capo and CAGED shapes.

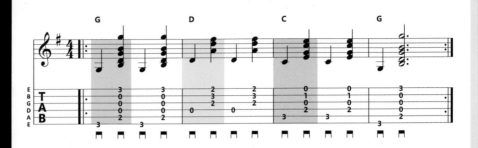

■ **Play the G chord.** Make sure each string rings out clearly: the first guitar's part needs to sound bold.

■ **Play the D chord.** Don't strum the 1st and 2nd strings by accident: the result will be an undesirable muddy sound.

■ **Move to C.** There's some finger-swapping when moving from D to C; practice slowly before increasing your speed.

PRACTICE AND PROGRESS

Consider your role whenever you play with another guitarist. Here, you're performing the chord progression's foundation using big, open-string chord shapes, so you may wish to play with an enhanced thick tone. You can do this on an electric guitar by selecting the neck pickup.

GUITAR 2: CAPO AT 5TH FRET

Guitar 2 plays higher up the fretboard with a capo fitted at the 5th fret. It duplicates the chords played by guitar 1, making CAGED shapes to reflect the new nut position. The two guitars together should produce a really full, satisfying sound.

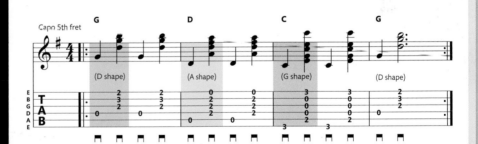

■ **Play G.** Make the chord by forming the D major shape with the capo at the 5th fret. Make sure all the notes sound clearly.

■ **Play D.** Use the A major shape with the capo at the 5th fret. Arch your 4th finger away from the 1st string so as not to mute it.

■ **Play C.** Use the G major shape to form this C major chord with the capo at the 5th fret. Notice the rich sound of this chord.

PRACTICE AND PROGRESS

Use your CAGED knowledge to position the capo. For example, a C chord can be played using the open A shape with the capo at the 3rd fret; open G shape (capo at the 5th fret); open E shape (capo at the 8th fret); and open D shape (capo at the 10th fret).

CHAPTER 3

Using a capo can transform a guitar's sound, giving it a quite different, fresher tone. It can also change a song's key, making the vocal melody possible. While many guitarists use capos, very few use them exclusively. Other than Albert Collins, the following four guitarists have used them for famous songs, but not necessarily throughout their careers.

❶ ALBERT COLLINS

Texan blues legend Albert Collins had a fiery guitar soloing style. His bright tone came from his snappy finger plucks, energized vibrato, and a capo at high fretboard positions.

ESSENTIAL TRACKS *Frosty* ◆ *The Freeze* ◆ *Delfrost* ◆ *Don't Lose Your Cool* ◆ *Ice Pickin'*

SIMILAR ARTISTS Guitar Slim ◆ Lightnin' Hopkins ◆ T-Bone Walker ◆ Clarence "Gatemouth" Brown

❷ GLENN FREY

Most famous for cofounding The Eagles with drummer Don Henley, Frey has been a successful solo artist since the 1980s. He used a 7th fret capo for the chord picking in *Hotel California*.

ESSENTIAL TRACKS *Desperado* ◆ *Hotel California* ◆ *Tequila Sunrise* ◆ *The Heat Is On* ◆ *Smuggler's Blues*

SIMILAR ARTISTS Joe Walsh ◆ Bryan Adams ◆ Neil Young ◆ Stephen Stills ◆ Steve Miller

❸ PAUL SIMON

Primarily an acoustic fingerpicker, Simon's style features busy rhythms and evocative chords. He used a 7th fret capo for Simon and Garfunkel's version of *Scarborough Fair*.

ESSENTIAL TRACKS *Sounds Of Silence* ◆ *Homeward Bound* ◆ *For Emily* ◆ *Scarborough Fair* ◆ *The Boxer*

SIMILAR ARTISTS Bob Dylan ◆ James Taylor ◆ Glenn Campbell ◆ John Denver ◆ Roy Harper

❹ GEORGE HARRISON

Harrison's playing encompasses many notable traits from chord strumming to slide guitar solos, via sitar and ukelele playing. He wrote *Here Comes The Sun* with a capo at the 7th fret.

ESSENTIAL TRACKS *Here Comes The Sun* ◆ *While My Guitar Gently Weeps* ◆ *Something* ◆ *My Sweet Lord*

SIMILAR ARTISTS John Lennon ◆ Donovan ◆ Eric Clapton ◆ Jeff Lynne ◆ Tom Petty

SESSION
4·9
DVD

MILESTONE PIECE

This piece is designed to develop your chord versatility, and packs in much of the variation explored in this session: sus, add9, and slash chords; broken strumming and arpeggiating; chords that are initiated simply by changing one finger within a chord shape; and chords that use only two fingers. Notice that towards the end, palm muted alternate picking is used. Don't rush to learn the piece: take your time, and tackle it bar by bar to achieve the best results.

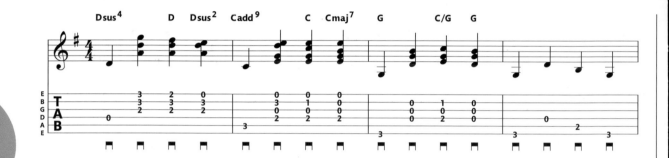

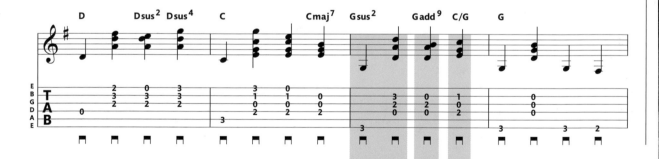

Use a new fingering for the Gsus2 chord here; this works more fluently with the chords played before and after.

Change to Gadd9 from Gsus2 by simply lifting your 4th finger from the fretboard. Keep the low G sustained.

Change to C/G by moving your 2nd finger to the 4th string, and your 1st finger to the 2nd string.

CHAPTER 3

Down pick the 4th string to sound the E note within the Em arpeggio. This is played using alternate picking.

An Esus4 chord occurs briefly in this passage as the 4th finger is placed quickly on, then off, the 3rd string at the 2nd fret.

PRO TIP
SOUND CHOICES

Guitar and tone choices can change the mood of a piece. If you have an acoustic and an electric guitar, compare the sound of this exercise when played on both. On an electric guitar, try selecting the bridge pickup for a bright sound, then the neck pickup for a warmer tone.

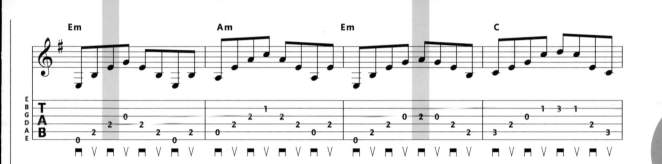

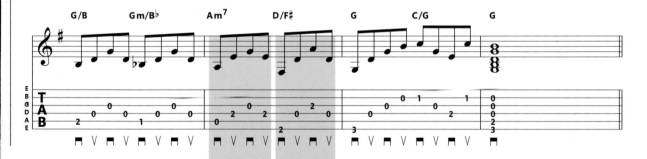

CHAPTER 3

Play this small fragment of Am7 in bar 14. Only a few strings are played, so you don't need to form the full shape.

Play this rich-sounding D/F# chord after Am7; avoid muting the 4th string with your 1st finger.

NEW SCALES AND BENDS

A scale is a collection of different notes (usually five, six, or seven) that are drawn on to make music. In this session you will learn about the three main scales used in rock, blues, and pop music: the five-note minor pentatonic, the five-note major pentatonic, and the six-note blues scale. After you've looked at these scales and how to play them at any point on the fretboard, you'll be well prepared to create your own riffs and lead solos. Later, you'll learn a new technique to embellish those solos and give them voice: string bending. This is a fundamental technique for playing expressively on the electric guitar.

SESSION 5·1

BLUES BASICS

Much of today's guitar playing, from rhythmic chords to single-note soloing, is based on styles derived from blues music. From its origins in Afro-American culture, the blues form emerged following recordings from the 1920s by artists such as Blind Lemon Jefferson and Charley Patton. In the 1930s and 40s, blues artists such as T-Bone Walker and Muddy Waters began using electric guitars and cultivated the sound of Chicago Blues. The blues style has a number of distinctive components: it makes extensive use of pentatonic scales (*see below*), which are great for melodic soloing, and is often embellished with slides and string bends. "Bluesy"-sounding 7th chords feature in preference to regular major or minor chords, and pieces often use just three chords, put together in repeating 12-bar structures for singing or guitar soloing over. The timing used is either 4/4 (a straight rhythmic feel, such as that featured in Cream's *Crossroads*) or 12/8 (a swing triplet-based rhythmic feel that can be heard on The Allman Brothers' version of *Stormy Monday*). These typical blues components are introduced on these pages.

INTRODUCING PENTATONIC SCALES

The blues makes extensive use of five-note pentatonic scales and the six-note blues scale. These scales have an intrinsic "bluesy" sound and offer the player many melodic possibilities. The diagram below allows you to compare the notes in these scales in the key of A (A minor pentatonic, A blues scale, and A major pentatonic) with the two seven-note scales you already know (A natural minor and A major). The diagram shows how these scales appear when played on the 5th (A) string.

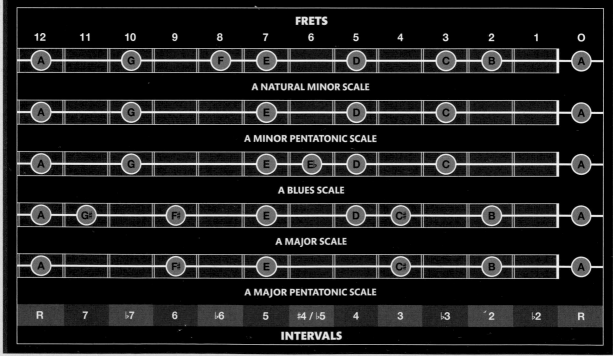

EXERCISE 5.1.1 – BLUES TIME SIGNATURES

BLUES RIFF IN 4/4

This **blues riff** in the key of A uses the common 4/4 time signature. The bluesy sound is augmented by the ♭7 note (G) in bar 1 and the ♭3 to 3 (C to C♯) played as a hammer-on in bar 2.

BLUES RIFF IN 12/8

This is the **same riff** as above, played not with a straight 4/4 feel but with a triplet (1-2-3, 1-2-3) swing rhythm. It is important to be able to play straight and with swing when playing the blues.

■ **Fret the A5 chord.** Use your 1st finger on the 2nd fret, 4th string. Down strum this together with the open 5th string.

■ **Sound F♯ and A.** Use your 3rd finger at the 4th fret, 4th string for F♯ and the open 5th string for A.

■ **Sound G and A.** Use your 4th finger to fret the higher G (5th fret, 4th string). Down strum this with the open 5th string (A).

■ **Hammer-on to C♯.** Pick the C note (3rd fret, 5th string) then hammer-on to C♯ (4th fret) to end bar 2.

 WHAT'S THE THEORY?
12-BAR BLUES STRUCTURE

Much blues music consists of just three chords in a 12-bar structure. The three chords are I, IV, and V (*see pp.48–49*) and they may be drawn from either the natural minor or the major scale. A blues in A minor would involve the chords of Am, Dm, and Em; a blues in A major would feature A, D, and E. To add color, the chords are often turned into 7th chords, so a minor progression would feature Am7, Dm7, and Em7. For a major blues, the 7ths don't adhere to major scale harmonization (Amaj7, Dmaj7, and E7) but use dominant 7th chord types instead—A7, D7, and E7. These 7th chords sound typically bluesy when put together.

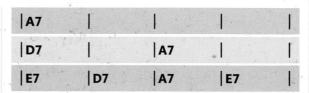

The diagram above shows a 12-bar blues in A major using 7th chords. The last four bars (or sometimes the last two bars) are known as the "turnaround," preparing you to return to bar 1. A popular variation is the "quick change"—instead of playing A7 for four bars at the start, play D7 in bar 2 then revert back to A7 in bar 3.

CHAPTER 3

5.1 5.2 5.3 5.4 5.5 5.6 5.7

SESSION 5·2 DVD
MINOR PENTATONIC SCALE

The minor pentatonic scale is one of the most popular scales in rock, blues, and jazz, and it's essential for soloing. Here you'll concentrate on learning the A minor pentatonic scale, which can be played along the fretboard using the five shapes of the CAGED system. Shown below are the five shapes of the

A minor pentatonic scale and the related Am chord shape found at the same fretboard position (A notes in white). Each of these scales uses the same five notes (A, C, D, E, and G) but is built on a different low note each time. Practise them often so you can use them instinctively when improvising.

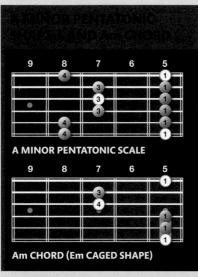

A MINOR PENTATONIC SHAPE 1 AND Am CHORD

A MINOR PENTATONIC SCALE

Am CHORD (Em CAGED SHAPE)

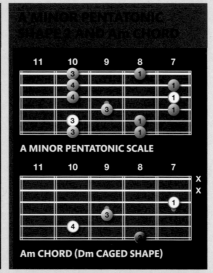

A MINOR PENTATONIC SHAPE 2 AND Am CHORD

A MINOR PENTATONIC SCALE

Am CHORD (Dm CAGED SHAPE)

WHAT'S THE THEORY?
PENTATONIC PATTERNS

As its name suggests, the minor pentatonic scale contains just five different notes: root, minor third, fourth, fifth, and minor seventh. In the examples shown here, the root note of A is highlighted in white. Compared to the seven-note major and minor scales, the five-note pentatonic scale is relatively easy to learn; even more so because you always play only two notes on each string in a repeating pattern. Once you have learned the scale patterns for the A minor shape, you can transfer, or transpose, these to all keys (*see pp.216–17*), so you can play lead solos in all keys, anywhere on the fretboard.

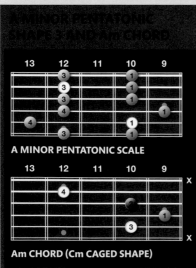

A MINOR PENTATONIC SHAPE 3 AND Am CHORD

A MINOR PENTATONIC SCALE

Am CHORD (Cm CAGED SHAPE)

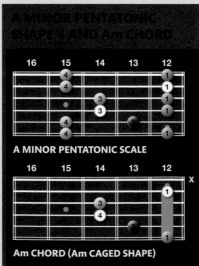

A MINOR PENTATONIC SHAPE 4 AND Am CHORD

A MINOR PENTATONIC SCALE

Am CHORD (Am CAGED SHAPE)

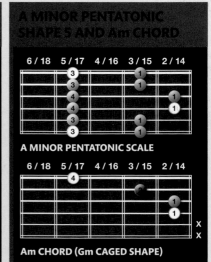

A MINOR PENTATONIC SHAPE 5 AND Am CHORD

A MINOR PENTATONIC SCALE

Am CHORD (Gm CAGED SHAPE)

CHAPTER 3

EXERCISE 5.2.1 – UP AND DOWN THE A MINOR PENTATONIC SCALE

This exercise will help you form a bond between the chord and the scale. Play the Am chord (using the Em CAGED shape, shown opposite) then play the A minor pentatonic scale, shape 1.

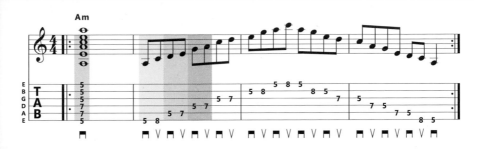

Play the Am chord.
Strum the full six-string Am chord using the Em shape from the CAGED system, then begin the scale.

Play the first two notes on the 6th string. Use a down pick for A (5th fret) then an up pick for C (8th fret).

Play the D and E notes on the 5th string. Use a down pick for D (5th fret) then an up pick for E (7th fret).

Play the G and A notes on the 4th string. Use a down pick for G (5th fret) then an up pick for A (7th fret).

PRACTICE & PROGRESS

Practice the chord and scale pairings slowly. Once you have mastered shape 1, move on to the other four shapes. Try to master them all: don't get "stuck" playing just one or two shapes, as this will ultimately limit versatility.

EXERCISE 5.2.2 – A MINOR PENTATONIC SCALE: A-TO-A OCTAVE SEGMENTS

Each shape of the A minor pentatonic scale (*opposite*) extends over more than one octave, but many guitarists use notes from within just one octave of the scale to concentrate on melodic riffs or soloing. In this exercise, split the shape 1 to two one-octave segments (from a low A to a higher A). Later, try applying this approach to the other minor pentatonic shapes. Like shape 1, shape 5 has two A-to-A octave segments. Shapes 2, 3, and 4 only have one, so play octaves from other notes instead (eg A minor pentatonic shape 4 has two E-to-E octaves).

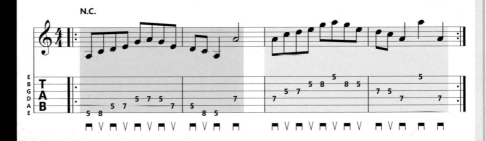

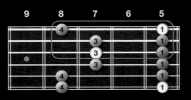

Play the lower octave segment.
The delineated area shows the notes of the A minor pentatonic scale, shape 1, played in the lower A-to-A octave segment.

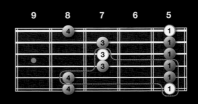

Play the upper octave segment.
The delineated area shows the notes of the A minor pentatonic scale, shape 1, played in the higher A-to-A octave segment.

CHAPTER 3

Now you have the five A minor pentatonic shapes at your fingertips, put them into practice in four exercises. In each one, A minor pentatonic shape 1 is used with various note combinations and picking options. Once fluent, duplicate the same notes with different pentatonic scale shapes.

EXERCISE 5.2.3 – DOUBLE PICKING WITHIN ONE OCTAVE OF A MINOR PENTATONIC

Double picking notes within one octave is a great approach for fast, single-note sequences, and it is favored by numerous guitarists, such as John Frusciante and Slash. Try this exercise with A minor pentatonic shape 1 first, then with shapes 2 and 4.

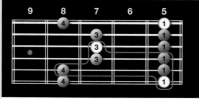

Play the exercise using A minor pentatonic, shape 1 (shown in the tab). The outlined area corresponds to the one-octave segment.

Repeat the exercise using A minor pentatonic, shape 2. Play notes from the one-octave segment outlined above.

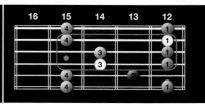

Use A minor pentatonic, shape 4 to perform the exercise again, playing notes from the one-octave segment outlined above.

EXERCISE 5.2.4 – PLAYING TRIPLETS WITHIN ONE OCTAVE OF A MINOR PENTATONIC

Triplet rhythm patterns (*see p.88*) in the minor pentatonic have featured in the lead playing of rock and metal guitarists such as Jimmy Page and Kirk Hammett. For this rhythmic exercise, use the triplet count of three: "straw-ber-ry."

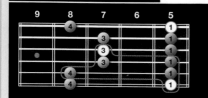

Play the exercise using A minor pentatonic, shape 1 (shown in the tab). Use notes from the one-octave segment outlined above.

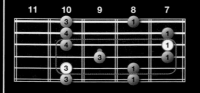

Repeat the exercise using A minor pentatonic, shape 2. Play notes from the one-octave segment outlined above.

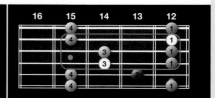

Use A minor pentatonic, shape 4 to perform the exercise again, playing notes from the one-octave segment outlined above.

EXERCISE 5.2.5 – "80s ROCK" PATTERN WITHIN ONE OCTAVE OF A MINOR PENTATONIC

This exercise features a classic pentatonic pattern before going up and down the scale to finish. Practice with both picking directions shown under the tab. Try accenting the first of every four notes with a louder pick-stroke.

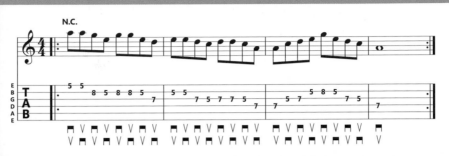

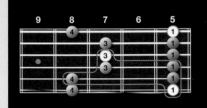

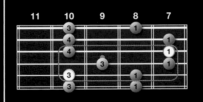

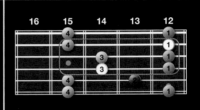

Play the exercise using A minor pentatonic, shape 1 (this is used in the tab). Use only the notes shown in the one-octave segment outlined above.

Repeat the exercise using A minor pentatonic, shape 2; the alternative scale shape opens up the fretboard. Use notes from the one-octave segment outlined above.

Use A minor pentatonic, shape 4 to perform the exercise again; the alternative scale shape opens up the fretboard. Use notes within the one-octave segment outlined above.

EXERCISE 5.2.6 – DESCENDING GROUPS OF SIX: FULL A MINOR PENTATONIC SHAPE

Going straight up or down a scale is fine, but it's good to break it up to create interest, as shown in this exercise. Once you've mastered two notes per beat, try playing it with three, four, and six notes per beat.

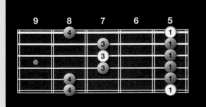

Play the exercise using A minor pentatonic, shape 1 (the tab uses this shape). Notice that the music finishes on an A-to-A octave jump, to emphasize the root note.

Repeat the exercise using A minor pentatonic, shape 4, as shown here. For your final note, opt for the A note at the 14th fret, 3rd string.

Use A minor pentatonic, shape 5 to play the piece again. To finish, opt for the A note at either the 14th fret, 3rd string or (if playing this shape lower) at the 2nd fret, 3rd string.

CHAPTER 3

SESSION 5•3 DVD MAJOR PENTATONIC SCALE

The major pentatonic is another great scale to use when improvising solos over chords. It has a brighter, more country-infused flavor than the bluesy minor pentatonic and is ideal over major chords. Like the minor pentatonic, it is a five-note scale, but made up of the root note, second, major third, fifth, and sixth.

When applied to the A major pentatonic (which you'll focus on in this lesson), the notes are A, B, C#, E, and F#. Shown below are the five A major pentatonic shapes alongside their parent A major chord shapes (A notes in white), derived from the CAGED system. Practice these scales often to memorize their patterns.

A MAJOR PENTATONIC SHAPE 1 AND A CHORD

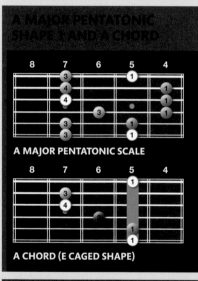

A MAJOR PENTATONIC SCALE

A CHORD (E CAGED SHAPE)

A MAJOR PENTATONIC SHAPE 2 AND A CHORD

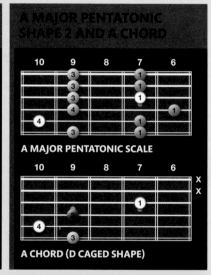

A MAJOR PENTATONIC SCALE

A CHORD (D CAGED SHAPE)

? WHAT'S THE THEORY?
SCALE COMPARISONS

The major and minor pentatonic scales both use five notes and share the same root and fifth notes (in A, the A and E notes). In the minor pentatonic there is a minor third and minor seventh (in A, the C and G notes); in the major pentatonic there is a major third and a major sixth (in A, the C# and F# notes). Interestingly, both pentatonics feature the same five shapes but in a different order. For example, A major pentatonic's shape 1 (5th fret position) is A minor pentatonic's shape 2 (8th fret position). As you progress, observe how these shapes change their function depending on the musical minor/major context.

A MAJOR PENTATONIC SHAPE 3 AND A CHORD

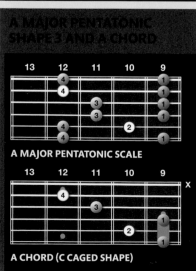

A MAJOR PENTATONIC SCALE

A CHORD (C CAGED SHAPE)

A MAJOR PENTATONIC SHAPE 4 AND A CHORD

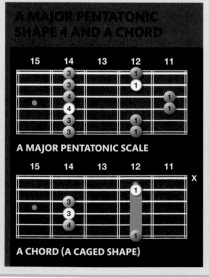

A MAJOR PENTATONIC SCALE

A CHORD (A CAGED SHAPE)

A MAJOR PENTATONIC SHAPE 5 AND A CHORD

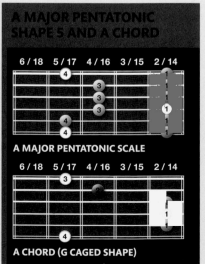

A MAJOR PENTATONIC SCALE

A CHORD (G CAGED SHAPE)

EXERCISE 5.3.1 – UP AND DOWN A MAJOR PENTATONIC

This exercise will help to cement the bond between the A chord and the scale. Practice carefully and then take the same approach with the remaining four scale shapes and chords.

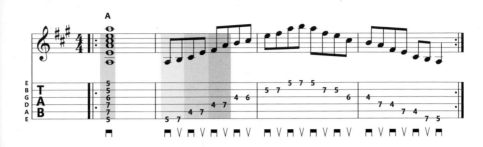

■ **Play the A chord.**
Strum the full six-string A chord using the E shape from the CAGED system, then begin the scale.

■ **Play A and B** on the 6th string. Use a down-pick for the A (5th fret) then an up-pick for the B (7th fret).

■ **Play C♯ and E** on the 5th string. Use a down-pick for the C♯ (4th fret) then an up-pick for the E (7th fret).

■ **Play F♯ and A** on the 4th string. Use a down-pick for the F♯ (4th fret) then an up-pick for the A (7th fret).

PRACTICE & PROGRESS

Don't try to learn all five shapes in one practice session. Play one shape slowly and repeatedly on each of five nights to develop precision. Afterward, try it a little quicker to focus instead on fluency.

CHAPTER 3

EXERCISE 5.3.2 – A MAJOR PENTATONIC: A-TO-A OCTAVE SEGMENTS

Each shape of the A major scale (*opposite*) extends over more than one octave, but many guitarists use notes from within just one octave. In this exercise, you'll split the shape 1 scale into two one-octave segments (from low A to a higher A note). Later, try applying this octave approach to the other major pentatonic shapes. Like shape 1, shape 5 has two A-to-A octave segments. Shapes 2, 3, and 4 only have one, so play octaves from other notes instead (for instance, A major pentatonic shape 4 contains two C♯-to-C♯ octaves).

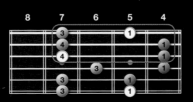 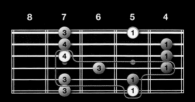

■ **Play the lower octave segment.**
The delineated area shows the notes of the A major pentatonic scale, shape 1, played in the lower A-to-A octave segment.

■ **Play the upper octave segment.**
The delineated area shows the notes of the A major pentatonic scale, shape 1, played in the higher A-to-A octave segment.

Although major pentatonic scales aren't quite as popular in rock and blues soloing as the minor pentatonic, they will boost your ability to improvise.

The four exercises here use A major pentatonic, first in shape 1, then in two other shapes, to play the same notes in other areas of the fretboard.

EXERCISE 5.3.3 – DOUBLE PICKING WITHIN ONE OCTAVE OF A MAJOR PENTATONIC

Double picking notes within one octave of the major pentatonic scale is a technique used by many country players. Try this exercise with shape 1, using the two picking options shown below the tab, and then with shapes 2 and 4.

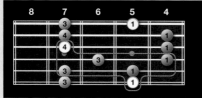

Play the exercise using A major pentatonic, shape 1 (used in the tab). Play notes from the one-octave segment outlined.

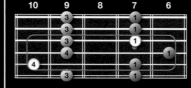

Repeat the exercise using A major pentatonic, shape 2. Play notes from the one-octave segment outlined above.

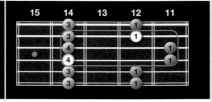

Use A major pentatonic, shape 4 to perform the exercise again. Use notes from the one-octave segment outlined above.

EXERCISE 5.3.4 – PLAYING TRIPLETS WITHIN ONE OCTAVE OF A MAJOR PENTATONIC

Experiment with triplet major pentatonic patterns in this exercise. These common rhythmic variations can be heard in the music of Bob Marley and Stevie Wonder. Play this first with alternate picking, then try a few hammer-ons and pull-offs.

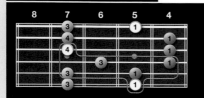

Play the exercise using A major pentatonic, shape 1 (used in the tab). Use notes from the one-octave segment outlined.

Repeat the exercise using A major pentatonic, shape 2. Play notes from the one-octave segment outlined above.

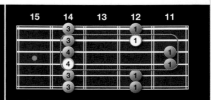

Use A major pentatonic, shape 4 to perform the exercise again. Use notes from the one-octave segment outlined above.

GREAT PENTATONIC PLAYERS

Almost every smouldering blues song or raucous rock performance features a lead guitar solo that relies on pentatonic scales. Iconic tracks such as *Smoke On The Water*, *Stairway To Heaven*, and *Sunshine Of Your Love* are just the tip of a giant musical iceberg. Here are four guitarists considered to be among the world's best pentatonic players.

❶ ANGUS YOUNG

Fuelled by a Gibson SG and Marshall amps, this Australian knows how to wring the most out of the minor pentatonic with his band, AC/DC.

ESSENTIAL TRACKS *Back In Black* ◆ *Whole Lotta Rosie* ◆ *Hells Bells* ◆ *For Those About To Rock (We Salute You)* ◆ *Highway To Hell*

SIMILAR ARTISTS Kelly Jones (Stereophonics) ◆ Paul Kossoff (Free) ◆ Bernie Marsden (Whitesnake)

❷ STEVIE RAY VAUGHAN

With a strong, explosive technique, the late Texan's tone, string bends, and authoritative pentatonic soloing remain revered today.

ESSENTIAL TRACKS *Pride And Joy* ◆ *Couldn't Stand The Weather* ◆ *Crossfire* ◆ *Scuttle Buttin'*

SIMILAR ARTISTS Albert King ◆ Jimi Hendrix ◆ Chris Duarte ◆ Kenny Wayne Shepherd ◆ Philip Sayce

❸ ZAKK WYLDE

Ozzy Osbourne's former guitarist, Wylde now heads up his own band, Black Label Society. Prodigiously fast, Wylde is a pentatonic master.

ESSENTIAL TRACKS With Ozzy: *Miracle Man* ◆ *Mama I'm Coming Home* ◆ *Perry Mason* ◆ With Black Label Society: *Suicide Messiah* ◆ *Low Down*

SIMILAR ARTISTS Frank Marino ◆ Randy Rhoads ◆ Eddie Van Halen ◆ Gary Moore ◆ John Sykes

❹ BILLY GIBBONS

With his Gibson Les Paul (nicknamed Pearly Gates) and Marshall amps, Gibbons' pentatonic soloing for ZZ Top can be both soulful and full of fire.

ESSENTIAL TRACKS *Tush* ◆ *La Grange* ◆ *Sharp Dressed Man* ◆ *Gimme All Your Loving* ◆ *Rough Boy*

SIMILAR ARTISTS Bo Diddley ◆ Eric Clapton ◆ Walter Trout ◆ Robin Trower ◆ Johnny Winter

SESSION 5·4 DVD
THE BLUES SCALE

The blues scale is essentially the same as the minor pentatonic scale (*see pp.148–49*) but with an added note, sometimes called the "blue note." The five notes shared with the minor pentatonic are the root, minor third, fourth, fifth, and minor seventh, while the exotic additional note is the diminished fifth (♭5), which creates the tension typical of a "bluesy" sound. Shown below are the five shapes of the A blues scale that cover the fretboard alongside their parent chord of Am. Practice these scales often to memorize their patterns, then compare with the minor pentatonic to appreciate the unique sound of a diminished fifth.

A BLUES SCALE SHAPE 1 AND PARENT A MINOR CHORD

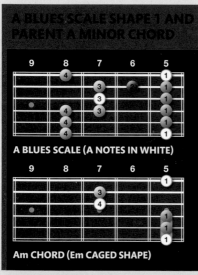

A BLUES SCALE (A NOTES IN WHITE)

Am CHORD (Em CAGED SHAPE)

A BLUES SCALE SHAPE 2 AND PARENT A MINOR CHORD

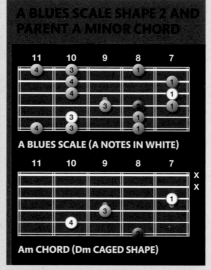

A BLUES SCALE (A NOTES IN WHITE)

Am CHORD (Dm CAGED SHAPE)

WHAT'S THE THEORY?
THE BLUES SOUND

What makes the minor pentatonic and blues scales sound bluesy is the minor third. This note provides melancholy—it's the "sad" note. Alongside the minor third is the softer-sounding minor 7th; this note sounds quite sophisticated over a minor chord. Intriguingly though, it's playing either of these two scales over a major chord (or a 7th such as A7) that generates what we deem as the most "bluesy" sounds. On paper, the opposing equation of a minor pentatonic (or blues scale) over a major chord is strikingly odd. But in practice, an accomplished guitarist can make it work wonderfully with tasteful phrasing and varied string bending.

A BLUES SCALE SHAPE 3 AND PARENT A MINOR CHORD

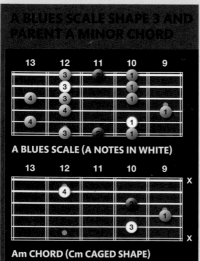

A BLUES SCALE (A NOTES IN WHITE)

Am CHORD (Cm CAGED SHAPE)

A BLUES SCALE SHAPE 4 AND PARENT A MINOR CHORD

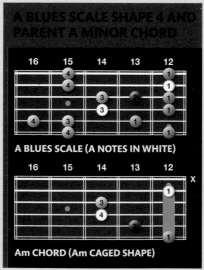

A BLUES SCALE (A NOTES IN WHITE)

Am CHORD (Am CAGED SHAPE)

A BLUES SCALE SHAPE 5 AND PARENT A MINOR CHORD

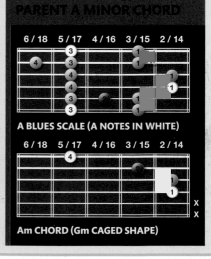

A BLUES SCALE (A NOTES IN WHITE)

Am CHORD (Gm CAGED SHAPE)

EXERCISE 5.4.1 – UP AND DOWN THE A BLUES SCALE

Establish the bond between the Am chord and the A blues scale through this exercise. Then use the same approach to become familiar with the other four chord and scale shapes.

■ **Play the Am chord.** Strum the full six-string Am chord using the Em shape from the CAGED system, then begin the scale.

■ **Play A and C** on the 6th string. Use a down pick for the A (5th fret) then an up pick to sound the C (8th fret).

■ **Play D, E♭, and E** on the 5th string. Down pick for D (5th fret), up pick for E♭ (6th fret), and down pick for E (3rd finger, 7th fret).

■ **Play G and A** on the 4th string. Use a down pick for the G (5th fret) then an up pick to sound the A (7th fret).

PRACTICE & PROGRESS

Try incorporating the diminished fifth when you improvise—add it between the fifth and fourth notes (e.g. E♭ between E and D over Am), resolving to C for a good blues lick. Don't overdo it, though—it's more effective when used sparingly.

CHAPTER 3

EXERCISE 5.4.2 – A BLUES SCALE: A-TO-A OCTAVE SEGMENTS

Each shape of the A blues scale (*opposite*) extends over more than one octave, but many guitarists use notes from within just one octave when building a solo. In this exercise, you will split the A blues scale shape 1 into two segments of one octave each (from a low A to a higher A note). After you have completed the exercise, try applying this octave approach to the other blues scale shapes.

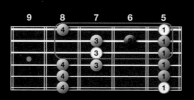

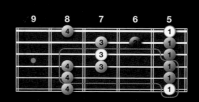

■ **Play the lower octave segment.** The delineated area shows the notes of the A blues scale, shape 1, played in the lower A-to-A octave segment.

■ **Play the upper octave segment.** The delineated area shows the notes of the A blues scale, shape 1, played in the higher A-to-A octave segment.

Experiment with the blues scale using the exercises below. Try playing them with both clean and distorted guitar tones to explore, respectively, a blues ballad sound and an energized rock sound. The notation for each exercise uses the A blues scale, shape 1; try using other shapes to repeat the exercise.

EXERCISE 5.4.3 – DOUBLE PICKING WITHIN ONE OCTAVE OF THE A BLUES SCALE

Double picking the blues scale can be very powerful, as the blue note (the diminished fifth) adds considerable attitude to the sound. Try each picking pattern with shape 1 of the A blues scale, before moving on to shapes 2 and 3.

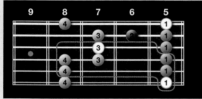

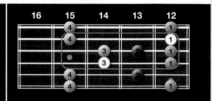

Play the exercise using the A blues scale, shape 1 (shown in the exercise tab). Use the one-octave segment outlined above.

Repeat the exercise using the A blues scale, shape 2. Use notes from the one-octave segment outlined above.

Use the A blues scale, shape 4 to perform the exercise again. Work within the one-octave segment outlined above.

EXERCISE 5.4.4 – PLAYING TRIPLETS WITHIN ONE OCTAVE OF THE A BLUES SCALE

In this exercise, you use alternate picking and a triplet rhythm. The usual two-notes-per-string pattern is altered, with three notes on the 3rd string. Going from the 3rd to the 2nd string can prove tricky, so practice carefully.

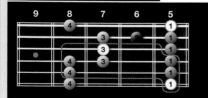

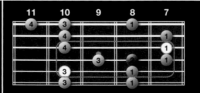

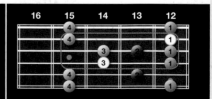

Start with the A blues scale, shape 1 (shown in the exercise tab). Use notes from the one-octave segment outlined above.

Repeat the exercise with the A blues scale, shape 2. Work within the one-octave segment outlined above.

Use the A blues scale, shape 4 to perform the exercise again. Work within the one-octave segment outlined above.

EXERCISE 5.4.5 – "80s ROCK" PATTERN WITHIN ONE OCTAVE OF THE A BLUES SCALE

Try turning up the distortion on this one-octave sequence for a very Slashlike sound. There are two picking patterns shown under the tab; start with the first (down pick to start). Once comfortable, try the second one (up pick to start).

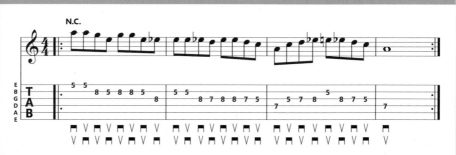

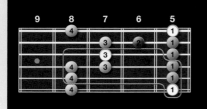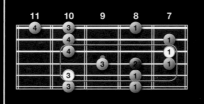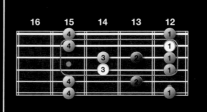

Start with the A blues scale, shape 1 (shown in the exercise tab). Use notes from the outlined area shown above to play the one-octave exercise.

Repeat the exercise using A blues scale, shape 2, to open up the fretboard. Use notes from the one octave segment outlined above.

Use A blues scale, shape 4 to perform the exercise again, using this alternative scale shape to open up the fretboard. Work within the one-octave segment shown above.

EXERCISE 5.4.6 – DESCENDING GROUPS OF SIX: FULL A BLUES SCALE SHAPE

This blues scale has been tweaked so that it can be played with a two-notes-per-string pattern. The diminished fifth (E♭, the "blue note") has been retained but the fourth (D) discarded. Omitting notes from scales can generate a unique soloing sound.

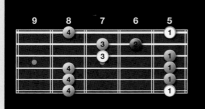

Start with the A blues scale (altered), shape 1. Play the exercise through using shape 1 (see 1, 2, 3; right), then try it again using the other four shapes.

Play the scale notes for shape 1. Notice that three notes sound exotic when played in this sequence: (1) the fifth (E note, 1st finger); (2) the diminished fifth (E♭ note, 4th finger); and

(3) the minor third (C note, 1st finger). Repeat the exercise several times to get used to the sound and to become accustomed to the large stretch involved.

STRING BENDING

Unique to the guitar, string bending is a great technique to give your solos a "vocal" quality. Using your fretting hand to bend a string and change its pitch can create another note (or sometimes several) without placing a finger at another fret, so it sounds smoother than hammer-ons or pull-offs (*see pp.80–81*).

Successful string bending requires practice; this is the only way to develop both the hand strength necessary to bend the strings, and the accuracy to make the bend sound neither sharp nor flat. What follows is an explanation of how to bend a string by a tone and semitone, and two string-bending exercises.

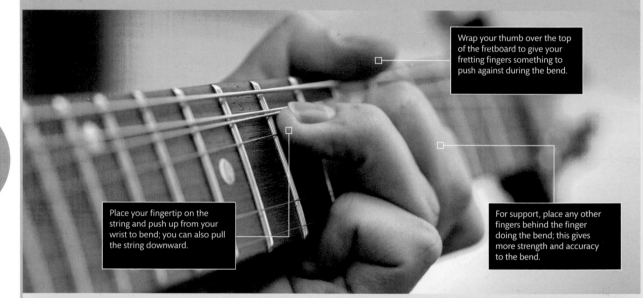

Wrap your thumb over the top of the fretboard to give your fretting fingers something to push against during the bend.

Place your fingertip on the string and push up from your wrist to bend; you can also pull the string downward.

For support, place any other fingers behind the finger doing the bend; this gives more strength and accuracy to the bend.

To bend the 3rd string through one tone from D to E, place your 3rd finger at the 7th fret and add your 1st and 2nd fingers behind it for support. Pick the 3rd string, then bend it up to E (think of this as a "virtual" 9th fret). Keep your thumb over the fretboard so that your grip is strong and secure.

To bend the 3rd string through a semitone from D to E♭, place your 3rd finger at the 7th fret, supported by your 1st and 2nd fingers. Pick the 3rd string, then bend it so that the D note rises to E♭ (a "virtual" 8th fret). This semitone bend requires less movement and effort than the tone bend.

EXERCISE 5.5.1 – STRING BENDS: ACCURACY AND INTONATION

Build your accuracy at string bending with this exercise. Sound a note, then move down two frets (for one tone) or one fret (for a semitone). Sound the note at the lower fret, then bend the string to match the tone of the note just fretted.

■ **Sound the E note.** Pick the 3rd string with your 3rd finger at the 9th fret. Listen carefully: this is your reference note.

■ **Bend up a tone.** With your 3rd finger at the 7th fret, 3rd string (D note), bend up to replicate the reference note, E.

■ **Sound the E♭ note.** Pick the 3rd string with your 3rd finger at the 8th fret. Listen carefully: this is your reference note.

■ **Bend up a semitone.** With your 3rd finger at the 7th fret, 3rd string (D note), bend up to replicate the reference note, E♭.

EXERCISE 5.5.2 – A MAJOR SCALE WITH TONE AND SEMITONE BENDS (ONE STRING)

Practice bending intonation with this exercise. Descend the seven-note A major scale, fretting each note then bending up to it from a lower fret.

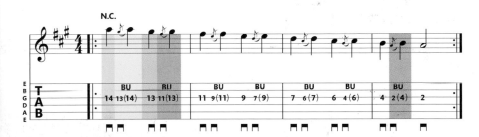

■ **Play the A note.** Place your 3rd finger at the 14th fret, 3rd string and play A. Listen well to this reference note for the next bend.

■ **Bend from G♯ to A.** Place your 3rd finger at the 13th fret, 3rd string, and perform a precise semitone bend up from G♯ to A.

■ **Play the G♯ note.** Place your 3rd finger on the 3rd string, 13th fret and play G♯. This is your reference note for the next bend.

■ **Bend from F♯ to G♯.** Place your 3rd finger on the 3rd string, 11th fret, and perform a tone bend from F♯ to G♯ (virtual 13th fret).

■ **Bend from A to B.** Use your 2nd finger, supported by your 1st, to bend the note to match the previous B note.

SESSION
5·6
STRING-BENDING LICKS

Here you will combine the minor pentatonic and blues scales with string bends to create licks (short lead phrases) featuring tone and semitone string bends.

The exercises below are typical blues rock licks: you can improvise by playing them slower or faster, or by rearranging and/or repeating the notes.

CHAPTER 3

EXERCISE 5.6.1 – A MINOR PENTATONIC (SHAPE 1) LICK WITH TONE BENDS

You'll probably recognize this lick, which has been played in various guises since the 1950s. Using A minor pentatonic (shape 1), it has two instances of tone bends; bend accurately, paying close attention to pitch intonation.

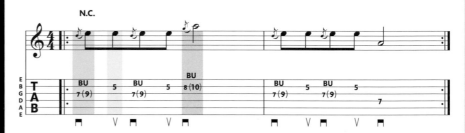

■ **Bend a tone** from D to E. Place your 3rd finger at the 7th fret, 3rd string. Bend up by a tone.

■ **Play the E note.** Reference the bend's intonation by playing E on the 5th fret, 2nd string.

■ **Bend a tone** from G to A. Use your 3rd finger at the 8th fret, 3rd string to bend (G) to A.

PRACTICE & PROGRESS

Remember to use the strength of the supporting fingers to make string bending more accurate and comfortable. If you find it very difficult, try switching to a lighter string-gauge such as .009 or .010 (see p.294).

EXERCISE 5.6.2 – A BLUES SCALE (SHAPE 1) LICK WITH SEMITONE AND TONE BENDS

This gritty blues lick features three different bends: one semitone bend (D to Eb) and two full tone bends (G to A and D to E).

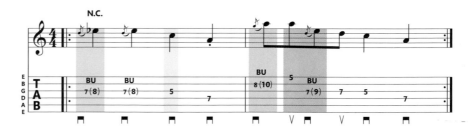

■ **Bend from D to Eb.** Use your 3rd finger for the semitone bend.

■ **Play the C note.** Place your 1st finger at the 5th fret, 3rd string for C.

■ **Bend from G to A.** Use your 3rd finger for the tone bend.

■ **Play the A note.** Place your 1st finger at the 5th fret, 1st string for A.

■ **Bend from D to E.** Use your 3rd finger for the tone bend.

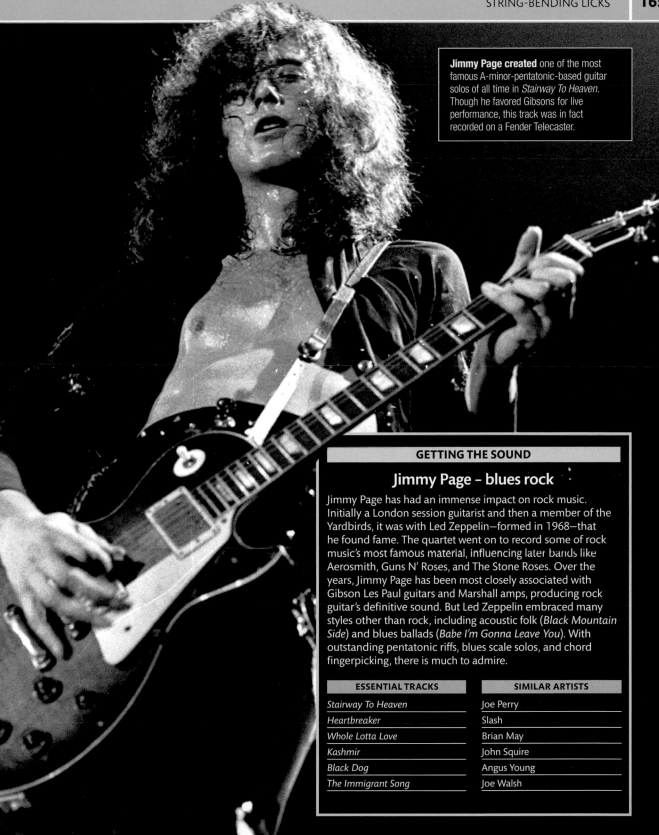

Jimmy Page created one of the most famous A-minor-pentatonic-based guitar solos of all time in *Stairway To Heaven*. Though he favored Gibsons for live performance, this track was in fact recorded on a Fender Telecaster.

GETTING THE SOUND

Jimmy Page – blues rock

Jimmy Page has had an immense impact on rock music. Initially a London session guitarist and then a member of the Yardbirds, it was with Led Zeppelin—formed in 1968—that he found fame. The quartet went on to record some of rock music's most famous material, influencing later bands like Aerosmith, Guns N' Roses, and The Stone Roses. Over the years, Jimmy Page has been most closely associated with Gibson Les Paul guitars and Marshall amps, producing rock guitar's definitive sound. But Led Zeppelin embraced many styles other than rock, including acoustic folk (*Black Mountain Side*) and blues ballads (*Babe I'm Gonna Leave You*). With outstanding pentatonic riffs, blues scale solos, and chord fingerpicking, there is much to admire.

ESSENTIAL TRACKS	SIMILAR ARTISTS
Stairway To Heaven	Joe Perry
Heartbreaker	Slash
Whole Lotta Love	Brian May
Kashmir	John Squire
Black Dog	Angus Young
The Immigrant Song	Joe Walsh

MILESTONE PIECE

This milestone consolidates the skills you learned in Session 5. It is a 16-bar piece that uses A minor pentatonic scale (A, C, D, E, G) for the first four bars of Am; D blues scale (D, F, G, A♭, A, C) for four bars of Dm; and then A major pentatonic (A, B, C♯, E, F♯) for the four bars of A. In the last four bars it uses D major pentatonic (D, E, F♯, A, B) for the two bars of D, followed by E major pentatonic (E, F♯, G♯, B, C♯) for one bar of E, and then A minor pentatonic—with string-bending—for the last bar of A. The final note, C♯, resonates well against the A chord.

CHAPTER 3

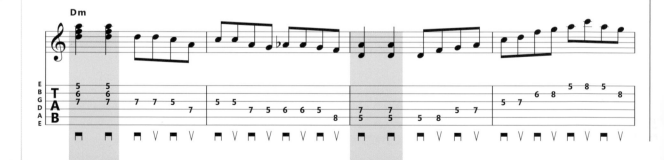

Play a small Am chord (Em shape, CAGED system). Press your 1st finger on the 1st, 2nd, and 3rd strings, 5th fret.

Play a small Dm chord (Am shape, CAGED system) on the 1st, 2nd, and 3rd strings with your 1st, 2nd, and 3rd fingers.

The D5 chord needs just two fingers: 1st finger (5th fret, 5th string) and 3rd finger (7th fret, 4th string).

Play a small A chord with your 1st finger at the 5th fret, 1st and 2nd strings, and 2nd finger at the 6th fret, 3rd string.

Form an A chord with your 1st finger (5th fret, 2nd string), 2nd finger (6th fret, 3rd string), and 3rd finger (7th fret, 4th string).

 PRO TIP
PLAYING BY EAR

It's not necessary to know every scale to become a good player. Spend time playing a new piece and detecting general minor and major sounds. Acquiring a good ear for these, especially while you're improvising, is a first step to great lead soloing.

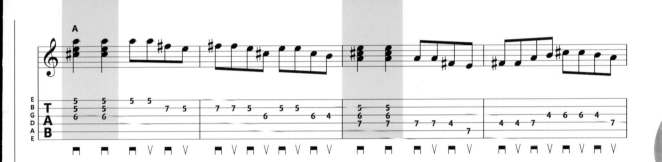

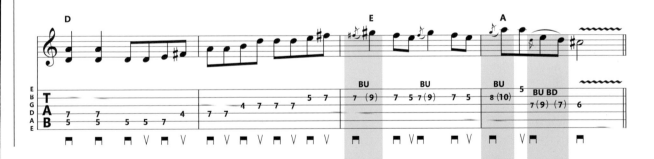

CHAPTER 3

Tone-bend from F♯ to G♯ using your 3rd finger to bend from F♯ (7th fret, 2nd string) to G♯ ("virtual" 9th fret).

Tone-bend from G to A using your 3rd finger to bend from G (8th fret, 2nd string) to A ("virtual" 10th fret).

Tone-bend from D to E using your 3rd finger to bend from D (7th fret, 3rd string) to E ("virtual" 9th fret).

PLAYING WITH EXPRESSION

Playing expressively is a quality that all musicians hope to possess. Expression goes beyond just notes and rhythms; it's the way you present your music and it's what makes others want to listen to you. One of the things you can most easily learn is how to alter expression through technique. This session looks at expressive techniques including blues curls, finger vibrato, slides, natural harmonics, and whammy-bar technique. Using these will give your playing an injection of drama—they will transform your scales and chords, and your playing will begin to sound less like practice drills and more like real music.

THE BLUES CURL

It's time to learn the blues curl—a simple technique to subtly enhance your blues and rock soloing. The curl is a very small string bend (*see pp.162–63*) that is applied to certain notes to create a mournful, bluesy sound. When you perform a blues curl, you first fret the original note, then bend it to become slightly sharp, but nowhere near the tone bends of session 5: aim for somewhere between the note you have fretted and the next half-tone (the next fretted note up). It's often referred to as a "quarter-tone bend,"

and it is signified in notation by an arrow curving upwards with the fraction sign: ¼. No one knows precisely when or where blues curls originated, but you can hear them on many old blues recordings by guitarists such as Robert Johnson and T-Bone Walker that date back to the 1930s and 40s. Musicians like these used blues curls instinctively, adding a rootsy appeal to the music. Since then, everyone uses them when soloing in almost every style, from blues to country, rock, and pop.

Many guitarists use the minor pentatonic (*see pp.148–49*) as their standard scale. Our ears have become accustomed to recognizing minor scales played over major chords as "bluesy" playing. To enhance minor pentatonic soloing over major chords, many guitarists apply a blues curl to a pentatonic's minor third note, implying the major third without ever getting there: the fourth note often gets the blues curl treatment too. So, for example, with the A minor pentatonic scale—A, C, D, E, G—blues curls are favored on C (minor third) and D (fourth). The photos below show the notes suitable for blues curls, before the bend has been applied (*above*) and after (*below*).

The A minor pentatonic scale: white-circled numbers are A (the root note) and bracketed circles are ideal blues curl notes.

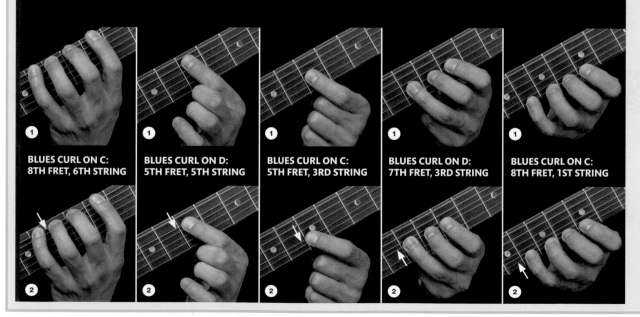

| **BLUES CURL ON C:** 8TH FRET, 6TH STRING | **BLUES CURL ON D:** 5TH FRET, 5TH STRING | **BLUES CURL ON C:** 5TH FRET, 3RD STRING | **BLUES CURL ON D:** 7TH FRET, 3RD STRING | **BLUES CURL ON C:** 8TH FRET, 1ST STRING |

EXERCISE 6.1.1 – A MINOR PENTATONIC LICK WITH BLUES CURLS

This exercise uses A minor pentatonic, shape 1, featuring three different blues curls: one on a high C (minor third); one on D (fourth); and one on a lower C. This lick, which can be played on top of Am or A chords, is a typically bluesy one.

■ **Play the C note curl.** Fret at the 8th fret, 1st string. Pick C and then apply a blues curl with your 4th finger.

■ **Play the A note.** Press the pad, rather than the tip, of your 1st finger on the 5th fret, 1st string, and pick to sound the note.

■ **Play the E note.** From the A note, roll your 1st finger forwards onto the 5th fret, 2nd string to play E. Fret with your fingertip.

■ **Play the D note curl.** Apply a blues curl with your 3rd finger, using your 1st and 2nd fingers to support it, if required.

EXERCISE 6.1.2 – BLUES CURLS WITH EXPRESSIVE PLAYING

This is a more animated A minor pentatonic lick, using a mixture of tone bends, pull-offs, and blues curls to finish. Although blues curls aren't as "showy" as bigger tone bends (*see pp.162–63*), they draw the listener in with their softer intimacy.

■ **Tone-bend from D to E.** Bend from D (7th fret, 3rd string) to E ("virtual" 9th fret) with your 3rd finger, supported by your 2nd.

■ **Tone-bend from G to A.** Bend with your 4th finger from G (8th fret, 2nd string) to A ("virtual" 10th fret).

■ **Play the D blues curl.** Use your 3rd finger at the 7th fret, 3rd string. Bend up with your 3rd finger supported by the first two.

■ **Play the C blues curl.** Apply a blues curl to C at the 5th fret, 3rd string. Bend the string down toward the floor.

CHAPTER 3

SESSION
6·2
DVD

FINGER VIBRATO

Vibrato is a technique used to add texture and emotion to guitar solos. It involves varying the pitch of a sustained note by oscillating a string to produce a "warbling" tone. Finger vibrato can be used on any string with any finger (including the fourth); there's great variety in the effect, depending on the pitch variation, speed of movement, and the moment at which it's applied during a note's sustain. Here, you'll learn to apply vibrato in two ways—classical, and blues rock—and how to combine it with string bends.

PRACTICE & PROGRESS

Get accustomed to playing vibrato with each of your fingers at different depths and speeds. For example, set a metronome to 90 bpm. Place your 3rd finger at the 5th fret, 3rd string and bend the string up by a semitone on the first click. For the second click, release the bend. Repeat this for eight clicks. Then do the same with each finger in turn. Then increase the metronome to 100 bpm and repeat.

TWO TYPES OF FINGER VIBRATO

Along the string (classical). This subtle type of vibrato is favored by nylon-string guitarists. Occasionally, steel-string guitarists use it for chords and slow solos. Sustain a fretted note then push/pull along the string as indicated by the arrows.

Along the fretwire (blues/rock). This vibrato offers greater pitch variation for electric guitarists. Sustain a fretted note then push/pull it across the fretboard as shown. Shallow, slow vibrato suits tranquil playing; wide vibrato suits energetic soloing.

COMBINING STRING BENDS AND VIBRATO

First, bend up a tone. Hook your thumb over the fretboard and use your 3rd finger to bend from D (7th fret, 3rd string) to E ("virtual" 9th fret, 3rd string).

Apply vibrato. Once you've performed the tone bend (supported by the 1st and 2nd fingers), apply vibrato by releasing the bend so your pitch dips to an E♭ note.

Bend back up to the E note. Don't overshoot and go sharp—your bend should return to the point of the first bend. Repeat evenly for a good rock/blues vibrato.

CHAPTER 3

EXERCISE 6.2.1 – MELODY WITH CLASSICAL-STYLE VIBRATO

This exercise explores classical vibrato, which is applied along the string. You will apply it to several notes in this A minor pentatonic melody, making them sound more emotive. Note the wavy line that denotes vibrato in the notation.

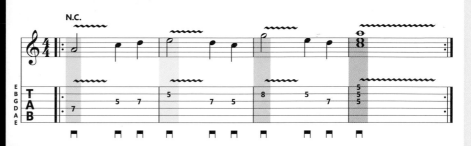

■ **Play the A note.** Place your 3rd finger at the 7th fret, 4th string; pick and apply along-the-string vibrato to the note.

■ **Play the E note.** Use your fretting 1st finger, at the 5th fret, 2nd string, to apply the vibrato effect.

■ **Play the G note.** Pick and apply vibrato with your 4th finger (or 3rd if your 4th is too weak) at the 8th fret, 2nd string.

■ **Play the Am chord.** To finish, place your 1st finger across the 1st, 2nd, and 3rd strings at the 5th fret and apply vibrato to all.

EXERCISE 6.2.2 – BLUES ROCK LICK

Match an energetic lick with wide blues-rock vibrato in this exercise. Make sure that the tone string bend in bar 1 doesn't waver too much from its central E note.

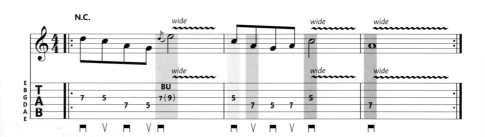

■ **Tone-bend with vibrato.** Place your 3rd finger at the 7th fret, 3rd string; pick, bend up from D to E, then apply vibrato.

■ **Play the C note.** Place your 1st finger at the 5th fret, 3rd string. Keep your thumb in position over the fretboard.

■ **Play the A note.** Place your 3rd finger at the 7th fret, 4th string and support it with your other fingers.

■ **Apply vibrato to C.** Bend the 3rd string a little towards the floor and then release. Repeat the action evenly.

■ **Apply vibrato to A.** Bend the 4th string towards the floor and then release. Repeat the action evenly.

CHAPTER 3

FRETBOARD SLIDES

CHAPTER 3

The fretboard slide is a technique widely used by all guitarists when performing. It involves using one finger (or more) to slide one or more notes up or down the same string. Its appeal is the sound the finger makes as it travels along the string, catching other frets as it goes; the bigger the slide, the more noticeable the effect. Many guitarists like its simplistic melodic strengths, breaking away from pentatonic box shapes to explore notes along the string. Slide guitar using metal or glass slides has spawned a whole style of playing, but here you will concentrate on learning finger slides and play two simple exercises.

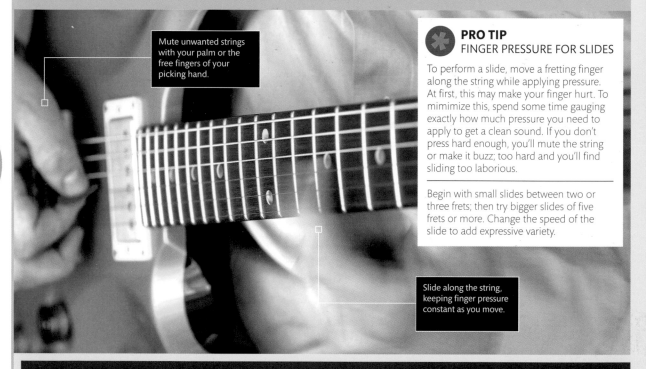

Mute unwanted strings with your palm or the free fingers of your picking hand.

Slide along the string, keeping finger pressure constant as you move.

PRO TIP
FINGER PRESSURE FOR SLIDES

To perform a slide, move a fretting finger along the string while applying pressure. At first, this may make your finger hurt. To minimize this, spend some time gauging exactly how much pressure you need to apply to get a clean sound. If you don't press hard enough, you'll mute the string or make it buzz; too hard and you'll find sliding too laborious.

Begin with small slides between two or three frets; then try bigger slides of five frets or more. Change the speed of the slide to add expressive variety.

SLIDING WITH ONE FINGER

Play the C note. Place your 1st finger at the 5th fret, 3rd string, positioning it just behind the fretwire.

Pick the 3rd string. Use a confident down stroke with your pick to strike the 3rd string's C note cleanly.

Slide up. With the 3rd note sustaining, slide your 1st finger up to the 7th fret's D note. Keep the finger pressure even.

Slide down. Once you've reached the D note, slide your 1st finger from the 7th fret back to the 5th fret.

① ② ③ ④

EXERCISE 6.3.1 – A MINOR PENTATONIC MELODY USING SLIDES

See how different A minor pentatonic can sound when using slides, by doing this exercise. Note that a slide is denoted by an inclined straight line linking notes together.

■ **Slide from C to D to C.** Begin by placing your first finger at the 5th fret, 3rd string, to play C.

■ **Pick the string** with a down stroke and slide up to the 7th fret to D.

■ **Slide from the 7th** fret to the 5th. Don't apply too much pressure or the note will go out of tune.

■ **Slide from G to E.** Begin by placing your 4th finger at the 8th fret, 2nd string for G.

■ **Pick the note** then slide your fretting finger down to the 5th fret for E.

EXERCISE 6.3.2 – A MINOR PENTATONIC WITH BIG SLIDES

Here you play within a familiar scale, but using a very different approach to sound the notes. Use one finger on the 3rd string, sounding notes with small and big slides.

■ **Play the C note.** Place your 1st finger at the 5th fret, 3rd string. Down-pick strongly.

■ **Slide up to the D note** on the 7th fret with your 1st finger.

■ **Slide back.** Slide down to the C note at the 5th fret, keeping finger pressure consistent.

■ **Slide to the E note.** Carry out this big slide by moving from the 5th fret up to the 9th fret.

■ **Slide to the G note.** Finish the first phrase with another big slide from the 9th to the 12th fret (G).

GREAT EXPRESSIVE PLAYERS

Being an expressive guitarist means having the ability to affect an audience; to play in a way that seems to bring out the true "voice" of your instrument. The best, like the four guitarists below, use a variety of techniques—string-bending, slides, hammer-ons, pull-offs, volume dynamics, and even moments of silence—to create music that communicates.

① JEFF BECK

Jeff Beck's influential sound includes a unique style of string bending, use of the whammy bar with harmonics, and fingerpicking.

ESSENTIAL TRACKS *Cause We've Ended As Lovers* ◆ *Freeway Jam* ◆ *Where Were You?* ◆ *Brush With Blues* ◆ *Somewhere Over The Rainbow*

SIMILAR ARTISTS Tommy Bolin ◆ Larry Carlton ◆ Eric Clapton ◆ David Gilmour ◆ Steve Lukather

② STEVE VAI

If guitar shred has an icon, it is Steve Vai, who combines both jaw-dropping speed and virtuoso technique with truly imaginative playing.

ESSENTIAL TRACKS *The Attitude Song* ◆ *For The Love Of God* ◆ *Tender Surrender* ◆ *Bad Horsie* ◆ *Ladies Night In Buffalo* (with David Lee Roth)

SIMILAR ARTISTS Joe Satriani ◆ Yngwie Malmsteen ◆ Mike Keneally ◆ Paul Gilbert ◆ Guthrie Govan

③ ALBERT KING

A blues legend and master string-bender, King's left-handed, upside-down stinging lead style made his signature Gibson Flying V guitar, "Lucy", sing.

ESSENTIAL TRACKS *Born Under A Bad Sign* ◆ *Oh Pretty Woman* ◆ *Laundromat Blues* ◆ *Crosscut Saw* ◆ *The Sky Is Crying*

SIMILAR ARTISTS Albert Collins ◆ Robert Cray ◆ Kenny Wayne Shepherd ◆ Stevie Ray Vaughan

④ BRIAN MAY

Queen guitarist Brian May is renowned for his great string bending, tonal and dynamic range, and melodic phrasing, as well as for his gift for stacking multiple guitar parts in harmony.

ESSENTIAL TRACKS *Bohemian Rhapsody* ◆ *One Vision* ◆ *Killer Queen* ◆ *Tie Your Mother Down* ◆ *Hammer to Fall*

SIMILAR ARTISTS Jimmy Page ◆ Nuno Bettencourt ◆ Steve Vai ◆ Steve Lukather ◆ Tom Scholz

SESSION

6•4 DYNAMICS

Just as you raise and lower your voice as you speak, to add emphasis and convey emotion, so you should use volume as an expressive tool in your guitar-playing. You can achieve this by controlling your picking. "Dynamics" is the word used for volume and timbre (sound) variations that add color to your performance. In this session you will explore how to vary your playing dynamics. The two exercises will give you a good understanding of when and where to apply dynamic control.

Choose a medium-thickness pick; it will help you coax the full dynamic range from your guitar.

Expose more of the the surface of the pick to bring out more tonal presence.

PLAYING QUIETLY

Playing quietly entails picking with a lighter touch. This not only means using less force with your hand as you pick, but also letting less of the pick make contact with the string. Use the very tip of the pick to really turn down the volume.

PLAYING LOUDLY

When you need to project your playing, such as when making it louder for a climactic solo, pick harder and use a deeper pick-stroke. Using picks of varying thickness will help influence the volume and tone of your playing (*see pp.26–27*).

EXERCISE 6.4.1 – CHANGING VOLUME WITH ONE NOTE

Practice varying dynamics on one note in this exercise. There are two 2-bar phrases: the first requires quiet-to-loud picking; and the second asks for loud-to-quiet. In the notation, "p" is short for *piano* (soft) and "f" is short for *forte* (loud).

EXERCISE 6.4.2 – PICKING DYNAMICS AND HAMMER-ONS

Compare the tonal dynamics of hammer-ons with alternate picking in this exercise, using an ascending A minor pentatonic phrase. Listen to the differences between the two (*see box below*).

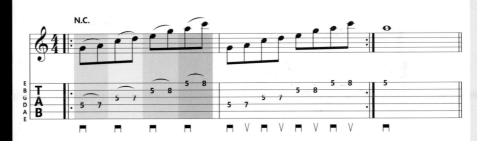

■ **Hammer-on to A.** Pick G (5th fret, 4th string) then hammer-on to the A note (7th fret).

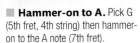

■ **Hammer-on to D.** Pick C (5th fret, 3rd string) then hammer-on to the D note (7th fret).

■ **Hammer-on to G.** Pick E (5th fret, 2nd string) then hammer-on to the G note (8th fret).

■ **Hammer-on to C.** Pick A (5th fret, 1st string) then hammer-on to the C note (8th fret).

❓ WHAT'S THE THEORY?
VOLUME AND TONE DYNAMICS

When you sound a note on the guitar, there's more to consider than just pure volume. Tone dynamics are also important. Notice that simple picking has a percussive element as well as the ability to vary volume; a hammer-on can produce less variation in volume but sounds smoother and softer than picking. A pull-off can be loud—louder even than the original note—because you pluck the string as you pull off, but it retains a smoother tone than a picked stroke. Achieving a good guitar tone is as much about understanding dynamics as it is about chords and scales.

✳ PRO TIP
ELECTRIC DYNAMICS

While an acoustic guitar's dynamics are solely generated by the player's interactions with the guitar, electric guitar dynamics are also dependent on the amplifier. Many guitarists look for an amp with lots of "headroom"—that is, the ability to complement both soft playing (with a clean tone) and aggressive playing (with a distorted tone). Amps of around 50 watts are usually loud enough for both clean(ish) and distorted sounds in band performances. But if you favor loud, clean tones (like Stevie Ray Vaughan), Fender amps—among others—are a good choice. If you like distortion, try amps from Marshall (like Ritchie Blackmore) or Vox (like Brian May).

CHAPTER 3

SESSION 6·5 ACCENTS

A great musical performance is always much more than flawlessly executed notes. It depends upon creating variety in expression and incorporating accents—stand-out moments that energize a piece. These occur as a result of something unusual, like a discordant chord, a sudden high note, or several loud notes among quieter notes. Here we look at three different examples of accents. The first focuses on volume accents (shown on the tablature as >) with chord-strumming; the second features pitch accents, with jumps to exclamatory high notes; and the last focuses on a mixture of pitch accents and palm-muted/unmuted playing. Play the exercises with and without the accenting to compare the effectiveness of using these techniques.

PRO TIP
ACCENTING WITH THE WAH-WAH

An electric guitarist has many sound effects at his or her disposal. One of the most effective for adding drama is the wah-wah foot pedal. This has a movable treadle: rock it forward and backward to sweep through low to high frequencies.

For great wah-wah guitar rhythms, check out Isaac Hayes's *Theme from Shaft* or Curtis Mayfield's *Superfly* theme. Here, the wah-wah drastically changes the guitar's tone, accenting the strumming as the pedal rocks forward and back to create bright (pedal down) and dull (pedal up) tones. For wah-wah soloing, listen to Jimi Hendrix at the start of *Voodoo Chile* and Steve Vai's "talking guitar" intro to David Lee Roth's *Yankee Rose*.

EXERCISE 6.5.1 – ACCENTING WITH CHORD STRUMS

Here you strum a regular rhythm using three different chords. On beats 2 and 4, strum louder with a more confident down stroke. These accents evoke a drummer's snare drum playing a backbeat on beats 2 and 4 in every bar.

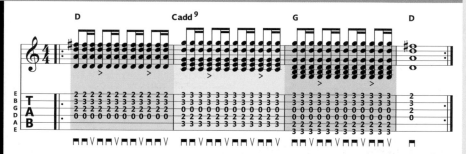

■ **Play the D chord.** This occurs in the first and last bars of the exercise. Position your fingers as shown above.

■ **Play the Cadd9 chord.** This sophisticated C chord (consisting of a C major with an added D note) occurs in bar 2.

■ **Play the G chord.** This is a fingering favored by folk and rock guitarists (the 2nd string is fretted, not open).

PRACTICE & PROGRESS

Break down your practice for this exercise into specific goals. Your first goal is to get the D chord sounding good: get the shape fretted then tackle the rhythm ("dum-dada") that repeats on every beat using one down strum, a silent up strum (ghost strum), a down strum, and then an up strum. Once you can strum this evenly for several bars, practice the two other chords: Cadd9 and G. Take time to get them right individually before moving on.

EXERCISE 6.5.2 – ACCENTING WITH STRING RAKING AND HIGH NOTES

This exercise shows how to create soloing accent points using raking and high notes. The opening C (with blues curl) features a string rake—a quick down pick across muted strings—to add percussive interest before the finish.

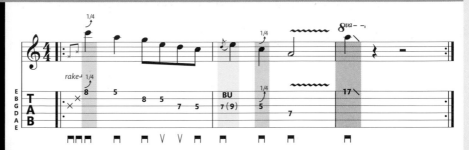

■ **Play C.** Place your 4th finger at the 8th fret, 1st string. Drag the pick over the 3rd and 2nd strings; sound the C, then do a blues curl.

■ **Tone bend from D to E.** Place your 3rd finger at the 7th fret, 3rd string (D), and bend up a tone to E ("virtual" 9th fret).

■ **Play the C note.** Place your 1st finger at the 5th fret, 3rd string (C), and bend the string downward for a blues curl.

■ **Slide the A.** Fret the 1st string with the 4th finger at the 17th fret; pick, then slide the note right down until it fades to silence.

EXERCISE 6.5.3 – ACCENTING WITH PITCH AND PALM MUTING

This exercise uses pitch jumps and palm muting to provide unique accents. Pitch accents—where you jump suddenly to a higher note—are favored by heavy rock players.

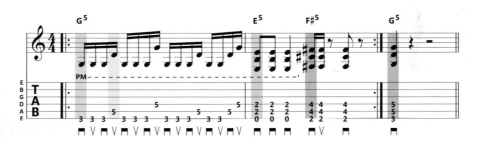

■ **Play the low G.** Pick with a down stroke on the 6th string. Use palm muted picking through to the middle of bar 2.

■ **Play the D note.** Up pick the 5th string fretted at the 5th fret to play this rhythmically accented high note.

■ **Move to the E5 chord.** Change quickly from G5 to E5, using only your 1st finger to fret the 5th and 4th strings.

■ **Play the F♯5 chord.** Use your 1st finger on the 2nd fret and your 3rd and 4th fingers on the 4th fret to play F♯5.

■ **Move to the G5 chord.** Move the chord shape you fretted for F♯5 up by one fret, to sound G5.

CHAPTER 3

SESSION
6·6
DVD

USING A WHAMMY BAR

The whammy bar is perhaps the most powerful sound-shaping guitar tool. It is capable of producing all manner of expressive pitch-based sounds, from subtle vibrato on sustained notes (hear Hank Marvin on The Shadows' *Wonderful Land*) to manic warbling (Steve Vai on *The Attitude Song*).

As its name suggests, the whammy bar is a bar attached to a movable bridge; when you push down on the bar, you lower the bridge so the strings slacken. Pulling up on the bar raises the bridge, so the strings tighten. Here you'll be introduced to just a few of the effects that can be produced by a whammy bar.

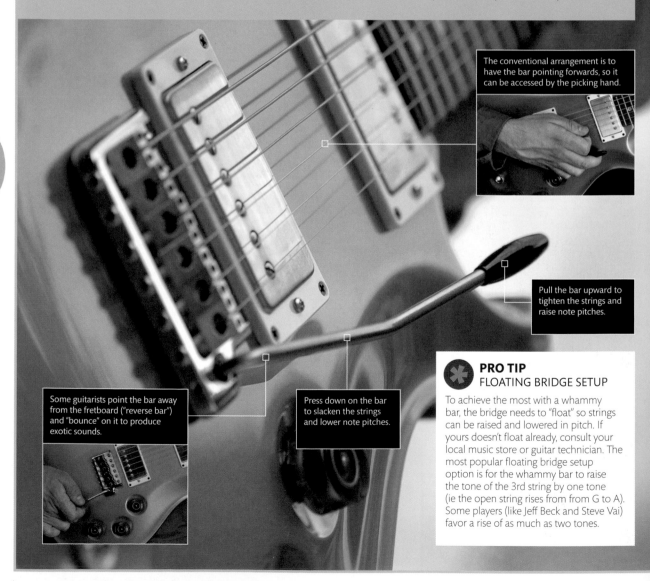

The conventional arrangement is to have the bar pointing forwards, so it can be accessed by the picking hand.

Pull the bar upward to tighten the strings and raise note pitches.

Some guitarists point the bar away from the fretboard ("reverse bar") and "bounce" on it to produce exotic sounds.

Press down on the bar to slacken the strings and lower note pitches.

PRO TIP
FLOATING BRIDGE SETUP

To achieve the most with a whammy bar, the bridge needs to "float" so strings can be raised and lowered in pitch. If yours doesn't float already, consult your local music store or guitar technician. The most popular floating bridge setup option is for the whammy bar to raise the tone of the 3rd string by one tone (ie the open string rises from from G to A). Some players (like Jeff Beck and Steve Vai) favor a rise of as much as two tones.

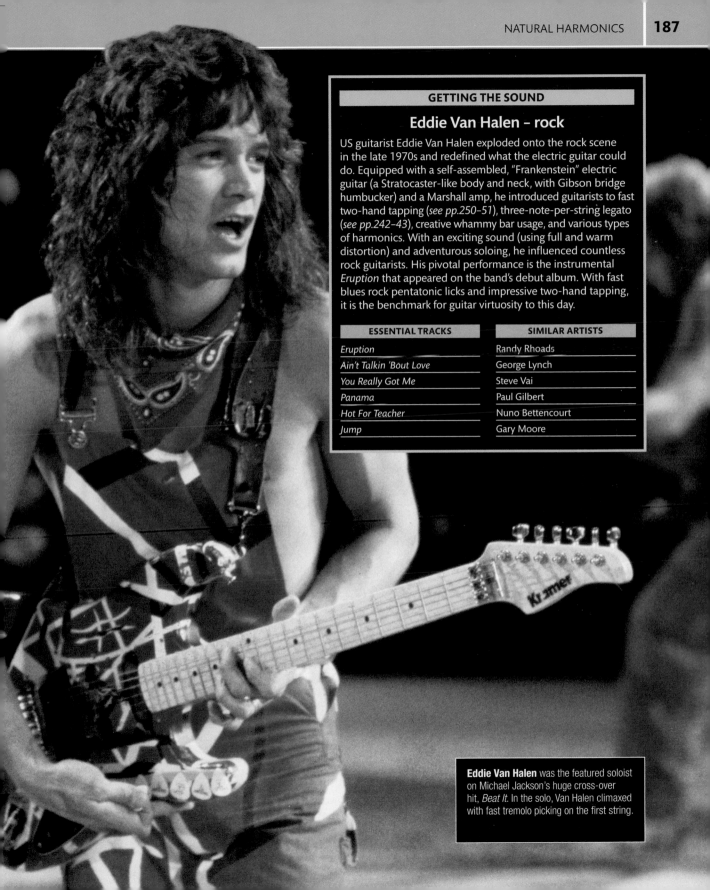

GETTING THE SOUND

Eddie Van Halen – rock

US guitarist Eddie Van Halen exploded onto the rock scene in the late 1970s and redefined what the electric guitar could do. Equipped with a self-assembled, "Frankenstein" electric guitar (a Stratocaster-like body and neck, with Gibson bridge humbucker) and a Marshall amp, he introduced guitarists to fast two-hand tapping (*see pp.250–51*), three-note-per-string legato (*see pp.242–43*), creative whammy bar usage, and various types of harmonics. With an exciting sound (using full and warm distortion) and adventurous soloing, he influenced countless rock guitarists. His pivotal performance is the instrumental *Eruption* that appeared on the band's debut album. With fast blues rock pentatonic licks and impressive two-hand tapping, it is the benchmark for guitar virtuosity to this day.

ESSENTIAL TRACKS	SIMILAR ARTISTS
Eruption	Randy Rhoads
Ain't Talkin' 'Bout Love	George Lynch
You Really Got Me	Steve Vai
Panama	Paul Gilbert
Hot For Teacher	Nuno Bettencourt
Jump	Gary Moore

Eddie Van Halen was the featured soloist on Michael Jackson's huge cross-over hit, *Beat It*. In the solo, Van Halen climaxed with fast tremolo picking on the first string.

MILESTONE PIECE

This piece uses the A natural minor scale (A, B, C, D, E, F, G) and draws on many of the expressive techniques you've learned in this session. It features slides and vibrato in the first three bars, string rakes and bends in bars 5–7, and whammy bar scoops/vibrato in bars 11–14. Lastly, there is a quick descending A minor pentatonic (A, C, D, E, G) scale pull-off lick to close.

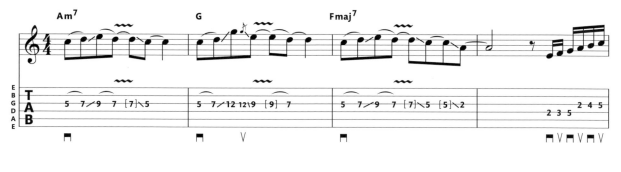

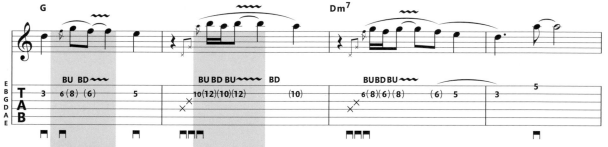

Place your 3rd finger at the 6th fret, 2nd string. Sound the F note and bend up a tone to G ("virtual" 8th fret).

Tone bend from A to B with your 3rd finger at the 10th fret, 3rd string; use your 1st and 2nd fingers as support.

CHAPTER 3

Fret C at the 8th fret, 1st string; down pick then hammer-on from C to D with your 3rd finger at the 10th fret.

Sound B with a hammer-on: starting a new string with a hammer-on is shown as a squared note and fret number.

PRO TIP
COPY AND EXPERIMENT

When you play a piece you like, pick out the best phrases and use them to form your own solo. Experiment with simple one- or two-bar phrases and augment them with techniques such as hammer-ons, pull-offs, slides, bends, or string rakes.

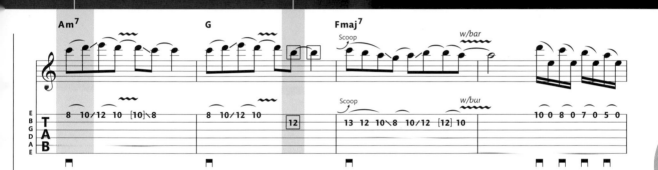

Sound B with your 1st finger, then place your 2nd finger at the 8th fret, 2nd string (G) and let it sustain alongside B.

Sound A with your 1st finger at the 5th fret, 1st string. Hammer-on for C (4th finger, 8th fret), then pull-off to A.

Finish the piece using whammy-bar vibrato on the A note at the 7th fret on the 4th string.

ACOUSTIC FINGERSTYLE

So far, you have learned to play the guitar using a pick, which is well suited to the clean, loud, and fast sounds characteristic of rock and pop. In this session, you will learn a style of playing closely associated with the acoustic guitar—using your fingers to pluck the strings. Called fingerstyle, this technique is a must for all classical guitarists, as well as folk and Delta blues players; it is also used by a small but growing group of electric guitarists inspired by the likes of Mark Knopfler and Jeff Beck. You will start the session using just your thumb and first finger to pick and strum chords you already know, then add your second, third, and fourth fingers—and even a pick—to pluck different string groupings and create interesting arpeggio sounds.

CHAPTER 3

SESSION 7·1 DVD

THUMB AND ONE FINGER

You'll begin your journey into fingerstyle by picking strings with your thumb (picking downward from the lowest joint of the thumb, toward the floor) and first finger (picking upward from the base joint of the finger, toward your face). You can achieve a lot with just these two digits, from jumping between strings with ease to playing two notes simultaneously. Notice the playing instructions under the exercise tabs: the thumb is labeled as "p" and the first or index finger as "i."

PRO TIP
LEARNING FINGERSTYLE

Using your fingers instead of a plectrum to pick allows for more variety in tone and volume. You can also fingerpick two or more strings simultaneously, while a pick can only strum across strings. For nylon-string acoustic (classical guitar) playing, you might want to grow your picking-hand nails slightly longer; this is less important for steel-string acoustic playing.

THUMB STROKE

Pick the 6th string with your thumb. Keep your thumb relatively straight throughout the motion and contact the string with both your skin and the tip of your nail.

Rest your thumb on the 5th string. This is known as a "rest stroke," and it's ideal for single notes. For busier picking, perform a "free stroke," by moving your thumb away after picking.

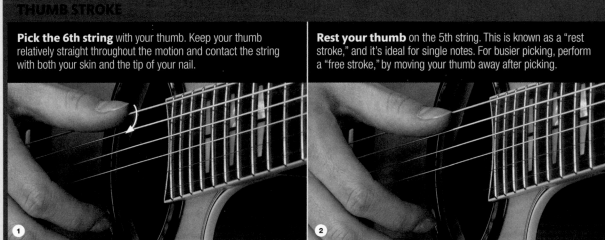

FINGER STROKE

Pick the 1st string with your 1st finger. Use an upward motion generated from the bottom finger joint and contact the string with both your skin and the tip of your nail.

Rest your 1st finger on the 2nd string. This is ideal for strong single notes. For chord picking, move your finger away after picking; this is a free stroke.

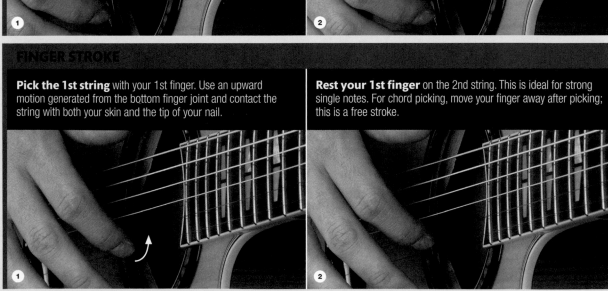

EXERCISE 7.1.1 – ALTERNATING BETWEEN THUMB AND 1ST FINGER

In this exercise you switch between low notes (played free stroke) by the thumb, and high notes (also played free stroke) by the 1st finger. Look out for a 5th string hammer-on in bar 2. The 6th and 1st strings are picked together to finish.

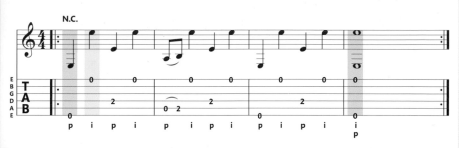

■ **Perform a free stroke** with your thumb. Sound the 6th string; aim to make contact with both skin (for tonal warmth) and nail (for note clarity).

■ **Sound the repetitive E note.** Use a free stroke with the 1st finger on the 1st string. As with the thumb, make contact with both skin and nail for the best sound.

■ **Play the E notes in the final bar.** Use both your thumb and 1st finger to pick the 6th and 1st strings. Sound both notes with free strokes so they ring out.

EXERCISE 7.1.2 – THUMB AND 1ST-FINGER PICKING, COUNTRY STYLE

The G and C chords of this exercise are played with a thumb-picked bassline and fingerpicked higher notes (using the 1st finger). Some of the higher notes are played simultaneously with a bass note.

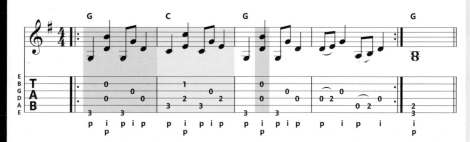

■ **Fret a small G chord.** In bar 1, make a small G chord using only your 3rd finger at the 6th string's 3rd fret as shown (stretched finger posture shown for clarity).

■ **Change from G to C** in bar 2. Make the full shape of the C chord, placing your 3rd, 2nd, and 1st fingers on the frets as shown above. Press down firmly on the strings.

■ **Pick the 4th and 2nd** strings together. You need to do this on the second beat in each of the first three bars. Pick with your thumb and 1st finger only.

SESSION 7·2
DVD

CARTER PICKING

Here you will develop your thumb and first finger skills by including strums performed by your first finger on the higher strings. These strums are performed in both down and up movements using your fingernail to create a bold and bright sound. This picking style is commonly known as Carter picking, named after the guitarist Maybelle Carter (*see box*), and has proved popular with many guitarists. Johnny Cash used it in many songs, including *I Walk The Line*.

WHAT'S THE THEORY?
CARTER PICKING

In the distinctive sound of Carter (or "scratch") picking, the melody is typically played on the bass strings, while the first finger performs rhythm strumming on the higher strings. It was developed from a banjo-playing style by Maybelle Carter, a guitarist born in Virginia, who played with the Carter Family country music group from the 1920s to the 1950s.

1ST-FINGER DOWN-STRUM

Position your 1st finger on the 4th string. Rest your nail against the string and bend the finger slightly so the finger can uncurl during the downward strum.

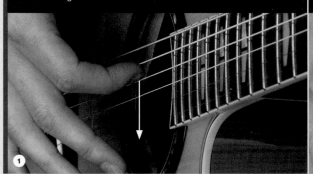

Strum the higher strings. In one movement, move your 1st finger quickly across all four strings, making contact with the nail. Experiment with the volume of your strums.

1ST-FINGER UP-STRUM

Position your 1st finger at the 1st string. Rest your fingertip or nail against the 1st string and slightly curl the finger. Keep your other fingers relaxed and away from the strings.

Strum the four higher strings. Bring your 1st finger back towards your body. Most of the movement should come from your finger joint, not your hand.

EXERCISE 7.2.1 – THUMB-PICKING BASS AND 1ST-FINGER STRUMS

In this exercise you use your thumb to play the bass notes, and your 1st finger for the down-and-up, four-string strums. Look out for the 4th string hammer-on in bar 2—this provides contrast to the other low notes.

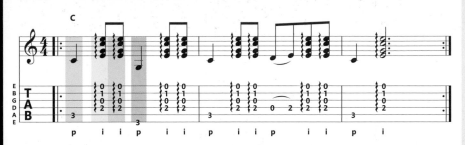

■ **Fret the C chord.** Use your 1st, 2nd, and 3rd fingers to fret. Pick the low C on the 5th string with your thumb.

■ **Down strum the four higher strings.** Start with the nail of your 1st finger (4th string) and perform a down strum.

■ **Up strum the four higher strings.** Use your 1st finger to up strum the four higher strings.

■ **Play the low G note.** From the C chord position, move your 3rd finger to the 3rd fret, 6th string and pick with your thumb.

EXERCISE 7.2.2 – THUMB-PICKING AND 1ST-FINGER STRUMMING PLUS HAMMER-ONS

Practise the Carter picking technique here with some added low note hammer-ons. The exercise features two chords—Am and Em—that are linked by descending bass notes.

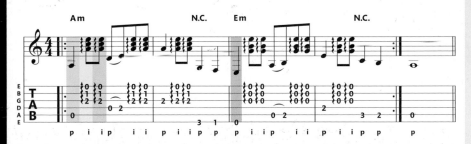

■ **Fret the Am chord.** Use your 1st, 2nd, and 3rd fingers to fret. Pick the low A on the open 5th string with your thumb.

■ **Down strum the three higher strings.** Start with the nail of your 1st finger on the 3rd string.

■ **Up strum the three higher strings.** Use your 1st finger again, this time to up strum the three higher strings.

■ **Play E minor.** Change to this new chord and perform the picking in the patterns indicated.

CHAPTER 3

SESSION
7•3
DVD

ARPEGGIO FINGERPICKING

Increase your picking versatility by introducing another finger—the second. This also opens the way to playing more varied arpeggio patterns, some of which you learned to play in Session 4 (*see pp.132–33*) using a pick. Fingerpicking will give them an almost harplike quality. Arpeggiating involves fretting the chord shape, while your picking hand sounds the strings in various down and up patterns. In this lesson, you will practise the skill of picking with your thumb and two fingers before applying it to some simple chord shapes. Notice in the musical notation that the second finger appears as "m" under the tab.

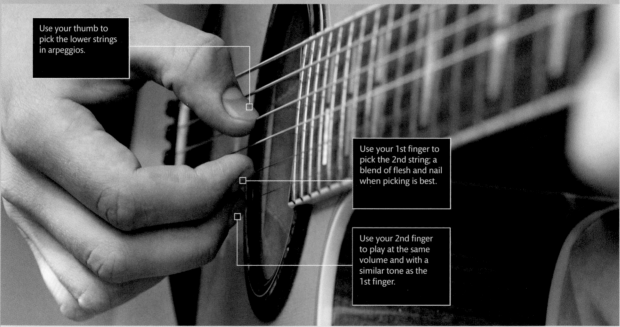

Use your thumb to pick the lower strings in arpeggios.

Use your 1st finger to pick the 2nd string; a blend of flesh and nail when picking is best.

Use your 2nd finger to play at the same volume and with a similar tone as the 1st finger.

PICKING WITH THE THUMB, 1ST, AND 2ND FINGERS

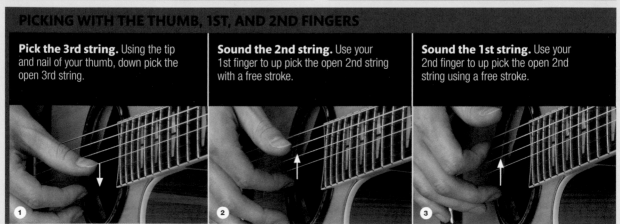

Pick the 3rd string. Using the tip and nail of your thumb, down pick the open 3rd string.

Sound the 2nd string. Use your 1st finger to up pick the open 2nd string with a free stroke.

Sound the 1st string. Use your 2nd finger to up pick the open 2nd string using a free stroke.

1   2   3

EXERCISE 7.3.1 – Em ARPEGGIO WITH THE THUMB, 1ST, AND 2ND FINGERS

Practice picking sets of three strings here. Move your thumb between the 6th and 3rd strings on each beat for an ascending and descending bass; use the 1st and 2nd fingers on the top two strings only.

■ **Fret the Em chord.** Use your thumb to pick the low E. Each of the triplets starts with a bass note on the beat.

■ **Pick with your 1st finger.** After each thumb-picked low note of the arpeggio, pick the open 2nd string with your 1st finger.

■ **Pick with your 2nd finger.** Sound the last note of each triplet on the 1st string, using your 2nd finger.

■ **Pick with your thumb** and two fingers. To finish, pick the 6th, 2nd, and 1st strings together as shown above.

EXERCISE 7.3.2 – ARPEGGIO PICKING USING FOUR CHORD SHAPES

In this exercise you will fingerpick two groups of three strings for each of four chord shapes: Em, G, Am, and C. First learn the exercise, then increase your speed.

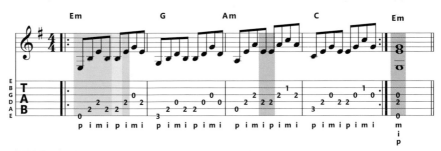

■ **Begin the first Em arpeggio.** Use your thumb and first two fingers to arpeggiate the lowest three strings.

■ **Play the second Em arpeggio.** After picking the 5th string with your 1st finger, pick it again with your thumb.

■ **Pick with your 1st finger.** After the thumb-pick on the 5th string, perform a free stroke on the 4th string.

■ **Play the Am arpeggio.** After picking the 4th string with your 1st finger, pick it again with your thumb.

■ **Play the final Em chord.** Pick the 6th, 4th, and 3rd strings with your thumb and first two fingers.

CHAPTER 3

SESSION
7·4
DVD

THUMB AND THREE FINGERS

Many acoustic guitarists use just the thumb and two fingers in their fingerstyle, but adding the third finger opens up many new musical possibilities.

Using the third finger requires precise coordination, and one popular playing option is to allocate one digit to each string in four-string groupings. This allows you to play rippling arpeggios that sound complex but are very economical for the picking hand. You can also pick four notes simultaneously, creating an almost pianolike sound.

The thumb and three-finger approach is favoured by all classical guitarists (try Andres Segovia, John Williams, and Julian Bream), as well as sophisticated acoustic guitarists such as Chet Atkins, Earl Klugh, and Tommy Emmanuel. Excellence in fingerpicking with thumb and three fingers takes a lot of practice, especially to make the action of your third finger as precise as the other two.

Two of the exercises shown here feature advanced arpeggio patterns and picking sequences. These will help to strengthen the action of your third finger, so you can use it for picking as effectively as the other fingers. The third exercise combines chords with arpeggios for a very full-sounding performance. Note that in the musical notation, the third finger is shown as "a" below the tab.

EXERCISE 7.4.1 – THUMB AND THREE-FINGER ARPEGGIOS ON THE HIGHEST FOUR STRINGS

This simple exercise introduces the 3rd finger into your fingerpicking. There is no chord shape to fret, so you can focus your attention on the picking pattern. Learn it very slowly, breaking the piece into one-bar segments.

■ **Sound the 4th string.**
Begin the picking pattern of bar 1 by performing a free stroke with your thumb. The thumb is used once in bars 1, 3, and 4, and twice in bar 2.

■ **Play the second note.**
Pick the 3rd string with your 1st finger using a free stroke. Take care not to brush other strings. The 1st finger is used twice in bars 1–3, and once in bar 4.

■ **Play the third note.**
Pick the 2nd string with your 2nd finger, using a free stroke. Use your 2nd finger three times in bars 1 and 3, twice in bar 2, and once in bar 4.

■ **Play the fourth note.**
Pick the 1st string with your 3rd finger using a free stroke. Using the 3rd finger can feel awkward at first, so repeat the exercise until it feels comfortable.

EXERCISE 7.4.2 – PIANO-LIKE ARPEGGIOS WITH THUMB AND THREE FINGERS

A varied picking pattern creates a sophisticated sound here using just two chords: C and G7/B. The 3rd (a) and 2nd (m) fingers are used extensively to build strength.

■ **Pick the 1st string.** Fret the C chord and play the first note in bar 1 with your 3rd finger, using a free stroke.

■ **Pick the 2nd string.** For the next note in bar 1, use a free stroke to pick the 2nd string with your 2nd finger.

■ **Pick the 3rd string.** For the penultimate note in bar 1, pick the 3rd string with your 1st finger, using a free stroke.

■ **Pick the 4th string.** Complete bar 1 by using your thumb to pick the 4th string. Avoid brushing adjacent strings.

■ **Move to bar 2.** Pick the 5th string using your thumb, in a free stroke. The next note (E) is also thumb picked.

EXERCISE 7.4.3 – CHORD AND ARPEGGIO PICKING WITH THUMB AND THREE FINGERS

In this exercise you'll practice sounding a chord by picking several strings simultaneously, and picking staggered arpeggios. It uses two chords: Am and Em.

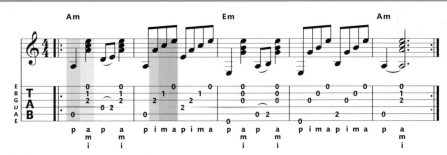

■ **Pick the open 5th string.** Begin bar 1 by fretting the Am chord, and picking the A note with your thumb.

■ **Pick with three fingers.** After playing the low A, use three fingers to pick the top three strings simultaneously.

■ **Move to bar 2.** After using your thumb to pick the 5th string, pick the 3rd string with your 1st finger to play the A note.

■ **Pick the 2nd string.** Perform a free stroke with your 2nd finger to sound the C note.

■ **Pick the open 1st string.** Perform a free stroke with your 3rd finger to sound the E note.

SESSION

7·5   CHORD INVERSIONS

So far you have learned many major and minor chords in which the root note is the lowest note in the chord: for example, the standard G major chord, made up of G, B, and A. The root and lowest note is G; the third is B; and the fifth is D. However, chords can be rearranged so that they have a nonroot note in the bass; these are called "chord inversions." For example, moving the G note in G major up by one octave makes the B (third) note the lowest note in the chord: B, D, G. This is called a "first inversion." For the second inversion, the fifth becomes the lowest note: D, G, B. In a 7th chord (*see pp.114–15*),

the additional note—the seventh—can provide a third inversion, where the seventh becomes the lowest note. Chord inversions are considered as slash chords (*see pp.130–31*) and they are written as the chord name separated by a slash from the bass note (the first inversion of G major is written as G/B).

Inversions inject variety into chord progressions and can help enhance a song's mood. They also smooth the transition from one chord to another, as there is a smaller movement between bass notes. Here you'll meet inversions of G7 and D7 chords and use various inversions to enhance a chord progression.

G7: ROOT POSITION AND THREE INVERSIONS

G7 (ROOT POSITION)
This is the basic six-string G7 chord. G notes are shown as white circled numbers or circled open strings.

G7/B (1ST INVERSION)
This five-string G7 chord has B instead of G as its lowest note: B is the third interval of the scale.

G7/D (2ND INVERSION)
This four-string G7 chord has D instead of G as its lowest note: D is the fifth interval of the scale.

G7/F (3RD INVERSION)
This four-string G7 chord has F instead of G as its lowest note: F is the seventh interval of the scale.

D7: ROOT VERSION AND THREE INVERSIONS

D7 (ROOT VERSION)
This is the basic four-string D7 chord with D as the bass note. The D note is a circled open string.

D7/F♯ (1ST INVERSION)
This five-string D7 chord has F♯ instead of D as its lowest note: F♯ is the third interval of the scale.

D7/A (2ND INVERSION)
This five-string D7 chord has A instead of D as its lowest note: A is the fifth interval of the scale.

D7/C (3RD INVERSION)
This final D7 chord has C instead of D as its lowest note: C is the seventh interval of the scale.

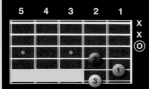
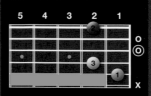
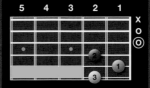
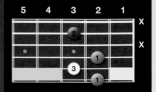

EXERCISE 7.5.1 – THREE-STRING CHORDS WITH INVERSIONS

This exercise shows that you can achieve great sophistication using only three strings, by playing inversions alongside root position chords.

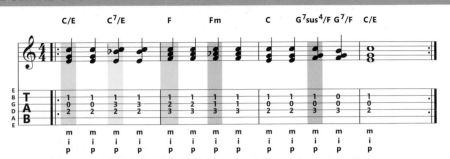

C/E   C7/E   F   Fm   C   G7sus4/F G7/F   C/E

■ **Play C/E.**
This is the first chord in the piece—a reduced form of C in first inversion, where E is the lowest note.

■ **Play C7/E.**
The fingering of this chord is the same as for the C/E chord, except that a B♭ note (the 7th) is also included.

■ **Play the F chord.**
This is in root position. I listen out for the smooth bass note change from the previous C7/E chord.

■ **Play the Fm chord.**
This minor chord directly follows the F chord and gives the progression a melancholy quality.

■ **Play G7sus4/F.**
F is the seventh of the chord and the lowest note (3rd inversion). Take the 1st finger off for G7/F.

EXERCISE 7.5.2 – FOUR-STRING CHORDS WITH INVERSIONS

This exercise uses four-string versions of chords. Notice the smooth bass movement with inversions and root position chords.

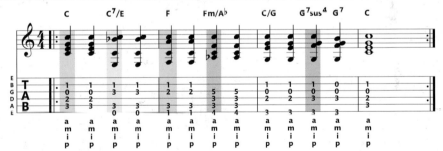

C   C7/E   F   Fm/A♭   C/G   G7sus4 G7   C

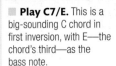

■ **Play the C chord.**
This is the first chord in the piece. Form it using the standard fingering shown in the picture.

■ **Play C7/E.** This is a big-sounding C chord in first inversion, with E—the chord's third—as the bass note.

■ **Play the F chord.**
This is in root position. Listen out for the smooth bass note change from the previous C7/E chord.

■ **Play the Fm/A♭ chord.** Fm is in first inversion because A♭ is the third of the chord, and the lowest note.

■ **Play the G7sus4 chord.** This is in root position because G is the lowest note in the chord.

CHAPTER 3

① **José Feliciano** has a phenomenal fingerpicking technique that incorporates arpeggios, fast single-note runs, and percussive slaps, along with sophisticated chords.

GREAT FINGERSTYLE PLAYERS

Fingerstyle is most closely associated with classical and flamenco players, but it has much wider applications too. From intricate Latin American grooves through to full-on folk guitar strumming, fingerpicking is fantastically versatile for all styles of music. Here are four guitarists who excel at the art of acoustic guitar fingerpicking.

① JOSÉ FELICIANO

Sublime fingerpicking on (mostly) a nylon-string guitar, and a great voice, brought José Feliciano fame in the late 1960s. He is as adept at rhythmic chord picking as virtuoso single-note soloing.

ESSENTIAL TRACKS *Light My Fire* ◆ *And I Love Her* ◆ *California Dreamin'* ◆ *Sunny* ◆ *Affirmation*

SIMILAR ARTISTS Chet Atkins ◆ Laurindo Almeida ◆ Antonio Carlos Jobim ◆ Djavan ◆ João Gilberto

② EARL KLUGH

This American fingerstyle player has an appealing smooth jazz sound. Inspired as much by Chet Atkins as George Benson, his playing is noted for its lyrical soloing and rippling arpeggios.

ESSENTIAL TRACKS *Living Inside Your Love* ◆ *Angelina* ◆ *Heart String* ◆ *Tropical Legs* ◆ *Dr Macumba*

SIMILAR ARTISTS Chet Atkins ◆ Jim Hall ◆ Larry Carlton ◆ Lee Ritenour ◆ Paul Jackson Jr.

③ KT TUNSTALL

Scottish singer-songwriter KT Tunstall is a confident singer and very musical guitarist. From chordal strumming to arpeggio picking, the acoustic guitar is pivotal in many of her songs.

ESSENTIAL TRACKS *Black Horse And The Cherry Tree* ◆ *Other Side Of The World* ◆ *Suddenly I See*

SIMILAR ARTISTS Sheryl Crow ◆ Joan Baez ◆ Joni Mitchell ◆ Joan Armatrading ◆ Tracy Chapman

④ JOHN WILLIAMS

From his classical guitar repertoire to pop forays with Sky and movie soundtracks, John Williams's fingerpicking combines precision with fluency.

ESSENTIAL TRACKS *Concierto De Aranjuez* ◆ *Memoirs De La Alhambra* ◆ *Cavatina* ◆ *Toccata in Dm* (with Sky) ◆ *Schindler's List* (for solo guitar)

SIMILAR ARTISTS Julian Bream ◆ Andrés Segovia ◆ David Russell ◆ Christopher Parkening

SESSION
7·6 BANJO ROLLS
DVD

The banjo roll is a picking technique characteristic of the approach developed by banjo players—notably Earl Scruggs—in the mid-1940s. This fast picking technique was soon adopted by guitarists, and became the signature quick and agile sound of bluegrass. It also added busy rhythmic color to country music.

A banjo roll is played by picking groups of three strings, using your thumb and first two fingers. The roll can be forwards (low to high strings), backwards (high to low strings), or a combination of the two. Banjo rolls are often played on chords with open strings so that notes can be sustained. In the following three exercises, you will learn how to use banjo rolls to organize scale playing, and perform various arpeggio patterns and melodic phrases, in combination with hammer-ons and pull-offs.

PRO TIP
BANJO ROLL TECHNIQUES

The banjo roll technique is often credited to the American banjo player Earl Scruggs, whose thumb and two-finger style made him popular in bluegrass music from the mid-1940s, with fast picking sequences that could create impressive accompaniment or lead performances.

Banjo rolls work best on chords with open strings, and for this reason certain keys are favoured over others: try G major and E major, both of which are banjo-roll friendly. You could also experiment with using metal fingerpicks (*see p.27*), which provide greater tonal brightness when playing banjo rolls.

EXERCISE 7.6.1 – BANJO ROLLS WITH HAMMER-ONS AND PULL-OFFS

This E major-based exercise uses forward banjo rolls with a descending melody line, and is played with hammer-ons and pull-offs. The open strings create a smooth sound as the fretting hand shifts position.

■ **Down pick with your thumb.** Sound the A note on the 3rd string, with your 1st finger at the 2nd fret.

■ **Hammer-on for B.** Use your 3rd finger to hammer-on to the 3rd string, 4th fret, to sound the B note.

■ **Pick with your 1st finger.** Sound the open 2nd string (another B note) and let the note ring out and sustain.

■ **Pick with your 2nd finger.** Complete the forward banjo roll by picking the open 1st string (E).

EXERCISE 7.6.2 – COUNTRY-BLUES LICK WITH BANJO ROLLS

Practice forward banjo rolls and hammer-ons with this exercise. Notice how the hammer-on notes (B, G, D, B) resolve the previous tension notes (B♭, F♯, C♯, B♭) played one fret lower.

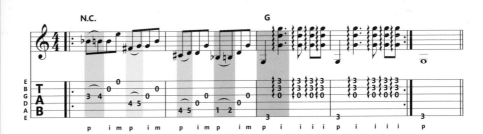

■ **Play B♭ and B.** Thumb-pick the 3rd string with your 1st finger on the 3rd fret (B♭), then hammer-on to the 4th fret.

■ **Play the F♯ and G notes.** Down pick with your thumb and use a hammer-on to move between the two notes.

■ **Play the C♯ and D notes.** Down pick with your thumb and play the two notes on the 5th string.

■ **Play the B♭ and B notes.** Down pick with your thumb and play the two notes on the 5th string.

■ **Fret the G chord.** Use your 2nd, 3rd, and 4th fingers to fret the chord; strum down and up with your 1st finger.

EXERCISE 7.6.3 – G MAJOR SCALE USING BANJO ROLLS AND OPEN STRINGS

This scale exercise features forward and forward/back banjo rolls. Aim to make the notes ring into each other wherever possible.

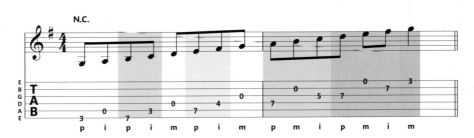

■ **Play the C and B notes.** The move from the 3rd and 4th notes (C and B) in bar 1 requires a long stretch between the 4th and 1st fingers.

■ **Play the E and F♯ notes.** This four-fret stretch using your 4th and 1st fingers is required for the 6th and 7th notes in bar 1.

■ **Play the A and C notes.** Use your 1st and 3rd fingers to fret the 1st and 3rd notes in bar 2. Notice the picking directions have changed (p, m, i).

■ **Play the F♯ and D notes.** Use your 3rd and 4th fingers (both at the 7th fret) for the 4th and 6th notes in bar 2.

■ **Play the final G note.** After the D note, reach back to the 3rd fret, 1st string, with your 1st finger for the final G.

CHAPTER 3

SESSION
7·7 HYBRID PICKING

Your newly developed fingerpicking skills are combined in this lesson with the use of a pick. This technique is known—not surprisingly—as "hybrid picking." Its great advantage over simply using a pick is that it is easier to move between strings, especially when making big string jumps. In addition, you can play several strings simultaneously, and your dynamics can be more varied (the pick can be loud/hard, the fingers quiet/soft). All this and you can still strum chords and pick lead lines too. Hybrid picking is beloved by country guitarists, and features in arpeggios, banjo rolls, and quick lead licks, but you'll also hear it in blues and rock. To begin, hold the pick as normal, between thumb and first finger, and use it to sound the lower strings; use your second and third fingers to pick the higher strings. The exercises here require you to sound two or more strings simultaneously, and to play hybrid-picked arpeggio patterns.

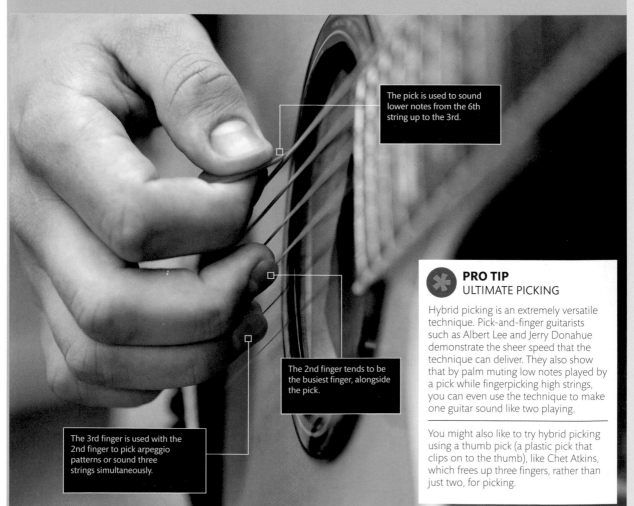

The pick is used to sound lower notes from the 6th string up to the 3rd.

The 2nd finger tends to be the busiest finger, alongside the pick.

The 3rd finger is used with the 2nd finger to pick arpeggio patterns or sound three strings simultaneously.

PRO TIP
ULTIMATE PICKING

Hybrid picking is an extremely versatile technique. Pick-and-finger guitarists such as Albert Lee and Jerry Donahue demonstrate the sheer speed that the technique can deliver. They also show that by palm muting low notes played by a pick while fingerpicking high strings, you can even use the technique to make one guitar sound like two playing.

You might also like to try hybrid picking using a thumb pick (a plastic pick that clips on to the thumb), like Chet Atkins, which frees up three fingers, rather than just two, for picking.

EXERCISE 7.7.1 – COUNTRY-STYLE CHORDS USING HYBRID PICKING

This exercise introduces hybrid picking in a short country-style piece. Once you can play the piece through, try adding palm muting for the low notes played with the pick.

■ **Play the C note.** Begin with a down stroke on the 5th string, while fingering the 3rd fret.

■ **Play the C chord.** Use the pick to sound the 4th string and then pick the 2nd and 3rd strings with your fingers.

■ **Play the higher C note.** Pick the 2nd string with your 3rd finger following the down stroke on the 6th string.

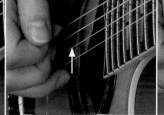

■ **Play the G note.** Pick the 3rd string with your 2nd finger following the down stroke on the 4th string.

EXERCISE 7.7.2 – ROCK-AND-ROLL RIFF USING HYBRID PICKING

This exercise is in two halves. Bars 1 and 2 feature low, picked strings, and two-string fingerpicking; bars 3 and 4 require big chord strums with the pick.

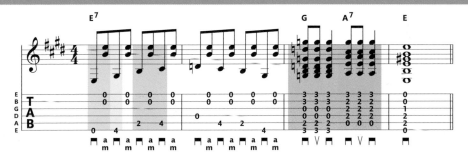

■ **Fret the E7 chord.** Play a down stroke on the 6th string, then use your 2nd and 3rd fingers to pick the top two strings.

■ **Play the G♯ note.** Place your 3rd finger at the 4th fret, 6th string. Use a down stroke to sound the G♯.

■ **Play the B and C♯ note.** Use your 1st finger (2nd fret) and 3rd finger (4th fret) on the 5th string.

■ **Play the G chord.** Fret the chord using all four fingers and sound it using down and up strokes of the pick.

■ **Play the A7 chord.** With your 4th finger on the 1st string, place your 1st finger across the 2nd fret, across three strings.

SESSION
7·8
DVD

FURTHER HYBRID PICKING

Hybrid picking is a powerful technique, but when you use a pick plus one or two fingers, you are still effectively one finger "down" on conventional fingerpickers, who have the thumb and three fingers at their disposal. To sound up to four strings simultaneously and maximize the potential of hybrid picking, you need to bring your fourth finger (or pinkie) into play. Notable hybrid pickers who use the fourth finger as well include Texan precision-picker Eric Johnson and the late Danny Gatton—"master of the Telecaster."

Your fourth finger is the weakest on your hand, so lots of practice is required to develop its strength and independence, even though it typically picks the highest (thinnest) string. The exercise below will get you started, and help you bring the technique into practice. Note that the fourth finger is shown in the musical notation as a "c" below the tab.

PRO TIP
DEVELOPING YOUR LITTLE FINGER

When you start picking with your fourth finger, you'll find that in comparison with your other fingers, it's lacking in control and strength. With focus and perseverance though, you will be able to improve its abilities.

Use your fourth finger when picking several strings simultaneously—it will copy the movement of the other fingers so won't be working in isolation. As it is picking the highest string, it will need less power than the other fingers that are picking thicker, lower strings. The first bar of the exercise below demonstrates this approach.

When hybrid-picking arpeggios with a pick and two fingers, include the next higher string by using the fourth finger. Slow your picking down to concentrate on maintaining the same volume for all strings. Bar 2 of the exercise below demonstrates this approach.

CHAPTER 3

EXERCISE 7.8.1 – HYBRID PICKING INCLUDING THE 4TH FINGER

The picking tasks in this exercise are split between a down stroke followed by three strings picked simultaneously, and some ascending arpeggios using a pick and three fingers.

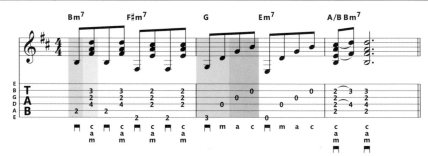

■ **Down stroke the 5th string** with a pick. Fret the Bm7 chord well, to produce a clear note.

■ **Fingerpick the chord.** Pick the three-string shape using your 4th, 3rd, and 2nd fingers as shown.

■ **Down pick the 6th string,** then use your 2nd finger to pick the open 4th string (D).

■ **Play the G note.** Use your 3rd finger to pick the 3rd string, to sound the G note.

■ **Play the B note.** Pick the open 2nd string with your 4th finger. Aim to make the sound as loud as with your other fingers.

GETTING THE SOUND

Joni Mitchell – singer-songwriter

Joni Mitchell stands alone in contemporary music, being as influential to singer-songwriters as to women looking for musical inspiration. Born in Canada, she taught herself to play guitar and performed on the local folk scene while at art college. Often surrounded by phenomenal musicians (band guitarists have included Pat Metheny and Robben Ford), her own guitar style has always been progressive. She favors fingerpicking and sophisticated chords and progressions, often more jazz-inflected than those used in folk. Mitchell has made use of unusual guitar tunings; early on she favored EBEG♯BE but other tunings include open G (DGDGBD) and DADFAD. In the 1990s she used modern technology (such as the Parker Fly guitar and Roland VG88 effects unit) to help make these tuning options easier to record and perform with.

ESSENTIAL TRACKS	SIMILAR ARTISTS
Big Yellow Taxi	Joan Baez
Woodstock	James Taylor
Coyote	Sarah McLachlan
Both Sides Now	Michelle Branch
Little Green	David Crosby
A Case Of You	Eva Cassidy

Joni Mitchell's alternate guitar tunings allow her to produce songs filled with consonances and dissonances—harmonies and conflicting tones—that gently play off one another. She claims to have used 51 different tunings.

MILESTONE PIECE

This piece, based in G major, features many of the fingerpicking and strumming patterns introduced in this session. In the first eight bars you will use variations on the banjo roll and thumb and first-finger strumming technique. These are in a call-and-response style, with single note picking in one bar, then chord strumming in the second. From bar 9, you shift to E minor and start fingerpicking using thumb, first, and second fingers with doublestops (two strings sounded simultaneously). From bar 12 there are more banjo rolls, before a G major scale passage leads to a final strummed G chord.

CHAPTER 3

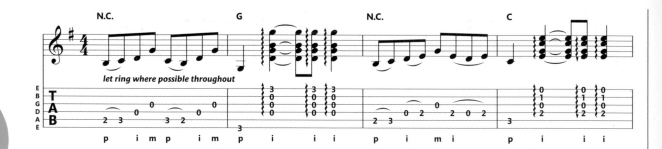

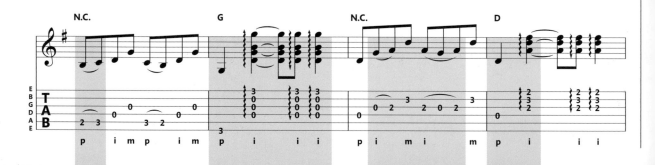

Use your 2nd and 3rd fingers to perform the hammer-ons and pull-offs involving B and C notes.

Fret the G chord and thumb pick the 6th string. Use your 1st finger to strum the higher strings of the G chord.

Using your 1st and 3rd fingers is the best way to perform the open-string hammer-ons and pull-offs.

Use your 2nd and 3rd fingers for the Em shape. You can then use your 4th finger for the low G note (bar 9, beat 2).

Use your first three fingers for the Am chord. You can then use your 4th finger for the lower C note (bar 11, beat 2).

Move your 2nd finger from the 2nd fret, 4th string to the 2nd fret, 6th string, to make the D7/F♯ shape.

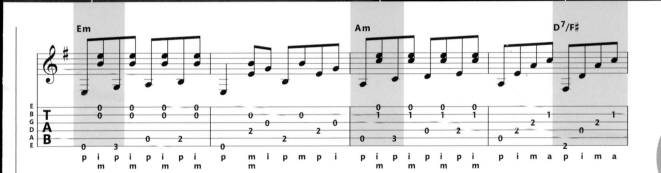

Use this fingering to make the D shape—it is the logical option following the D5 shape in the preceding bar.

Use your 4th finger for B (7th fret, 6th string) and your 1st finger for C (3rd fret, 5th string).

Use your 4th finger for E (7th fret, 5th string) and your 1st finger for F♯ (4th fret, 4th string).

CHAPTER 3

BLUES-ROCK SOLOING AND IMPROVISATION

Here you return to the electric guitar to develop your blues-rock soloing abilities with new skills and some exotic scales that take you beyond the realms of pentatonics. First, you'll learn how to play pentatonic scales horizontally—along the length, rather than width of the fretboard—opening up new soloing options. You'll discover which scales and notes are most effective when soloing over different keys, get to grips with the Dorian and Mixolydian modes (perfect for sophisticated soloing), and learn phrasing that will make you stand out from other guitarists. Finally, you'll consolidate your knowledge in two milestone pieces: a minor blues and a major blues.

SESSION

8·1 HORIZONTAL PENTATONICS

Here you will look at ways to broaden your use of the minor pentatonic scale. So far you have learned how to solo "vertically"—moving across the strings within one pentatonic shape. This is a fruitful approach for expressive soloing and is popular with blues rock guitarists because it minimizes hand movement. However, you may have noticed that many players like to solo horizontally—moving up and down the length of the fretboard. This skill opens up new approaches to soloing, allowing for hammer-ons, pull-offs, and longer slides, and delivering bigger pitch variations from fewer strings.

The three exercises shown here demonstrate how these new horizontal fretboard pathways can be used with the A minor pentatonic scale to produce fresh sounds that will give a new dimension to your soloing.

PRO TIP
PENTATONIC VARIATION

You may find that some guitarists look down on the minor pentatonic for its "fits all situations" simplicity. However, you don't need to move away from the pentatonic to more exotic scales to make your playing sound more sophisticated. Horizontal playing (as shown here) is one way to spice up your pentatonic soloing. Another is omitting one or two notes from the scale, or skipping over several strings for big note jumps. This not only tests your technique but also sounds fresh, stylistically shifting the scale from blues and rock into areas like fusion and jazz. Listen to the way that Eric Johnson, John Scofield, and the new blues hero Joe Bonamassa add variety and sophistication to pentatonic playing by skipping strings and omitting notes.

EXERCISE 8.1.1 – A MINOR PENTATONIC: ASCENT ACROSS ALL STRINGS

In this exercise you play A minor pentatonic using shape 5 (low strings), then shapes 1 and 2 (middle strings), before finishing with shape 3 (highest strings). Note how the sound is more colorful and expansive than when using just one shape of A minor pentatonic. The diagram (*below right*) shows the A minor pentatonic scale mapped out from the 2nd fret to the 13th fret, linking all of the shapes. The notes used in the exercise above are highlighted in white. Other notes from A minor pentatonic shapes are shown in orange.

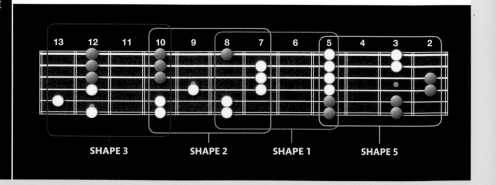

SHAPE 3   SHAPE 2   SHAPE 1   SHAPE 5

EXERCISE 8.1.2 – A MINOR PENTATONIC: ASCENDING TWO-STRING SEQUENCE

Only the top two strings are used in this exercise. You ascend using A minor pentatonic shapes 5, 1, and 2, for a sound favored by modern rock guitarists such as John Petrucci and Paul Gilbert. The diagram (*below right*) shows the A minor pentatonic scale mapped out from the 2nd fret to the 10th fret, linking the three shapes. The notes used in the exercise above are highlighted in white, with other A minor pentatonic notes shown in orange. Look at other two-string groupings for similar sequences.

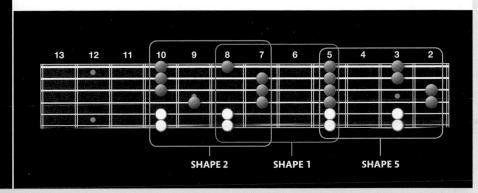

EXERCISE 8.1.3 – A MINOR PENTATONIC: ASCENDING WITH STRING-SKIPPING

This exercise takes a string-skipping idea (shown in bar 1) and then duplicates it with higher minor pentatonic shapes. Start each position shift with the 1st finger each time. The diagram (*below right*) shows only the A minor pentatonic notes used in the exercise above. Notice the omission of the second string—this is the string that is skipped over. As this is a very fruitful approach for getting new pentatonic sounds, try skipping other strings in each shape.

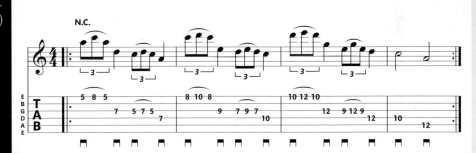

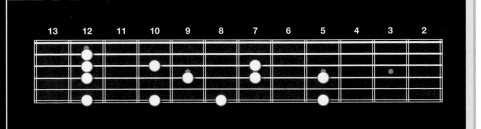

CHAPTER 3

SESSION 8·2 DVD OTHER PENTATONIC KEYS

So far, you have explored the potential of minor pentatonics for soloing only in the key of A. It is now time to extend your knowledge over the 11 other keys. These pages provide a reference guide for the other minor pentatonic scales, with each scale shown as a fretboard diagram.

In each case, the root notes of the scales are indicated by white circles. Spend time learning the scale in every key to be completely "pentatonic ready" by practicing daily.

Once you have become familiar with these scales, try improvising lead lines for songs you hear on the radio or favorites from your music collection. Try to identify the song key first, and then play along in its minor pentatonic.

WHAT'S THE THEORY?
11 OTHER MINOR PENTATONIC KEYS

Use this chart to see the notes that you will be playing for each minor pentatonic key.

D# minor pentatonic D# F# G# A# C#	
Bb minor pentatonic Bb Db Eb F Ab	E minor pentatonic E G A B D
B minor pentatonic B D E F# A	F minor pentatonic F Ab Bb C Eb
C minor pentatonic C Eb F G Bb	F# minor pentatonic F# A B C# E
C# minor pentatonic C# E F# G# B	G minor pentatonic G Bb C D F
D minor pentatonic D F G A C	G# minor pentatonic G# B C# D# F#

Bb MINOR PENTATONIC
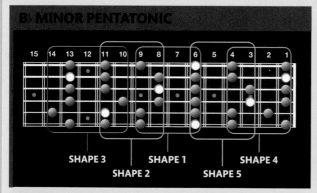

B MINOR PENTATONIC
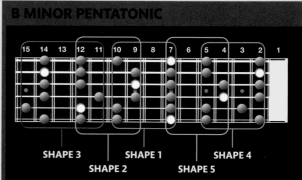

C MINOR PENTATONIC
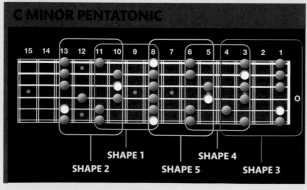

C# MINOR PENTATONIC
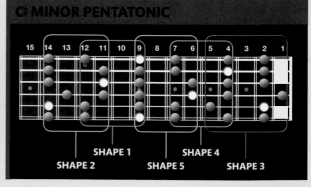

D MINOR PENTATONIC

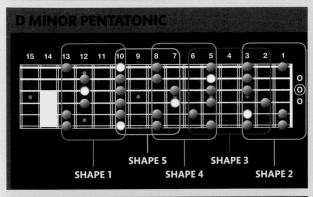

SHAPE 5 · SHAPE 3
SHAPE 1 · SHAPE 4 · SHAPE 2

D♯ MINOR PENTATONIC

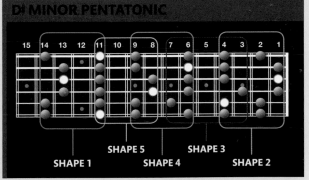

SHAPE 5 · SHAPE 3
SHAPE 1 · SHAPE 4 · SHAPE 2

E MINOR PENTATONIC

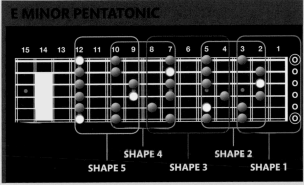

SHAPE 4 · SHAPE 2
SHAPE 5 · SHAPE 3 · SHAPE 1

F MINOR PENTATONIC

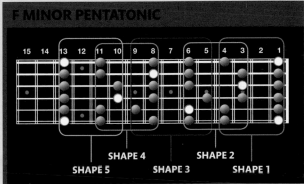

SHAPE 4 · SHAPE 2
SHAPE 5 · SHAPE 3 · SHAPE 1

F♯ MINOR PENTATONIC

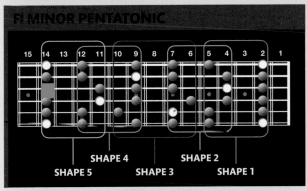

SHAPE 4 · SHAPE 2
SHAPE 5 · SHAPE 3 · SHAPE 1

G MINOR PENTATONIC

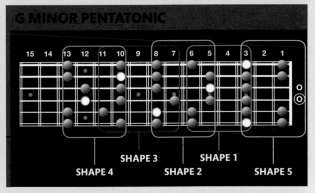

SHAPE 3 · SHAPE 1
SHAPE 4 · SHAPE 2 · SHAPE 5

G♯ MINOR PENTATONIC

SHAPE 3 · SHAPE 1
SHAPE 4 · SHAPE 2 · SHAPE 5

PRACTICE & PROGRESS

Gaining fluency in these scales takes time and discipline, so try planning your practice around a weekly schedule. Day one: start with shape 1, wherever it is on the fretboard. Practice ascending and descending this shape for 15 minutes. Day two: practice shape 2 for 15 minutes (and recap shape 1). Day three: shape 3 (and recap shapes 1 and 2), and so on until day five. Day six: focus on playing all five shapes without hesitation. Day seven: rest! With a one-scale-a-week practice plan, you will cover all 11 scales in just under three months. You are now pentatonic ready.

① **Jimi Hendrix** did not let his flamboyance as a showman distract from his technique. His entrancing pentatonic-based melodies and driving riffs outshone any onstage antics.

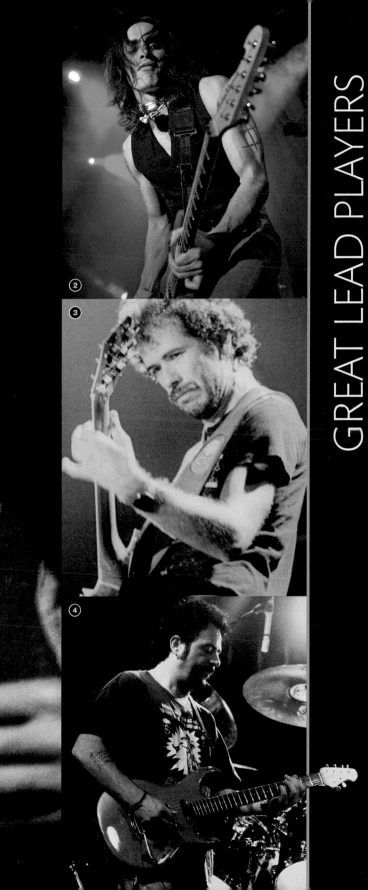

GREAT LEAD PLAYERS

Slow and tasteful or fast and exciting, the lead guitarist is the link between the vocalist and the band, taking the limelight when the vocals stop. Lead guitarists are found in various styles but all are intent on communicating great guitar playing and vibrant melodies to the audience. The following four guitarists are virtuoso lead guitar players.

❶ JIMI HENDRIX

Hendrix is the definitive guitar legend. He combined excellent riff and chord playing with fast bluesy pentatonic playing and varied guitar tones including fuzz and wah wah.

ESSENTIAL TRACKS *Hey Joe* ◆ *Purple Haze* ◆ *Voodoo Chile* ◆ *Little Wing* ◆ *Red House*

SIMILAR ARTISTS Stevie Ray Vaughan ◆ Robin Trower ◆ Eric Johnson ◆ Steve Vai ◆ Eric Gale

❷ NUNO BETTENCOURT

The lead guitarist of Boston rock band Extreme combines fast picking and legato, emotive bends, and impressive two-hand tapping.

ESSENTIAL TRACKS *Get The Funk Out* ◆ *He-Man Woman Hater* ◆ *Flight Of The Wounded Bumble Bee* ◆ *It's A Monster* ◆ *Cupid's Dead*

SIMILAR ARTISTS Eddie Van Halen ◆ George Lynch ◆ Paul Gilbert ◆ Reb Beach

❸ CARLOS SANTANA

With a warm distorted tone, Santana blends blues-rock with Afro-Cuban grooves. Mostly known for his soloing, he favors string bends, minor pentatonic phrases, and quick pull-offs.

ESSENTIAL TRACKS *Black Magic Woman* ◆ *Europa* ◆ *Evil Ways* ◆ *Oye Como Va* ◆ *Smooth*

SIMILAR ARTISTS Peter Green ◆ Eric Clapton ◆ Jimi Hendrix ◆ Stevie Salas ◆ Al Di Meola

❹ STEVE LUKATHER

With impressive speed, tasteful string bending, and soaring distorted tone, Toto's Steve Lukather's style combines blues-rock pentatonics with modern techniques such as harmonics and fast picking.

ESSENTIAL TRACKS *Hold The Line* ◆ *Roseanna* ◆ *Gypsy Train* ◆ *Song For Jeff* ◆ *Party In Simon's Pants*

SIMILAR ARTISTS Jeff Beck ◆ Neal Schon ◆ Joe Satriani ◆ Robben Ford ◆ Richie Kotzen

SESSION
8•3
DVD

SELECTING NOTES

Playing effective solos is a goal for most guitarists, but how do you choose the notes that sound "right" over a chord progression? At first glance it seems simple: first, establish the song's key by identifying the root chord (the one that sounds like "home" each time it's played). If this chord is major, play the major pentatonic scale based on that chord's root note; if it's minor, play the minor pentatonic scale. The longer, seven-note scales of the major scale or natural minor scale may work too.

While this is a good starting point, some notes may not sound good over some of the progression's chords. Spontaneously drawing on the scale template

to "play by ear" is a perfectly valid approach (countless guitarists do it), but results can be a little hit-or-miss, especially if you lack experience.

A more systematic approach for soloing is to analyze the chord progression in the song and then duplicate notes in the chords in your solo. These chord notes can be classed as "golden notes:" when chord and soloing notes are aligned, the results are stronger (especially when starting or ending a phrase).

Here you will apply this principle to two bluesy 7th chord progressions in the keys of A minor and A major. Look for the golden notes in relation to the chord each time.

EXERCISE 8.3.1 – Am7–Dm7–Em7–Am7 BLUES PROGRESSION

First, record yourself playing a simple chord progression in A minor (or ask a friend to play along with you). The progression runs as follows: Am7–Dm7–Em7. Use the A minor pentatonic

scale to solo over the progression. The "golden" notes—those that are also within the chords—are shown in orange; notes to avoid are indicated by circles containing an "X."

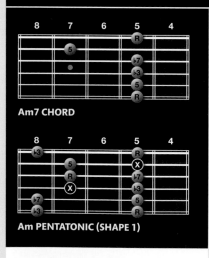

Am7 CHORD

Am PENTATONIC (SHAPE 1)

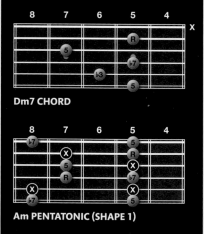

Dm7 CHORD

Am PENTATONIC (SHAPE 1)

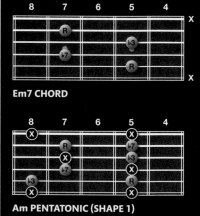

Em7 CHORD

Am PENTATONIC (SHAPE 1)

Improvise over Am7. Compare the notes in the chord and scale diagrams. The root, minor third, fifth, and minor seventh occur in both, so these are the golden notes.

Improvise over Dm7. Compare the notes in the chord and scale diagrams. The root, minor fifth, and minor seventh occur in both, so these are the golden notes.

Improvise over Em7. Compare the notes in the chord and scale diagrams. The root, minor third, and minor seventh occur in both, so these are the golden notes.

EXERCISE 8.3.2 – A MINOR PENTATONIC SOLO: GOLDEN NOTES OVER Am7, Dm7, AND Em7

This exercise demonstrates one possible soloing outcome using A minor pentatonic over the Am7, Dm7, and Em7 chords. The intervals in relation to the chord are shown above the tab.

EXERCISE 8.3.3 – Amaj7–Dmaj7–E7–Amaj7 POP BLUES

First, record yourself playing a simple chord progression in A major (or ask a friend to play along with you). The progression runs as follows: Amaj7–Dmaj7–E7. Use the A major pentatonic scale to solo over the progression. The golden notes—those that are also within the chords—are shown in orange; notes to avoid are indicated by circles containing an "X."

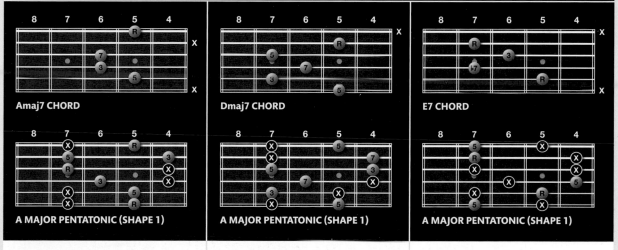

Amaj7 CHORD

Dmaj7 CHORD

E7 CHORD

A MAJOR PENTATONIC (SHAPE 1)

A MAJOR PENTATONIC (SHAPE 1)

A MAJOR PENTATONIC (SHAPE 1)

Improvise over Amaj7. Compare the notes in the chord and scale diagrams. The root, major third, and fifth occur in both, so these are the golden notes.

Improvise over Dmaj7. Compare the notes in the chord and scale diagrams. The major third, fifth, and seventh occur in both, so these are the golden notes.

Improvise over E7. Compare the notes in the chord and scale diagrams. Only the root and fifth occur in both, so these are the golden notes.

EXERCISE 8.3.4 – A MAJOR PENTATONIC SOLO: GOLDEN NOTES OVER Amaj7, Dmaj7, AND E7

This demonstrates one possible soloing outcome using A minor pentatonic over the Am7, Dm7, and Em7 chords. The intervals in relation to the chord are shown above the tab.

SESSION
8·4
DVD

MAJOR BLUES SOLOING

The conventional way to solo over major chords is to play a related major scale (*e.g.* the A major scale over a chord progression of A–D–E–A), but many guitarists choose a minor scale for a more "bluesy" sound. The minor pentatonic scale may seem at odds with major chords, but with good note selection, string bends, and blues curls, you can get great blues results.

Here, you'll play a blues progression in A major, with the A7, D7, and E7 chords. First you will use the A minor pentatonic scale, selecting the golden notes (*see p.220*) that relate to each chord; then you will repeat the progression using the A major pentatonic scale, with its golden notes, for the solo.

PRO TIP
GOLDEN NOTES AND PASSING NOTES

Sticking to golden notes in your soloing is safe but can be restrictive. In practice, great improvising guitarists blend "golden notes" with "passing notes"—notes that aren't directly related to a chord's notes—to provide color. From a structural perspective, the golden notes are used at key moments in a passage, such as at the beginning or end of a musical phrase or when a note is emphasized by sustaining it. The passing notes are used to link golden notes and are played at less important moments, such as in a run before settling on a golden note.

In the pentatonic scale exercises on these pages you are learning to play golden notes. At first, avoid the the notes shown as Xs; with more experience try including them as passing notes in your solos.

EXERCISE 8.4.1 – ROCK-AND-ROLL BLUES WITH MINOR PENTATONIC

First, record yourself playing a simple chord progression in A major (or ask a friend to play along with you). The progression runs as follows: A7–D7–E7–A7. Use the A minor pentatonic scale to solo over the progression. The "golden" notes—those that are also within the chords—are shown in orange; notes to avoid are indicated by circles containing an "X."

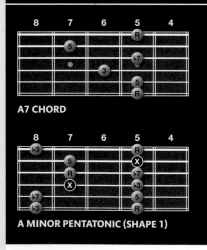

A7 CHORD

A MINOR PENTATONIC (SHAPE 1)

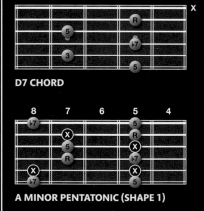

D7 CHORD

A MINOR PENTATONIC (SHAPE 1)

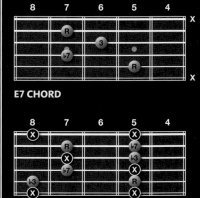

E7 CHORD

A MINOR PENTATONIC (SHAPE 1)

Improvise over A7. Notice that the root, fifth, and minor seventh occur in both diagrams. You'll need to do a blues curl bend on the minor third to suggest the chord's major third.

Improvise over D7. Compare the notes in the chord and scale diagrams. The root, fifth, and minor seventh occur in both diagrams, so these are the golden notes.

Improvise over E7. Notice that the root and minor seventh occur in both diagrams. You'll need to do a blues curl bend on the minor third to suggest the chord's major third.

EXERCISE 8.4.2 – A MINOR PENTATONIC SOLO: GOLDEN NOTES OVER A7, D7, AND E7

This solo uses A minor pentatonic over the A7, D7, and E7 chords. Notice the blues curls applied to C (bar 1) and G (bar 3) to imply the accompanying chord's major third (A7's C# note and E7's G# note).

EXERCISE 8.4.3 – ROCK-AND-ROLL BLUES WITH A MAJOR PENTATONIC

Play and record the same chord progression in A major as used in exercise 8.4.1 (or ask a friend to play along with you). It runs: A7–D7–E7–A7. Use the A major pentatonic scale to solo over the progression. The "golden" notes—those that are also within the chords—are shown in orange; notes to avoid are indicated by circles containing an "X."

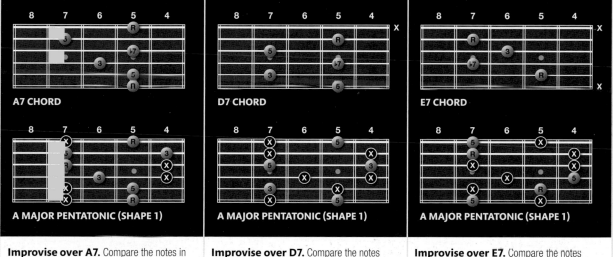

A7 CHORD

D7 CHORD

E7 CHORD

A MAJOR PENTATONIC (SHAPE 1)

A MAJOR PENTATONIC (SHAPE 1)

A MAJOR PENTATONIC (SHAPE 1)

Improvise over A7. Compare the notes in the chord and scale diagrams. The root, major third, and fifth occur in both, so these are the golden notes.

Improvise over D7. Compare the notes in the chord and scale diagrams. Only the major third and fifth occur in both, so these are the golden notes.

Improvise over E7. Compare the notes in the chord and scale diagrams. Only the root and fifth occur in both, so these are the golden notes.

EXERCISE 8.4.4 – A MAJOR PENTATONIC SOLO: GOLDEN NOTES OVER A7, D7, AND E7

Try this solo one using A major pentatonic over the A7, D7, and E7 chords. The intervals in relation to the chord are shown above the tab.

CHAPTER 3

PHRASING

Playing the guitar expressively requires that you develop your own approach to "phrasing"—considering not only what you play, but how you play it. Good phrasing—using tools like melody, rhythmic changes, and accents—will provide musical emphases and nuances that help you communicate with your audience and transform you from competent player to artist. Below are three exercises that demonstrate different phrasing ideas. The first exercise covers long, sustained notes—a confident, slower style of soloing that makes melodies memorable. The second exercise involves a quick blues-scale sequence with sustained notes to end. It's a popular combination (quick then slow playing) for creating solo contrast and puts your scale practice to good use. The last is a call-and-response phrase common in blues and rock music, starting with a riff (call) and ending with a lead lick (response).

WHAT'S THE THEORY?
PACE AND BALANCE

Phrasing is about making a piece of music your own: it provides shape and direction to musical statements and interest to the listener. Imagine playing a long, eight-bar musical statement. Chances are that it will sound "shapeless," but segmenting it into two four-bar phrases or four two-bar phrases can give the statement a clear beginning, middle, and end, just as sentences have when you speak.

Phrasing is used instinctively by vocalists, saxophone, and trumpet players because their breathing patterns set limits to the number of notes they can produce. Guitarists, who can play without such enforced breaks, need to think more consciously about shaping shorter note groupings—it's this that will produce memorable phrasing that enhances appeal to audiences.

EXERCISE 8.5.1 – PHRASING WITH SUSTAINED NOTES

This features a four-note lick that starts each two-bar phrase. A sustained string bend and three descending notes provide the phrase's payoff.

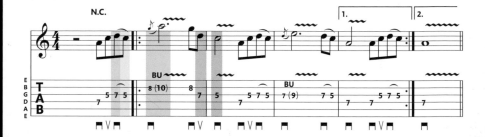

■ **Play the D note.** Place your 3rd finger at the 7th fret, 3rd string (D) and have your 1st finger ready at the 5th fret.

■ **Play the C note.** After picking D, use a pull-off to sound the 1st finger's C note, primed at the 5th fret.

■ **Tone bend from G to A.** Place your 3rd finger at the 8th fret, 2nd string, and bend from G to A ("virtual" 10th fret).

■ **Play the D note.** Following the G, use your 2nd finger to fret the D note at the 7th fret, 3rd string.

■ **Play the C note.** Following the D note, use a down-stroke to sound the C note (5th fret, 3rd string).

EXERCISE 8.5.2 – PHRASING WITH NOTE SEQUENCES AND SUSTAINED NOTES

This exercise starts with a fast A blues-scale sequence followed by string bends and sustained notes to provide additional interest.

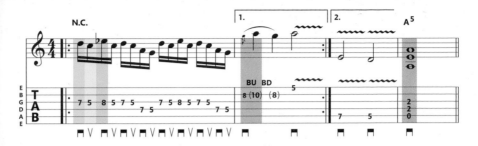

■ **Play the D note.** Place your 3rd finger at the 7th fret, 3rd string. Have your 1st finger ready at the 5th fret.

■ **Play the C note.** After using a down stroke for D, lift your 3rd finger and use an up stroke to sound the 5th-fret C note.

■ **Play the E♭ note.** With your 4th finger at the 8th fret, 3rd string, perform a down stroke to sound E♭.

■ **Tone bend from G to A.** Place your 3rd finger at the 8th fret, 2nd string and bend from G to A ("virtual" 10th fret).

■ **Play the A5 chord.** To finish, place your 1st finger across the 4th and 3rd strings at the 2nd fret for the A5 chord.

EXERCISE 8.5.3 – RIFF AND LEAD LICK PHRASING

This exercise will seem more complete than the others because you're fulfilling both rhythm and lead guitar duties. Once learned, create your own riff and lead lick statements.

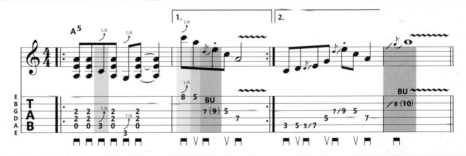

■ **Play the low C note** with a blues curl. After the A5 chord, use your 2nd finger to slightly bend the 5th string at the 3rd fret.

■ **Play the high C note** with a blues curl. Use your 3rd (or 4th) finger to slightly bend the 1st string at the 8th fret.

■ **Play the A note.** After the high C blues curl, place your 1st finger at the 5th fret, 1st string and sound the A note.

■ **Tone bend from D to E.** Place your 3rd finger at the 7th fret, 3rd string and bend from D to E (virtual 9th fret).

■ **Tone bend from G to A.** Slide up to the 8th fret, 2nd string with your 2nd finger then bend up a tone to A.

CHAPTER 3

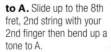

SESSION 8•6 DVD

THE DORIAN MODE

Many guitarists are happy to use only pentatonic scales, but venturing beyond these into other scales opens up new possibilities. The Dorian mode (*see box, right*) is great for soloing over minor chord progressions, giving a brighter sound than the natural minor scale.

On these pages you will learn two Dorian-based Am chords, then learn two full, seven-note A Dorian mode shapes, and five A Dorian pentatonic shapes, where the mode has been reduced to five notes to create two-note-per-string shapes.

A DORIAN ASSOCIATE CHORDS

Here are two Am7add6 chords to evoke A Dorian. Both are based on common Am7 shapes with the F♯ note (2nd fret, 1st string and 7th fret, 2nd string) providing the Dorian flavor.

Am7add6 (OPEN POSITION). The circled open string is the root note (A).

Am7add6 (FIFTH POSITION). White notes are the root (A).

A DORIAN MODE SHAPES

Here are two A Dorian shapes using the mode's seven notes (A, B, C, D, E, F♯, G). The first is based around the low frets and the second is at the fifth position.

A DORIAN (OPEN POSITION). White notes and circled open strings are the root (A).

A DORIAN (FIFTH POSITION). White notes are the root (A).

A DORIAN PENTATONIC SHAPES

Here are five A Dorian pentatonic shapes using five notes (A, C, D, E, F♯). Compare these two-note-per-string shapes to the A minor pentatonic shapes (*see p.148*).

A DORIAN PENTATONIC (SHAPE 1). White notes are the root (A).

A DORIAN PENTATONIC (SHAPE 2). White notes are the root (A).

A DORIAN PENTATONIC (SHAPE 3). White notes are the root (A).

A DORIAN PENTATONIC (SHAPE 4). White notes are the root (A).

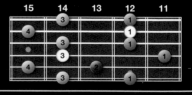

A DORIAN PENTATONIC (SHAPE 5). White notes are the root (A).

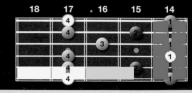

WHAT'S THE THEORY?
THE DORIAN VS THE NATURAL MINOR SCALE

The Dorian mode is the second of seven modes derived from the major scale. It contains seven different notes and has a minor sound (because it includes the minor third); it is more uplifting than the natural minor scale because it contains a major sixth (rather than the minor sixth found in the natural minor scale). Compare the intervals of A natural minor (A, B, C, D, E, F, G) and A Dorian (A, B, C, D, E, F#, G) played on the fifth string on the diagram (*see right*). When soloing over a minor chord or minor chord progression, you can use the Dorian mode as well as the minor pentatonic. In the diagram, "R" indicates the root.

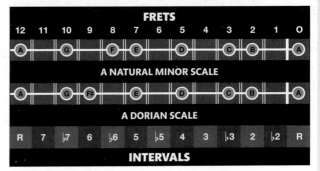

FRETS

A NATURAL MINOR SCALE

A DORIAN SCALE

R	7	♭7	6	♭6	5	♭5	4	3	♭3	2	♭2	R

INTERVALS

EXERCISE 8.6.1 – CHORDS AND SINGLE NOTES USING A DORIAN

This is a good first exercise in A Dorian because it strongly states the mode's sound with Am7 and D chords, plus lead licks featuring C (minor third) and F# (major sixth) notes.

EXERCISE 8.6.2 – BLUESY A DORIAN PENTATONIC LICK

This exercise is focused on soloing ideas using A Dorian. It features blues curls, hammer-ons, pull-offs, and string-bending. Notice where the F# notes are placed.

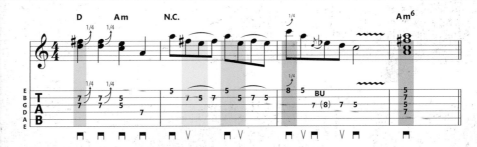

■ **Play the F# and D** notes simultaneously. Use your 3rd and 4th fingers for a blues curl on the 2nd and 3rd strings.

■ **Perform an F# to E pull-off.** Place your 3rd finger at the 7th fret, 2nd string, and pull-off to E at the 5th fret.

■ **Play the A and E notes.** Roll your 1st finger off the 5th fret, 1st string (A) to the 2nd string (E).

■ **Play a high C note blues curl.** Place your 4th finger at the 8th fret, 1st string and perform a blues curl.

■ **Play the Am6 chord.** To close, fret the Am6 chord with your 1st, 3rd, and 4th fingers as shown here.

CHAPTER 3

SESSION
8·7
DVD

UP AT THE DUSTY END

It's time to focus your attention on a neglected area of the fretboard—above the 12th fret. Many guitarists avoid it, perhaps because the frets are so close together, but once you've overcome your fears, you'll appreciate that high-fretboard soloing is both climactic and very expressive. Great rock and metal soloists favor high frets because they can soar above the band and play high string bends that really scream.

To hear high fretboard soloing, check out the following songs: the outro twin guitar harmonies in The Eagles' *Hotel California*, Jimmy Page's fast pentatonic pull-offs that finish his solo in Led Zeppelin's *Stairway To Heaven*, and Hugh Burns's screaming bends in Gerry Rafferty's *Baker Street*. The exercise below will get you working hard to dust off the high end of the fretboard.

EXERCISE 8.7.1 – HIGH FRETBOARD A MINOR PENTATONIC MELODY

This longer exercise is an expressive solo that uses notes from the A minor pentatonic scale. Playing from the 12th fret up to the 22nd fret, you will need to focus on sustaining notes, using hammer-ons, finger vibrato, and bending notes, all while watching your intonation. To finish, there is a quick descending pull-off run before the final A note.

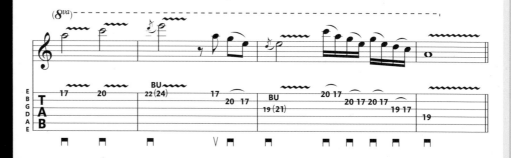

Use shape 4. The first five bars of the solo feature notes from shape 4 of A minor pentatonic.

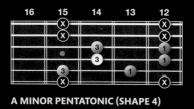

A MINOR PENTATONIC (SHAPE 4)

Use shape 1. The final five bars of the solo feature notes mostly from shape 1 of A minor pentatonic.

A MINOR PENTATONIC (SHAPE 1)

CHAPTER 3

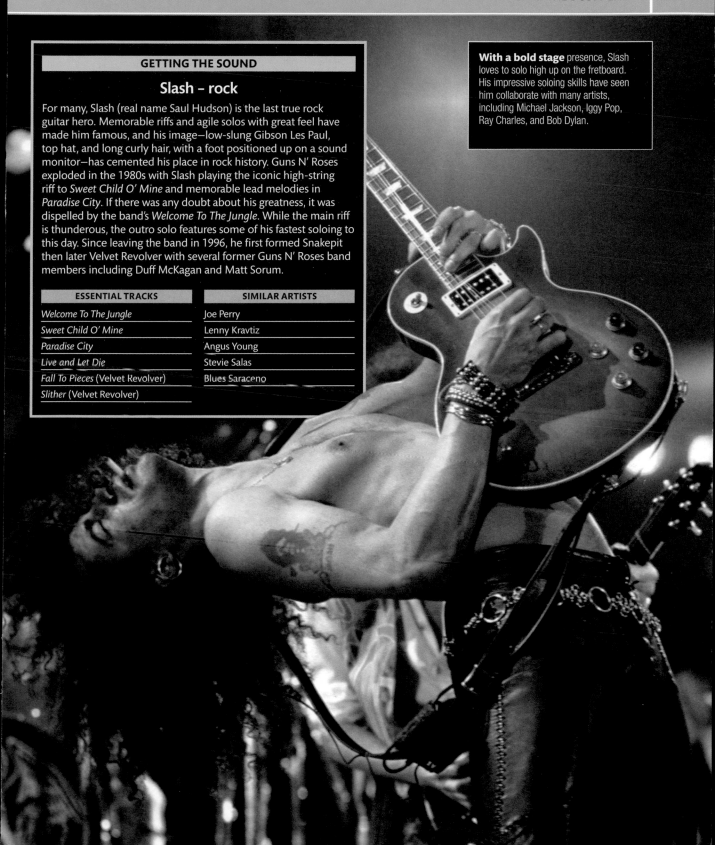

GETTING THE SOUND

Slash – rock

For many, Slash (real name Saul Hudson) is the last true rock guitar hero. Memorable riffs and agile solos with great feel have made him famous, and his image—low-slung Gibson Les Paul, top hat, and long curly hair, with a foot positioned up on a sound monitor—has cemented his place in rock history. Guns N' Roses exploded in the 1980s with Slash playing the iconic high-string riff to *Sweet Child O' Mine* and memorable lead melodies in *Paradise City*. If there was any doubt about his greatness, it was dispelled by the band's *Welcome To The Jungle*. While the main riff is thunderous, the outro solo features some of his fastest soloing to this day. Since leaving the band in 1996, he first formed Snakepit then later Velvet Revolver with several former Guns N' Roses band members including Duff McKagan and Matt Sorum.

ESSENTIAL TRACKS	SIMILAR ARTISTS
Welcome To The Jungle	Joe Perry
Sweet Child O' Mine	Lenny Kravtiz
Paradise City	Angus Young
Live and Let Die	Stevie Salas
Fall To Pieces (Velvet Revolver)	Blues Saraceno
Slither (Velvet Revolver)	

With a bold stage presence, Slash loves to solo high up on the fretboard. His impressive soloing skills have seen him collaborate with many artists, including Michael Jackson, Iggy Pop, Ray Charles, and Bob Dylan.

THE MIXOLYDIAN MODE

In this session you will be shown another new scale—the Mixolydian mode (*see box, right*)—suitable for soloing over major chord progressions. It can be thought of as a grittier version of the major scale. On these pages, you will learn two A-based chords to familiarize you with an A Mixolydian sound, then learn two full, seven-note A Mixolydian mode shapes and five A Mixolydian pentatonic shapes, where the mode has been reduced to five notes in order to create two-note-per-string shapes.

A MIXOLYDIAN ASSOCIATE CHORDS

Here are two A7 chords to evoke A Mixolydian. They're both common A7 chord shapes with the G note (open 3rd string and 5th fret, 4th string) providing the Mixolydian flavor.

A7 (OPEN POSITION). The circled open string is the root note (A).

A7 (FIFTH POSITION). White notes are the root (A).

A MIXOLYDIAN MODE SHAPES

Here are two A Mixolydian shapes using the mode's seven notes (A, B, C#, D, E, F#, G). The first is based around the low frets and the second is at the fifth position.

A MIXOLYDIAN (OPEN POSITION). White notes and circled open strings are the root (A).

A MIXOLYDIAN (FIFTH POSITION). White notes are the root (A).

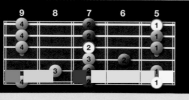

A MIXOLYDIAN PENTATONIC SHAPES

Here are five A Mixolydian pentatonic shapes using five notes (A, C#, D, E, G). The scales are structured using two notes per string (as are all pentatonics in this book).

A MIXOLYDIAN PENTATONIC (SHAPE 1). White notes are the root (A).

A MIXOLYDIAN PENTATONIC (SHAPE 2). White notes are the root (A).

A MIXOLYDIAN PENTATONIC (SHAPE 3). White notes are the root (A).

A MIXOLYDIAN PENTATONIC (SHAPE 4). White notes are the root (A).

A MIXOLYDIAN PENTATONIC (SHAPE 5). White notes are the root (A).

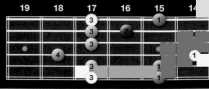

WHAT'S THE THEORY?
THE MIXOLYDIAN VS THE MAJOR SCALE

The Mixolydian mode is the fifth of seven modes derived from the major scale. The Mixolydian contains seven different notes and has a bluesy major sound, perfect for adding attitude and tension to a major chord progression. It differs from the standard major scale by containing a minor seventh. Compare the intervals of A major (A, B, C#, D, E, F#, G#) and A Mixolydian (A, B, C#, D, E, F#, G) played on the fifth string on the diagram (*see right*). When soloing over a major chord or major chord progression, you can use the Mixolydian mode as well as the major pentatonic. In the diagram, "R" indicates the root.

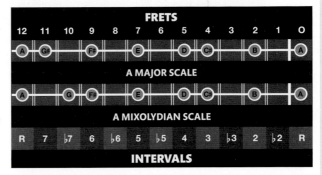

EXERCISE 8.8.1 – CHORDS AND SINGLE NOTES USING A MIXOLYDIAN

This exercise clearly states A Mixolydian with A7 and D chords, and has lead licks featuring C# (major third) and G (minor seventh) notes. Compare this with the earlier A Dorian exercise, 8.6.1 (*see p.227*).

EXERCISE 8.8.2 – BLUESY A MIXOLYDIAN PENTATONIC LICK

In this exercise you will use A Mixolydian pentatonic shape 1: notice this differs from A minor pentatonic shape 1 by one note (C has changed to C#). Also notice bar 2's sustained G note, implying A Mixolydian.

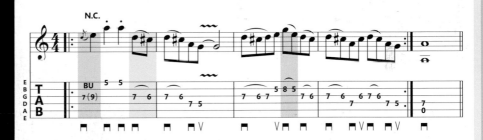

■ Tone-bend from D to E. Using your 3rd finger (7th fret, 3rd string) for D, bend up a tone to sound E ("virtual" 9th fret).

■ Play D and C#. Place your 3rd finger at the 7th fret, 3rd string and 2nd finger at the 6th fret, then pull off from D to C#.

■ Play G and E. Place your 4th finger at the 8th fret, 2nd string, and 1st finger at the 5th fret, then pull off from G to E.

PRACTICE & PROGRESS

As you practice soloing, remember all your options. When soloing over minor chords, choose from the minor pentatonic, the Dorian pentatonic, the blues scale, the natural minor scale, and the Dorian mode. For major progressions, you can use the major pentatonic, minor pentatonic (with blues curls on minor third notes), the major scale, or the Mixolydian mode.

CHAPTER 3

MILESTONE PIECE 1

This—the first of two milestone pieces to conclude Session 8—is a blues in
A minor. Riff and lead licks in a call-and-response arrangement form the piece's
structure, which is based around four chords—Am7, Dm7, Fmaj7, and Em7. In
the solo, you will use A minor pentatonic (A, C, D, E, G) throughout; an E♭ note
from the A blues scale (A, C, D, E♭, E, G) in bar 4; D minor pentatonic (D, F, G, A, C)
in bars 6–7; and notes from the chords of Fmaj7 (F, A, C, E) and Em7 (E, G, B, D) in
bars 10 (Fmaj7) and 11 (Em7).

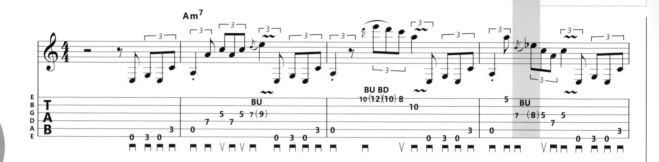

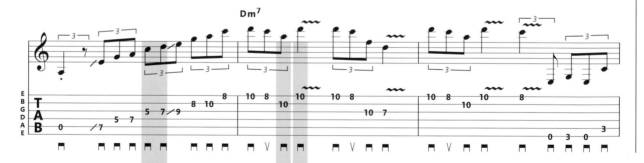

Play the C note with your 1st finger,
then D with your 3rd, before sliding up
to the 9th fret for E.

Sound the A note clearly using a down
stroke with your 3rd finger on the 10th fret,
2nd string.

From A, roll your 3rd finger across
to the 1st string's 10th fret, resting your
finger pad on the string to sound D.

Semitone-bend from D to E♭ using your 3rd finger at the 7th fret, supported by the 1st and 2nd fingers.

Quickly pull off and hammer on from A (2nd fret, 3rd string) to the open G and back. This action is called a "trill."

Tone-bend from D to E using your 3rd finger at the 7th fret, 3rd string, supported by the 1st and 2nd fingers.

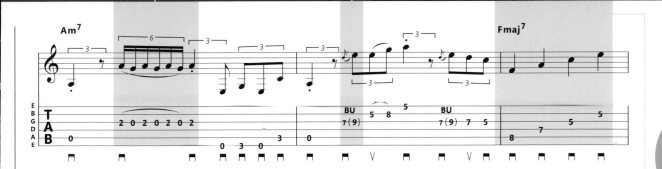

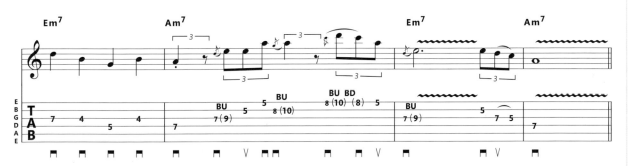

PRO TIP
VERSATILE SCALE

Notice how much you can achieve using mostly A minor pentatonic. When teamed with effective note placement, string bends, hammer-ons, pull-offs, and finger vibrato, this five-note scale provides big results.

Finger the Fmaj7 chord between the 5th and 8th frets, then sound each note in turn, from low to high.

MILESTONE PIECE 2

This second milestone piece for Session 8 is a blues in A major. It features single-note phrases that draw on the A Mixolydian mode (A, B, C♯, D, E, F♯, G), the A blues scale (A, C, D, E♭, E, G), A Mixolydian pentatonic (A, C♯, D, E, G), and A Dorian pentatonic (A, C, D, E, F♯). These scales work well with the three chords of A7 (A Mixolydian and A blues scale), D7 (A Dorian pentatonic), and E7 (a mixture of A major and A minor pentatonics).

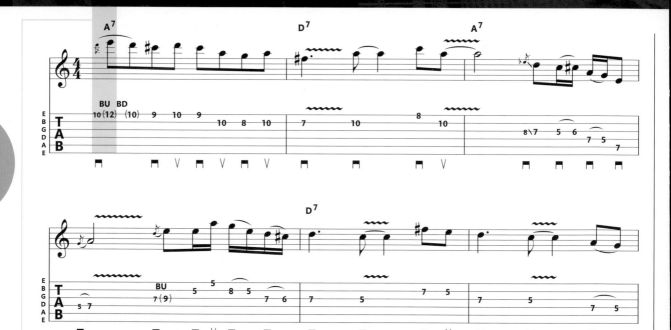

Tone-bend from D to E using your 3rd finger to bend up a tone from D (10th fret, 1st string) to E ("virtual" 12th fret).

PRO TIP
SCALES AND SHAPES

Bends and blues curls on the higher frets can give your solos urgency, cutting through the sound of a band. Focus on learning some "ready to go" licks that use each shape from a scale (*e.g.* five shapes of A minor pentatonic). You're sure to use them.

Tone-bend from B to C♯ using your 3rd finger on the 12th fret, 2nd string. Bend down then up again.

Play the B and A notes with your 3rd finger for the B note (12th fret, 2nd string) and 1st finger for the A note (10th fret).

Blues-curl the G note using your 2nd finger at the 12th fret, 3rd string, to bend slightly upward.

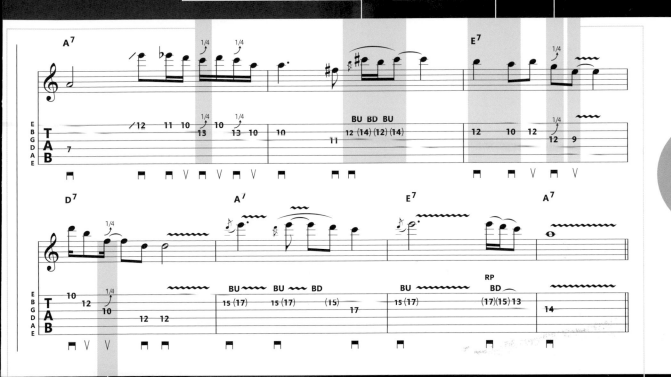

CHAPTER 3

Blues-curl the C note using your 4th finger at the 13th fret, 2nd string, to bend slightly upward.

Blues-curl the F note using your 1st finger at the 10th fret, 3rd string, to bend slightly downward.

Play the E note after the G blues curl; move your 1st finger down to the 9th fret, 3rd string, to play E.

ADVANCED SOLOING

In this penultimate session, you will learn about some of the more advanced aspects of guitar soloing. You will work on improving your technique and speed and be introduced to modern approaches favored by the world's most impressive lead guitarists. To start, you'll revisit string bends, looking at bends of more than one tone, the bend-and-fret technique, and the ghostly sound of prebends. You'll practice adding speed to familiar pentatonic scales, and then focus attention on the fretting hand—learning legato technique for fast and fluid lead phrases, and two-hand tapping, where you use both hands on the fretboard. To close, you will be introduced to sweep picking for arpeggio playing, and odd note sequences to add rhythmic interest to familiar scales. All this is then combined in an impressive—and ambitious—milestone piece.

SESSION 9·1 DVD

ADVANCED BENDS

Here you will develop the string-bending skills you learned in Session 5.5 (*pp.162–63*). In the first of the three exercises, you will perform big tone-and-a-half bends—equivalent to moving up by three frets—which you can hear in the playing of Albert King, Eric Clapton, and Jimmy Page, among others. Next, you'll learn pre-bends—essentially the reverse of regular bends—where you bend first, then pick the string and release the bend for a characteristic "crying" sound, and compound bends, where you bend a string once, and then bend it again to play two "bent" notes.

In the last exercise, you will look at the bend-and-fret technique made famous by Toto's Steve Lukather: bend and hold, then fret again with another finger. Like the other advanced string-bending techniques, this has a unique sound.

PRO TIP
TIPS FOR GUITAR SETUP

Good string-bending technique requires a guitar that is set up appropriately. This mainly involves setting the guitar's action (the distance between fretboard and strings) at an ideal height for string bending (*see pp.300–303*).

If the strings are too close to the fretboard, fretting is easy but bends can slip under your fingers. Conversely, if the strings are too high, you will have good finger contact for bends but your general playing will be more laborious. To optimize your string bending setup, take your guitar to a technician (visit your local music shop for guidance and recommendations).

EXERCISE 9.1.1 – TONE-AND-A-HALF AND TONE BENDS

This short A minor pentatonic lead line is enhanced with two string bends: a tone-and-a-half bend (bar 2) and a tone bend (bar 3). Notice the majestic, expressive sound as you swoop up to the higher note.

■ **Fret the E note.** At the start of bar 2, place your 3rd finger at the 9th fret, 3rd string. Place your 1st and 2nd fingers behind the 3rd finger for support.

■ **Bend from E to G.** Pick the E note, then bend up a tone and a half (equivalent to 3 frets) to a G note. Bring your thumb over the fretboard for more support.

■ **Fret the G note.** For the last note in bar 3, place your 2nd finger at the 8th fret, 2nd string. Use your 1st finger to support the 2nd finger in the bend.

■ **Bend from G to A.** Pick the G note, then quickly bend up a tone (equivalent to 2 frets) to sound A. Bring your thumb over the fretboard for more support.

C MAJOR SCALE (SHAPE 2)

Shape 2 starts on the scale's 2nd note: a low D (10th fret, 6th string). C notes are shown in white in the diagrams.

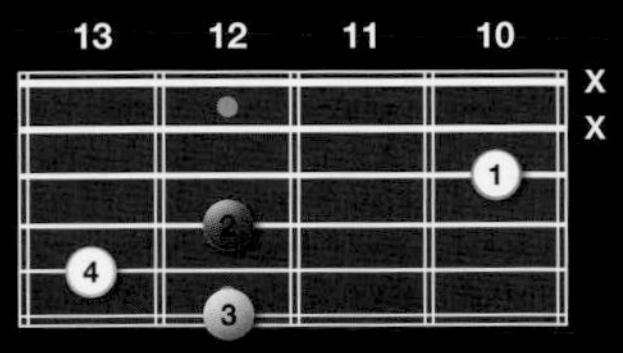

C CHORD (D SHAPE)

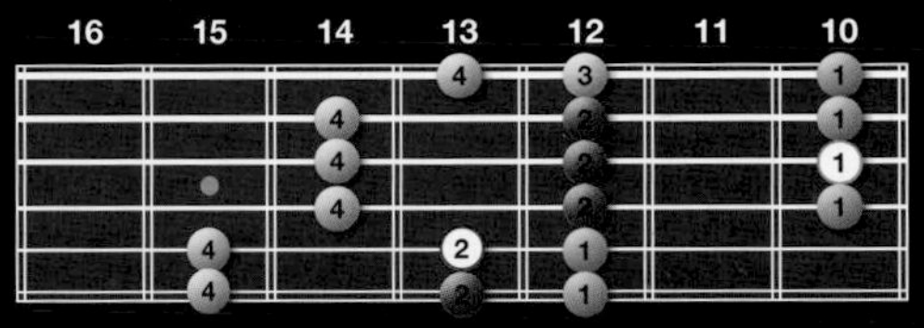

C MAJOR SCALE (SHAPE 2)

C MAJOR SCALE (SHAPE 3)

Shape 3 starts on the scale's 3rd note: a low E (12th fret, 6th string). C notes are shown in white in the diagrams.

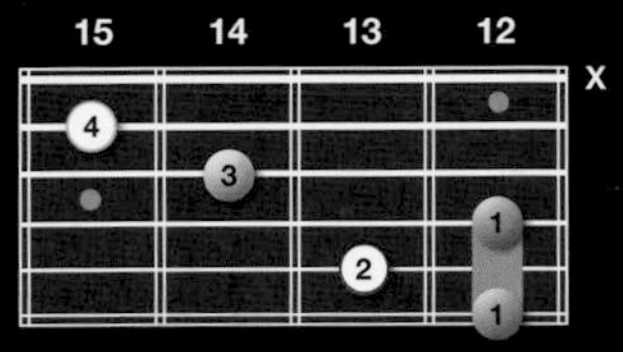

C CHORD (C SHAPE)

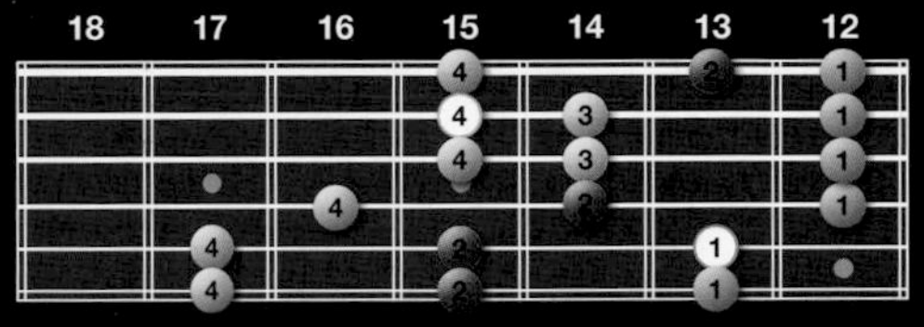

C MAJOR SCALE (SHAPE 3)

C MAJOR SCALE (SHAPE 4)

Shape 4 starts on the scale's 4th note: a low F (1st fret, 6th string). C notes are shown in white in the diagrams.

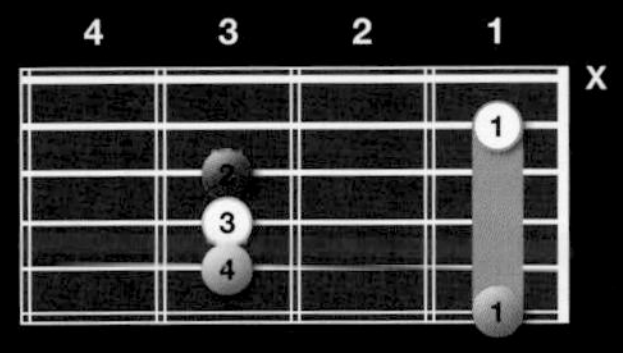

C CHORD (A SHAPE)

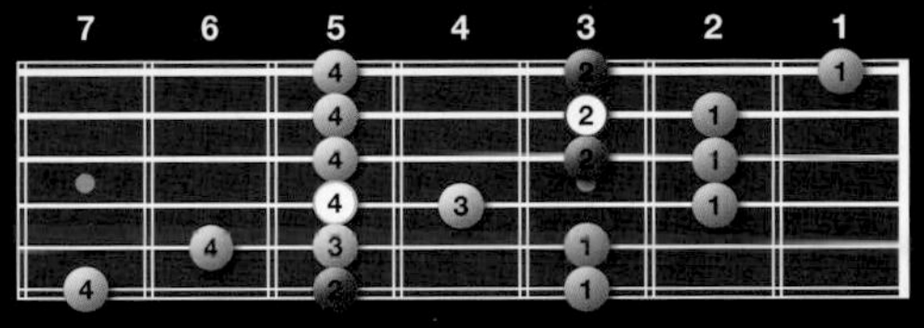

C MAJOR SCALE (SHAPE 4)

C MAJOR SCALE (SHAPE 5)

Shape 5 starts on the scale's 5th note: a low G (3rd fret, 6th string). C notes are shown in white in the diagrams.

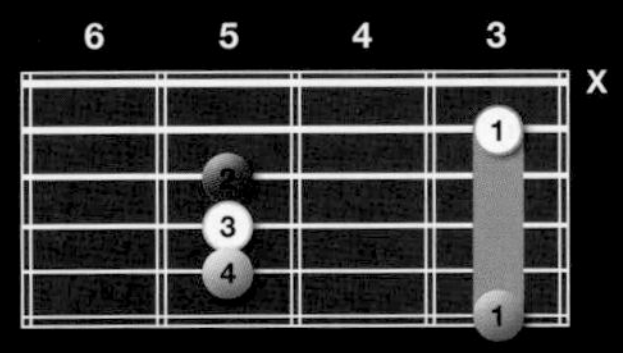

C CHORD (A SHAPE)

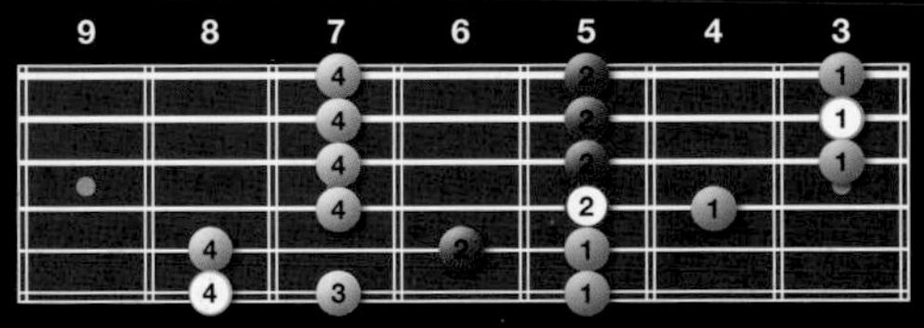

C MAJOR SCALE (SHAPE 5)

C MAJOR SCALE (SHAPE 6)

Shape 6 starts on the scale's 6th note: a low A (5th fret, 6th string). C notes are shown in white in the diagrams.

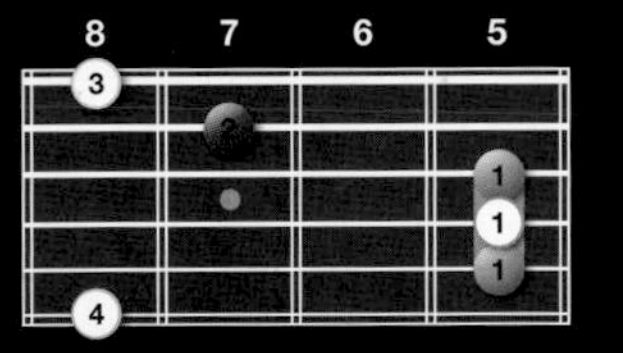

C CHORD (G SHAPE)

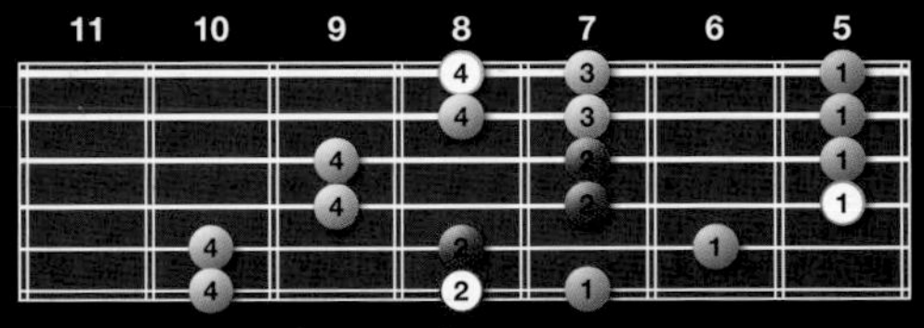

C MAJOR SCALE (SHAPE 6)

C MAJOR SCALE (SHAPE 7)

Shape 7 starts on the scale's 7th note: a low D (7th fret, 6th string). C notes are shown in white in the diagrams.

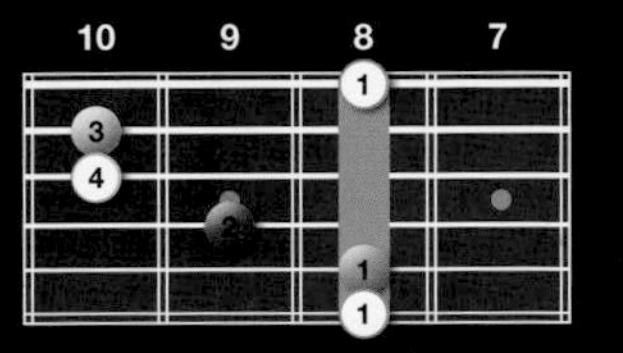

C CHORD (E SHAPE)

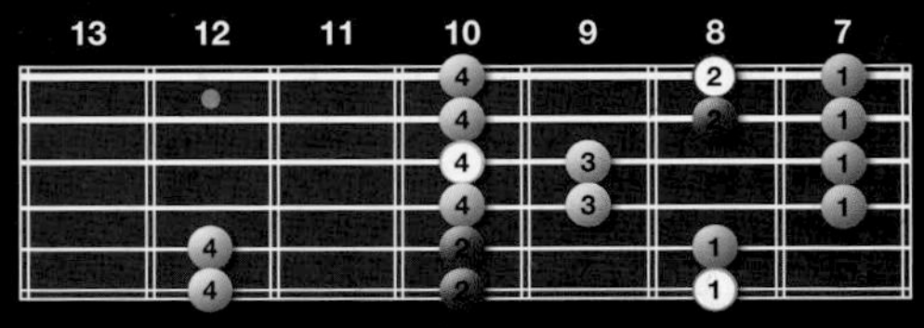

C MAJOR SCALE (SHAPE 7)

CHAPTER 3

Learning the seven shapes of the C major scale takes serious practice, which can at times seem somewhat removed from playing music. However, mastering 3-note-per-string scales is the key to exciting soloing, with fast fretting and plenty of hammer-ons and pull-offs. Such legato playing (*see pp.246–47*) has found favor with countless rock guitarists including Paul Gilbert, Richie Kotzen, and Nuno Bettencourt, and is as much a technical approach as a means of playing a wider range of notes. What follows here are four short exercises that demonstrate note patterns favored by many rock guitarists. They are in keeping with a lead guitarist's approach, favoring higher notes (and strings) over low ones—these are the pitches that have the clarity to cut through a band.

EXERCISE 9.3.2 – LEGATO TRIPLETS (SHAPE 1)

This exercise uses the 3-note-per-string C major scale, shape 1. Starting on the 4th string, it ascends across four strings using a pick–hammer-on–hammer-on sequence. It then descends two strings, culminating with a semitone bend from B (12th fret, 2nd string) to C ("virtual" 13th fret, 2nd string).

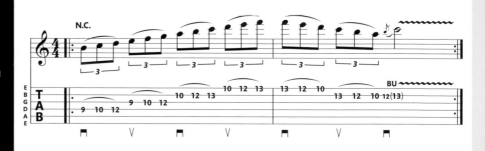

EXERCISE 9.3.3 – LEGATO TRIPLETS WITH STRING-SKIPPING (SHAPE 1)

Using the C major 3-note-per-string scale, shape 1, this exercise also employs hammer-ons and includes string-skipping—jumping a string to break up the strict note ordering of the scale, creating color and variety.

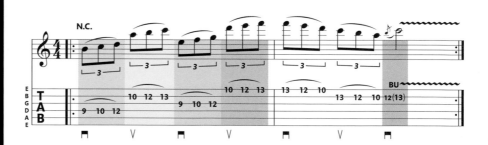

■ **Play the B, C, and D notes.** Use hammer-ons on the 4th string.

■ **Play the A, B, and C notes.** Use hammer-ons on the 2nd string.

■ **Play the E, F, and G notes.** Use hammer-ons on the 3rd string.

■ **Play the D, E, and F notes.** Use hammer-ons on the 1st string.

■ **Bend from B to C.** Bend from the 12th fret to the "virtual" 13th fret.

EXERCISE 9.3.4 – ASCENDING USING TWO STRINGS (SHAPES 7, 1, AND 2)

This involves playing notes from three different scale shapes on the 1st and 2nd strings, shifting fretboard position each time. The 1st finger starts each six-note grouping, so it's important that you can not only play each shape accurately but can "recover" well each time you shift position.

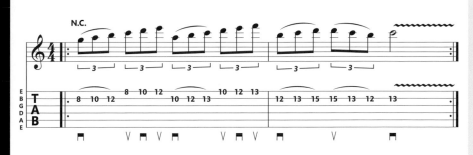

EXERCISE 9.3.5 – DESCENDING WHILE ASCENDING USING TWO STRINGS (SHAPES 7, 1, AND 2)

Rising cascades of notes form bar 1 of this exercise. The first two triplets are made up of descending notes. The second two also descend, but they are played higher up the fretboard, making an interesting sound.

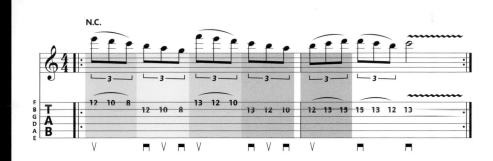

■ **Play the E, D, and C notes.** Finger the 12th, 10th, and 8th frets on the 1st string.

■ **Play the B, A, and G notes.** Finger the 12th, 10th, and 8th frets on the 2nd string.

■ **Play the F, E, and D notes.** Finger the 13th, 12th, and 10th frets on the 1st string.

■ **Play the C, B, and A notes.** Finger the 13th, 12th, and 10th frets on the 2nd string.

■ **Play the D, C, and B notes.** Finger the 15th, 13th, and 12th frets on the 2nd string.

PRACTICE & PROGRESS

There's more to 3-note-per-string playing than moving quickly up and down all six strings, one shape at a time. For example, try using the seven shapes to explore two-string groupings. The diagram opposite makes explicit what you learned in exercises 9.3.4 and 9.3.5, showing how shapes 7, 1, and 2 overlap one another on the top two strings. Apply string groupings of 6 and 5; 5 and 4; 4 and 3; and 3 and 2, in the same manner.

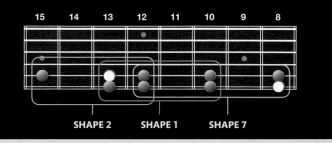

CHAPTER 3

SESSION 9·4 DVD
LEGATO PLAYING

Three-note-per-string playing isn't that new to guitarists—Chuck Berry was performing impressive three-note-per-string pull-offs in the 1950s. However, the technique was adopted more widely from the late 1970s and early 80s (listen to the ascending fast run that ends Eddie Van Halen's solo in *Jump*) and many rock guitarists now use three-note-per-string scale shapes to drive their soloing.

In a similar way to the two-note-per-string pentatonic approach (*see p.148*), the regularity of three notes played on one string can provide advantages in rhythmic patterns (often based in threes or sixes) and playing speed.

Using hammer-on and pull-off techniques in speedy licks means that the picking hand doesn't need to keep up with every fretted note. This approach is known as legato playing. It encourages long, flowing, scale-based phrases that are played as pick–hammer-on–hammer-on; or pick–pull-off–pull-off; or combinations of the two. It's a fast and impressive sound when using clean or (especially) distorted sounds, and when combined with a low action and light-gauge strings, such as .009 or .010, which are a primary choice for fast rock guitarists. The three exercises here—all based on the C major scale—will kick-start your legato playing.

EXERCISE 9.4.1 – TRIPLET LEGATO WITH FRETBOARD POSITION SHIFTS: C MAJOR (SHAPE 1)

This exercise is played on the 1st string. Each six-note grouping is played at one fretboard position, using hammer-ons and pull-offs. See if you can spot the larger three-note-per-string shape that each group of six notes is derived from.

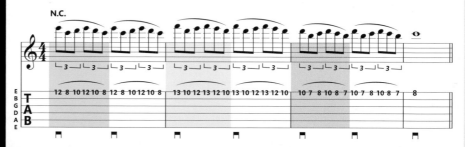

■ **Play the C, D, and E notes.** Use your 1st, 2nd, and 4th fingers at the 8th (C), 10th (D), and 12th (E) frets, respectively.

■ **Play the D, E, and F notes.** Use your 1st, 3rd, and 4th fingers at the 10th (D), 12th (E), and 13th (F) frets, respectively.

■ **Play the B, C, and D notes.** Use your 1st, 2nd, and 4th fingers at the 7th (B), 8th (C), and 10th (D) frets, respectively.

PRACTICE & PROGRESS

The exercise here develops legato technique. Break it down into small sections when you first begin. Try the first six notes alone, making your pull-off and hammer-on combinations sound dynamically and rhythmically even. If you find that one note is too slow or quiet, isolate the immediate area around it and practice repeatedly and very slowly to improve results.

EXERCISE 9.4.2 – TRIPLET LEGATO: DESCENDING C MAJOR (SHAPE 1)

This exercise uses the same six-note pattern as the previous exercise, but covers a wider spread of notes by using the fast and smooth sounding legato technique.

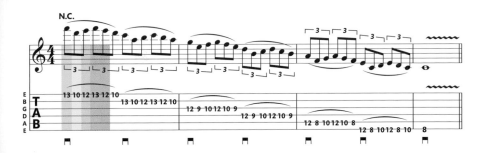

■ **Play F.** With your 4th finger at the 13th fret, pick the string. Have your 1st finger at the 10th fret ready for the D note.

■ **Pull-off to sound the D note.** Perform a strong pull-off from the F note to the 1st finger fretting D (10th fret).

■ **Hammer-on to E.** Following the D note, hammer-on at the 12th fret with your third finger to sound E.

■ **Hammer-on to F.** Following the E note, hammer-on at the 13th fret with your 4th finger to sound F.

■ **Pull-off to E.** Pull-off to the 3rd finger (12th fret) for E. Be ready to pull-off to the 1st finger (10th fret) to finish.

EXERCISE 9.4.3 – LEGATO IN GROUPS OF FOUR: C MAJOR (SHAPE 1)

While 3-note-per-string scale shapes encourage three- or six-note rhythmic groupings, they can also be applied to other groupings. Here you will explore C major shape 1, with the notes ordered in four-note groupings. You will play a four-note pattern on each string before moving to the next one. As before, take your time and watch out for "lazy fingers" which don't sound notes as loud or as perfectly in time as the other fingers.

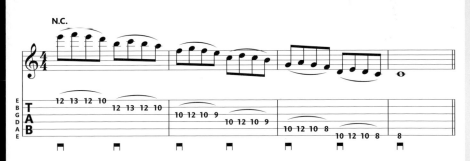

PRACTICE & PROGRESS

Once you have mastered the two exercises on this page using C major scale shape 1 (*shown right, with C notes as white circles*), try applying these same patterns to the other six three-note-per-string scale shapes to expand your knowledge of the fretboard.

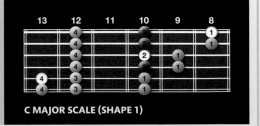

C MAJOR SCALE (SHAPE 1)

1 **French guitarist Django Reinhardt** had a staggering command of the guitar, despite damaging his fretting hand's third and fourth fingers in a fire in 1928.

JAW-DROPPING PLAYERS

There are guitarists of staggering ability in every musical genre, but many beginners seek their inspiration from jazz and rock guitarists, who have traditionally displayed the highest technical virtuosity. Artists like the four below have inspired many to perform with a wider note and chord vocabulary married to imaginative and fast playing styles.

❶ DJANGO REINHARDT

Reinhardt is the legend of gypsy jazz—he used an often uptempo style that had driving chord rhythms and melodic arpeggio-based soloing.

ESSENTIAL TRACKS *Nuages* ◆ *Minor Swing* ◆ *Djangology* ◆ *Honeysuckle Rose* ◆ *Ain't Misbehavin'*

SIMILAR ARTISTS Bireli Lagrene ◆ Gary Potter ◆ Martin Taylor ◆ Stochelo Rosenberg ◆ John Jorgenson

❷ STANLEY JORDAN

This Chicago-born guitarist uses two hands on the fretboard to produce pianolike chords and melodies (he is also a pianist). Primarily a jazz musician, he consistently astounds audiences.

ESSENTIAL TRACKS *Eleanor Rigby* ◆ *Stairway To Heaven* ◆ *Impressions* ◆ *The Lady In My Life*

SIMILAR ARTISTS Preston Reed ◆ Erik Mongrain ◆ Jennifer Batten ◆ Steve Lynch

❸ YNGWIE MALMSTEEN

Malmsteen's unique sound, which has been described as "rock meets Bach," features fast, exciting scale and arpeggio runs performed with flawless picking and legato techniques.

ESSENTIAL TRACKS *Blackstar* ◆ *Far Beyond The Sun* ◆ *I'll See The Light Tonight* ◆ *Gates Of Babylon*

SIMILAR ARTISTS Ritchie Blackmore ◆ Uli Jon Roth ◆ Paul Gilbert ◆ Chris Impellitteri

❹ PAUL GILBERT

Gilbert demonstrated his outrageously fast rock playing in the bands Racer X and Mr Big. His broad output, spanning instrumental rock, jazz, and fusion has inspired countless guitarists.

ESSENTIAL TRACKS *Scarified* ◆ *Addicted To That Rush* ◆ *Colorado Bulldog* ◆ *To Be With You* ◆ *I Like Rock*

SIMILAR ARTISTS Eddie Van Halen ◆ Randy Rhoads ◆ Nuno Bettencourt ◆ Andy Timmons

SESSION
9·5
DVD

TWO-HAND TAPPING

Advanced guitarists love to wow their audiences with impressive techniques like two-hand tapping. An extension of legato playing, two-hand tapping looks very different to conventional playing—both hands are on the fretboard—and it is also a popular choice for speed soloing. In this technique, one or more of the picking hand's fingers can hammer-on and pull-off notes on the fretboard in conjunction with the fretting hand, to produce smooth and fast note passages.

On these pages, you will be introduced to the technique, and you'll perform two exercises that will add speed and flash to your soloing.

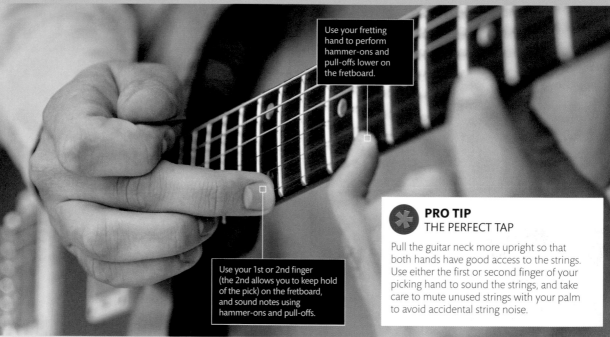

Use your fretting hand to perform hammer-ons and pull-offs lower on the fretboard.

Use your 1st or 2nd finger (the 2nd allows you to keep hold of the pick) on the fretboard, and sound notes using hammer-ons and pull-offs.

✳ PRO TIP
THE PERFECT TAP

Pull the guitar neck more upright so that both hands have good access to the strings. Use either the first or second finger of your picking hand to sound the strings, and take care to mute unused strings with your palm to avoid accidental string noise.

BASIC TAPPING TECHNIQUE

① **Fret the 1st string** at the 8th and 5th frets as shown. Start by hammering on at the 12th fret with your picking hand's 2nd finger to sound E.

② **Pull-off from the 12th fret** with a downward (or upward) flick. The pull-off will sound the 8th fret's C note, fretted by the 4th finger.

③ **Pull-off from the 8th fret** to the 5th fret (A note). Have your picking hand's finger ready to hammer-on to the 12th fret to begin the three-note sequence again.

CHAPTER 3

EXERCISE 9.5.1 – TAPPING AT THE 12TH FRET

This exercise is based on three-note rhythmic groupings using a pattern of tap–pull-off–hammer-on. In this instance, the picking-hand tap remains at the 12th fret (E note) while the fretting hand moves down and up the fretboard. Circles on the tab and notation indicate tapped notes.

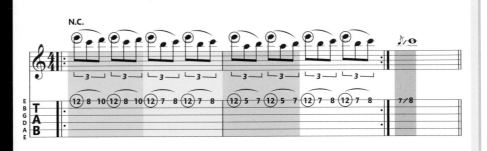

■ Play the first six-note run. Use your fretting hand's 1st and 3rd fingers and your picking hand's 2nd finger.

■ Play the second six-note run. Use your fretting hand's 1st and 2nd fingers and your picking hand's 2nd finger.

■ Play the third six-note run. Use your fretting hand's 1st and 3rd fingers and your picking hand's 2nd finger.

■ Slide to finish. Slide your fretting hand's 1st finger quickly up from the 7th to the 8th fret to conclude the exercise.

EXERCISE 9.5.2 – TAPPING ACROSS FOUR STRINGS

Playing on one string with two-hand tapping is a lot of fun and there are numerous note patterns to be had. Here, you'll go further, taking a simple one-string pattern and applying it across four strings. The phrases that result would be very difficult to duplicate in any other way. This exercise uses a simple tap–pull-off –hammer-on pattern, applied to A minor pentatonic scale, shape 1 (*see diagram right*). This creates a speedy and expansive sound, akin to a virtuoso pianist.

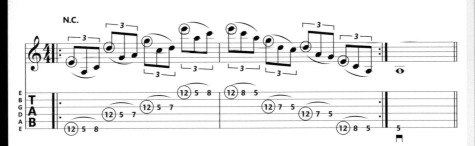

PRACTICE & PROGRESS

The diagram (*right*) shows the A minor pentatonic notes (from shape 1) used in this exercise. The 12th fret "T" represents a picking-hand tap. See what new two-hand tapping patterns you can create from this.

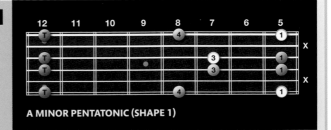

A MINOR PENTATONIC (SHAPE 1)

CHAPTER 3

SWEEP PICKING

Here you will be introduced to sweep picking, a demanding technique that can create patterns and speeds not easily possible with alternate picking. Although it has been around for many years—it was used by jazz guitarists like Django Reinhardt and Tal Farlow from the early 20th century—its popularity has risen as rock guitarists such as Yngwie Malmsteen and fusion players such as Frank Gambale adopted the style. Sweep picking involves moving your pick smoothly in one direction (up or down) across two or more strings and, importantly, making notes on adjacent strings sound separately. To make sure that notes don't ring together when moving to another string, lift your finger off the fretted note just before you pick the next string. This demands great coordination between the picking and the fretting hands. In these exercises you'll practice the hand movement required for sweep picking, before applying it to arpeggios on two and three strings.

PRO TIP
CLEAN SWEEPS

To develop an ideal sweep-picking technique, try visualizing yourself "pushing" the pick into down sweeps and "pulling" it backward for up sweeps. Avoid aggressive strokes, because these hinder the pick's fluid movement—visualize yourself ice-skating across the top of each string, moving with grace.

When crossing several strings with one stroke, apply light palm muting to the lower strings to reduce unwanted string noise and make each picked string sound clearly.

If you want to reduce the raspy tone often created by sweep picking, select your guitar's neck pickup—this is warmer and less bright-sounding than the bridge pickup.

EXERCISE 9.6.1 – PERFECTING PICKING-HAND MOVEMENT

This exercise focuses on picking—there's no fretting involved. Pick each group of three notes as down–down–up, repeatedly. The two down-strokes (the sweep) should be one smooth stroke. Spend some time getting the sweep stroke correct.

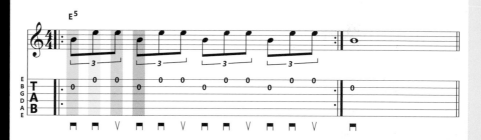

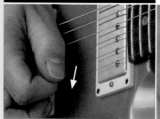

■ **Sound the open 2nd string.** Use a down stroke, angling the pick slightly in the direction of travel for a smooth movement.

■ **Follow through.** Continue the down stroke smoothly from the 2nd string to pick the open 1st string.

■ **Up-pick the 1st string.** Sound the open 1st string again, this time using an up stroke.

■ **Return to your original position.** Play the sweep repeatedly until you have a smooth, confident motion.

EXERCISE 9.6.2 – TWO-STRING SWEEP ARPEGGIOS

In this exercise you keep the simple sweep-picking approach of 9.6.1 but apply it to fretted notes. Sweep across the 1st and 2nd strings to spell out the arpeggios for Am, G, and F.

■ **Play the Am arpeggio.**
Use your 1st, 2nd, and 4th fingers between the 8th and 12th frets to play the A minor arpeggio.

■ **Play the G arpeggio.** Use your 1st, 2nd, and 4th fingers between the 7th and 10th frets to play the G arpeggio.

■ **Play the F arpeggio.** Use the same fingering shape as for G but two frets lower (between the 5th and 8th frets).

PRACTICE & PROGRESS

This technique requires really focused practice. When starting sweep picking, be sure to take your finger off one fretted note just before you pick (and fret) the next string, otherwise the notes will ring into one another. To succeed, you need to fret your notes accurately and synchronize your fretting hand perfectly with your picking hand.

EXERCISE 9.6.3 – TWO-STRING SWEEPS WITH PULL-OFFS

Sweep picking is often combined with hammer-ons or pull-offs to pack in lots of notes. Here you play the highest note of each run with an up stroke, then perform a pull-off before descending the arpeggio shape with one up stroke across two strings.

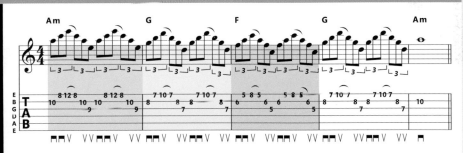

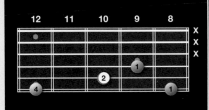

■ **Play the Am arpeggio.** The diagram above shows the Am arpeggio shape on the fretboard and indicates finger placements. The white circled note is the root note, A.

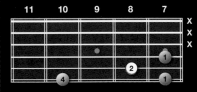

■ **Play the G arpeggio.** The diagram above shows the G arpeggio shape on the fretboard and indicates finger placements. The white circled note is the root note, G.

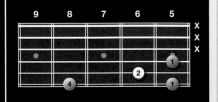

■ **Play the F arpeggio.** The diagram above shows the F arpeggio shape; notice that it looks the same as the G arpeggio but two frets lower. The white circled note is the root note, F.

CHAPTER 3

SESSION 9•7 DVD
RHYTHMIC INTEREST

Here you will discover that odd note groupings can create rhythmic and melodic interest when playing riffs and solos. Playing notes in groups of three (*see box, right*) may be considered odd, but even more unusual groupings can be made from sets of five or seven notes. Consider a piece of music in conventional 4/4 time that is two bars in length. You could play this using constant eighth notes (*see p.50*), grouping four notes in each phrase (a total of 16 notes over two bars). This conventional phrasing sounds even, but if you play the same notes in groups of three, then five, notes (3+5+3+5=16), you immediately create rhythmic tension. Introducing a few odd note groupings can create accents in unexpected places, especially when you play a constant stream of notes (slow or fast). The exercise below demonstrates a 3+5 approach in each bar.

WHAT'S THE THEORY?
GROUPS OF THREE

Odd note groupings tend to be used in solos where notes are improvised. One popular blues-rock approach is the "three against two" rhythm—three minor pentatonic notes repeated while maintaining an even two-notes-per-beat rhythm. The result sounds more complex than it really is, due to the tension between the notes and rhythm played. The result is shown below; bold numbers represent the main ¼ note beats in 4/4 time, and semicolons mark the start of a new bar:

"THREE AGAINST FOUR" RHYTHM
1 2 **3** 1 2 **3** 1 **2**; **3** 1 **2** 3 **1** 2 **3** 1; **2** 3 **1** 2 **3** 1 **2** 3; **1**

As you can see, the same three notes create a lot of rhythmic variety—over three bars—before the first note returns as the first beat of a new bar. Try four notes per beat for a "three against four" rhythm.

EXERCISE 9.7.1 – THREE- AND FIVE-NOTE GROUPINGS

This exercise features A minor pentatonic, shape 1 played with a constant eighth-note rhythm; each bar contains 3+5 note groupings. The melodic jump up at the fourth note (the first of the five-note group) creates immediate rhythmic interest.

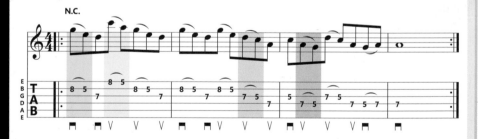

■ **Play the G and E notes.**
Place your 4th finger at the 8th fret, 2nd string (for G) and your 1st finger at the 5th fret, 2nd string (for E).

■ **Play the C and A notes.**
For the 4th and 5th notes of bar 1, use your 4th and 1st fingers at the 8th fret (C) and 5th fret (A) on the 2nd string.

■ **Play the D and C notes.**
For the 6th and 7th notes of bar 2, use your 3rd and 1st fingers at the 7th fret (D) and 5th fret (C) on the 3rd string.

■ **Play the A and G notes.**
Use your 3rd finger (7th fret) and 1st finger (5th fret) on the 4th string for A and G in bar 3.

9.1 9.2 9.3 9.4 9.5 9.6 **9.7** 9.8

GETTING THE SOUND

Larry Carlton – jazz rock

Although not a household name, the chances are that your music collection features the sound of Larry Carlton. In the 1970s and 80s, Larry used his musical vocabulary of rock, blues, and jazz in recordings with artists such as Steely Dan, Joni Mitchell, Michael Jackson, Christopher Cross, Olivia Newton John, and The Crusaders, and he worked on many TV themes and movie soundtracks. He has also enjoyed a solo career, favoring a Gibson ES335 guitar and Mesa Boogie amplifier and then a highly regarded (and scarce) Dumble Overdrive Special amplifier. His impeccable use of pentatonics, modes, and arpeggios, along with exquisite string bending, places him in the unique position of being a guitarist's guitarist, but also highly accessible and enjoyable.

ESSENTIAL TRACKS	SIMILAR ARTISTS
Kid Charlemagne (Steely Dan)	Lee Ritenour
Free As The Wind (The Crusaders)	Steve Lukather
It Was Only Yesterday	Carlos Rios
Room 335	Jay Graydon
Don't Give It Up	Johnny Smith
Last Nite	

Larry Carlton often uses smooth distortion in his performances and a volume pedal to fade in notes and chords. He is a master of prebends—they are an essential part of his unmistakable "sweet" sound.

SESSION
9.8
DVD

MILESTONE PIECE

In this piece, based in A minor, you will use the A minor pentatonic and A natural minor scales with a variety of advanced soloing techniques. Bars 2, 4, and 10 feature 3-note-per-string legato pull-offs. Bars 5, 10, and 11 have fast pentatonic phrases, and bar 15 features minor pentatonic "three against four" rhythmic interest. You'll perform two-hand tapping in bars 12 and 16, and sweep picking in bars 13–14 to spell out the arpeggios of G and F. There is a lot required of you here; practice one bar at a time before playing the whole piece.

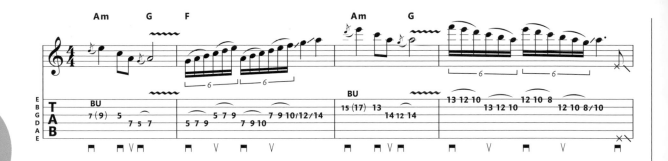

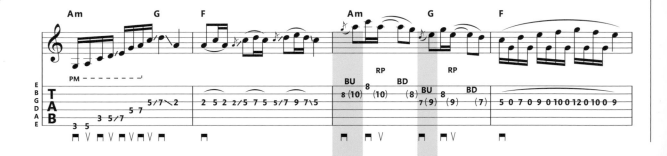

Tone-bend from G to A with your 3rd finger at the 8th fret, 2nd string. Keep your 4th finger in place for the next C.

Tone-bend from D to E with your 2nd finger at the 7th fret, 3rd string. Keep your 4th finger in place for the next G.

Start the G arpeggio with D, using your 4th finger at the 10th fret, 1st string. Pull-off to B (7th fret, 1st string).

Perform a three-note pull-off from D to C# then C with your fingers at the 7th, 6th, and 5th frets, 3rd string.

Perform a three-note pull-off from A to G# then G with your fingers at the 7th, 6th, and 5th frets, 4th string.

Perform a picking hand tap at the 12th fret, 6th string (E). Have the first finger ready at the 5th fret (A).

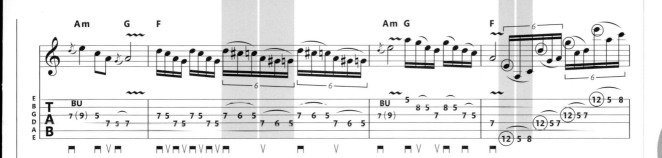

CHAPTER 3

Use an up stroke to sound G in the arpeggio, placing your 2nd finger at the 8th fret, 2nd string.

Continuing your up stroke from the previous G, play a D note at the 7th fret, 3rd string.

Play A with your 1st finger at the 5th fret, 6th string, then hammer-on to C at the 8th fret with your 4th finger.

MUSICAL GENRES

Now that you have mastered an extensive array of techniques and approaches fundamental to guitar playing, you're ready to be more selective with what you play and how you play it. This session provides a taster of ten popular guitar-based genres and their trademark playing styles. For each genre you will learn about the leading guitar icons, the famous songs, the essential techniques, and the classic equipment. You will then sample each genre through two short exercises—one riff- or rhythm-based, the other lead-orientated. These short actvities may inspire you to explore styles of playing that you had not considered before, or open your ears to sounds that you can adapt and incorporate into your own unique approach.

10·1 BLUES TRADEMARKS

10·2 ROCK TRADEMARKS

10·3 METAL TRADEMARKS

10·4 COUNTRY TRADEMARKS

10·5 R&B TRADEMARKS

10·6 FUNK TRADEMARKS

10·7 REGGAE TRADEMARKS

10·8 80s POP TRADEMARKS

10·9 JAZZ TRADEMARKS

10·10 JAZZ ROCK TRADEMARKS

SESSION 10·1 DVD

BLUES TRADEMARKS

Ask any blues guitarist to describe the blues, and you'll probably hear that it is all about emotion, expression, and playing from the heart. Great blues guitarists are able to affect an audience through dramatic runs, long sustaining notes, and by the creative use of space. From a technical perspective, blues players don't need as extensive a knowledge of scale and chord shapes as for other styles— pentatonic scales predominate—but they do possess a huge authority over what is played. Phrasing is crucial because it makes the vocal-like blues so memorable, and string bends are used widely to wring the most drama out of minor and major pentatonics.

ESSENTIAL LISTENING

Eric Clapton *Hideaway* ◆ *Crossroads* ◆ *Sunshine Of Your Love* ◆ *White Room* ◆ *Layla* ◆ *Bad Love* ◆ *Before You Accuse Me*

B.B. King *The Thrill Is Gone* ◆ *Every Day I Have The Blues* ◆ *How Blue Can You Get*

Albert King *Born Under A Bad Sign* ◆ *Crosscut Saw* ◆ *Laundromat Blues*

Stevie Ray Vaughan *Texas Flood* ◆ *Mary Had A Little Lamb* ◆ *Scuttle Buttin'* ◆ *Cold Shot*

Peter Green *The Stumble* ◆ *Black Magic Woman* ◆ *Need Your Love So Bad* ◆ *Shake Your Money Maker* ◆ *Rattlesnake Shake*

Gary Moore *Still Got The Blues* ◆ *Don't Believe A Word* ◆ *Stop Messin' Around*

KEY TECHNIQUES

String bends *See pp.162–63*

Blues scale *See pp.158–61*

Minor pentatonic *See pp.148–51*

Sustained notes *See pp.178–79*

Hammer-ons and pull-offs *See pp.80–81*

CLASSIC EQUIPMENT

Les Paul Excels at thick and warm sounds

Stratocaster Capable of creamy and biting tones

Gibson ES335 A warm, resonant semiacoustic

Fender Twin Rich, clean blues tones

Marshall Bluesbreaker Gutsy bass notes

When B.B. King stops singing, his guitar starts. His solos are full of memorable string bends and expressive, melodic pentatonics.

EXERCISE 10.1.1 – BLUES RIFF

This two-chord riff based in A features A7 (I) and D7 (IV). Notice the C to C♯ transition in bar 1—this transition from the minor third to the major third is a typically bluesy move.

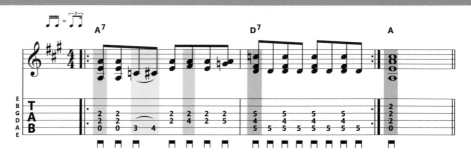

■ **Play the A7 chord.**
Place your 1st finger across the 4th and 3rd strings at the 2nd fret to play the chord.

■ **Hammer-on from C to C♯.** Use your 2nd finger for C then your 3rd finger for C♯ for this bluesy-sounding shift.

■ **Play F♯ and A.** With your 1st finger on the 2nd fret, reach up to the 4th fret with your 3rd finger; play the notes together.

■ **Change to the D7 chord.** In bar 2, change to the D7 chord, placing your 3rd, 2nd, then 4th fingers as shown.

■ **Play the final A chord.** Make a 1st-finger barre across the 4th, 3rd, and 2nd strings at the 2nd fret.

EXERCISE 10.1.2 – BLUES LEAD

This lead exercise can be played on its own or to complement the riff above. With string bends, pull-offs, hammer-ons, and triplet rhythms, A minor pentatonic sounds very bluesy.

■ **Bend from D to E.**
Place your 3rd finger at the 7th fret and bend up from D to E with support from your other fingers.

■ **Play the E note.** After bending to E on the 3rd string, place your 1st finger on the 2nd string, 5th fret and pick the E.

■ **Play the A note.** Fret the A note (5th fret, 1st string) by rolling onto the pad of your 1st finger rather than the tip.

■ **Play a C blues curl.** Use your 4th finger, supported by the others, to curl the C towards C♯— A major's third note.

■ **Hammer-on from C to D.** Perform the hammer-on on the 3rd string, 5th to 7th frets, and add finger vibrato.

CHAPTER 3

SESSION
10·2
DVD

ROCK TRADEMARKS

Rock is about loud and impressive playing. While it incorporates blues stylistics like pentatonics and string bending, its focus is on grand-scale bravado. Although the drums and bass are often prominent, rock is all about the guitar's sound. Memorable single-note or doublestop riffs create song "hooks" (pieces that make songs instantly recognizable), and solos—often long and elaborate—provide respite for the vocalist. Some players go for Chuck Berry-type licks played loud, fast, and distorted; others opt for Clapton-style blues licks mixed with exotic scales and speed techniques, such as legato, but in the end, rock's intention is to grab the audience's attention with volume and power.

Ritchie Blackmore, formerly of Deep Purple, excels at exotic scales mixed with speed and whammy bar use.

ESSENTIAL LISTENING

AC/DC *Back In Black* ◆ *Whole Lotta Rosie* ◆ *For Those About To Rock (We Salute You)*

Deep Purple *Smoke On The Water* ◆ *Speed King* ◆ *Highway Star* ◆ *Black Night*

Led Zeppelin *Whole Lotta Love* ◆ *Stairway To Heaven* ◆ *Immigrant Song* ◆ *Communication Breakdown* ◆ *Heartbreaker*

Queen *Tie Your Mother Down* ◆ *Bohemian Rhapsody* ◆ *Killer Queen* ◆ *Fat Bottomed Girls* ◆ *Hammer To Fall*

Van Halen *Ain't Talkin' 'Bout Love* ◆ *Jamie's Crying* ◆ *Eruption* ◆ *Panama* ◆ *Poundcake*

Guns N' Roses *Sweet Child O' Mine* ◆ *Paradise City* ◆ *Welcome To The Jungle* ◆ *Patience*

KEY TECHNIQUES

String-bends *See pp.162–63*

Power chords *See pp.70–71*

Minor pentatonics *See pp.148–51*

Low-string riffs *See pp.86–87*

Hammer-ons and pull-offs *See pp.80–81*

CLASSIC EQUIPMENT

Les Paul Produces thick and loud distortion

Stratocaster Ideal with the whammy bar

Marshall amp The definitive rock amp brand

Mesa Boogie Mark 4 Varied rock tones

Boss SD1 distortion The pro's choice for distortion

EXERCISE 10.4.1 – COUNTRY RIFF

This exercise features G and C chords played with hybrid picking (pick and three fingers). On beat 4 of each bar there are two low notes to make the chord change smoother. On the down picks, try some light palm muting.

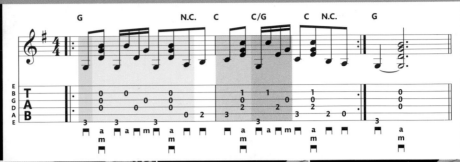

■ **Fret the G chord.** Make a reduced G chord shape with your 3rd finger on the 3rd fret, 6th string. Pick the G note.

■ **Hybrid-pick the G chord.** Use the pick for the 4th string, your 2nd finger (m) for the 3rd string, and 3rd finger (a) for the 2nd string.

■ **Fret the C chord.** Use your 3rd, 2nd, and 1st fingers to fret the C chord.

■ **Fret the C/G slash chord.** Change from the conventional C chord fingering by moving your 3rd finger to the 6th string.

EXERCISE 10.4.2 – COUNTRY LEAD

Two common country techniques featured in this exercise are doublestops (where two strings are played simultaneously) with the lower string bent, and hybrid picking.

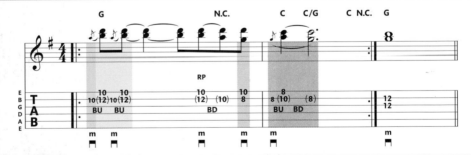

■ **Play the A and D doublestop.** At the 10th fret, place your 3rd finger on the 2nd string and 4th finger on the 1st string.

■ **Bend the string.** With the doublestop fretted, bend the 2nd string up by one tone to a "virtual" 12th fret with your 3rd finger.

■ **Play the G and D doublestop.** Place your 1st finger on the 2nd string, 8th fret, and 4th finger on the 1st string, 10th fret.

■ **Play the G and C doublestop.** At the 8th fret, place your 3rd finger on the 2nd string and 4th finger on the 1st string.

■ **Bend the string.** Bend the lower G note up a tone to A ("virtual" 10th fret), then drop the bend down and sustain.

CHAPTER 3

SESSION
10·5
DVD

R&B TRADEMARKS

Rhythm and blues, or R&B, is a generic term with various musical strands, but the mainstream involves 1950s artists like Bo Diddley, 60s artists such as The MGs and Otis Redding, and later 70s bands like The Meters. Initially a precursor to rock and roll, its guitar trademarks involve clipped rhythms, chord picking, hybrid picking, and memorable riffs and licks.

There is some soloing, often with bluesy doublestops and pentatonic notes, but the guitar's role here is mainly to accompany a singer within a band's rhythm section. For this reason, single-coil-pickup guitars like Telecasters, paired with clean and overdriven amps, have shaped R&B music.

CHAPTER 3

ESSENTIAL LISTENING

Booker T & the MGs *Time Is Tight* ◆ *Green Onions* ◆ *Soul Limbo* ◆ *Over Easy* ◆ *Melting Pot* ◆ *Hang 'Em High* ◆ *Heads Or Tails*

Ike Turner *A Fool In Love* ◆ *It's Gonna Work Out Fine* ◆ *Nutbush City Limits*

Isley Brothers *That Lady* ◆ *Summer Breeze* ◆ *Work To Do* ◆ *Harvest For The World* ◆ *Caravan Of Love*

The Meters *Cissy Strut* ◆ *Simple Song* ◆ *Lady Marmalade* ◆ *Look-Ka Py Py* ◆ *I Need More Time* ◆ *Handclapping Song*

Bo Diddley *Who Do You Love* ◆ *Say Man* ◆ *Roadrunner* ◆ *Before You Accuse Me* ◆ *You Can't Judge A Book By The Cover* ◆ *Pretty Thing* ◆ *Bring It To Jerome* ◆ *Bo Diddley*

KEY TECHNIQUES

Clipped chords	*See pp.134–35*
Up-tempo blues riffs	*See pp.86–87*
String bending	*See pp.162–63*
Hybrid picking	*See pp.206–07*
Mixolydian mode	*See pp.230–31*

CLASSIC EQUIPMENT

Telecaster	Sharp sounds for precise chords
Stratocaster	Great for clean tones
ES335	Good for thicker chord and solo work
Fender Twin	Loud amp for rhythm playing
Fender Bassman	Powerful clean tones

Bo Diddley, with his distinctive rectangular guitar, became known for his driving, hard-edged sound.

EXERCISE 10.5.1 – R&B RHYTHM

This typical 1950s/60s R&B rhythm guitar part features E, G, and A chords and the trademark Bo Diddley rhythm. Keep your strumming precise to bring out the best in this appealing mixture of on- and off-beat chords.

■ **Play the E chord.** Form the E chord as shown—down strum only the four low strings and avoid the two high open strings.

■ **Clip the E chord.** Stop the chord from sustaining by releasing fretting-hand pressure and muting the strings with your palm.

■ **Play the G chord.** Play the G as a barre chord with a 1st-finger barre at the 3rd fret.

■ **Play the A chord.** Play the A as a barre chord with a 1st-finger barre at the 5th fret.

EXERCISE 10.5.2 – R&B LEAD

This lead part uses a contrasting rhythm and doublestops to complement the chord riff above. Notice the blues curls (quarter-tone bends) that emulate the sound of a train.

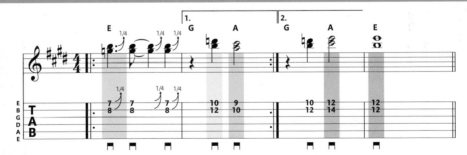

■ **Play the doublestop blues curl.** Fret G (8th fret, 2nd string) and B (7th fret, 1st string) then bend up slightly.

■ **Play the B and G doublestop.** Use your 3rd finger (12th fret, 2nd string) and 1st finger (10th fret, 1st string).

■ **Play the A and C♯ doublestop.** Use your 2nd finger (10th fret, 2nd string) and 1st finger (9th fret, 1st string).

■ **Play the C♯ and E doublestop.** Use your 3rd finger (14th fret, 2nd string) and 1st finger (12th fret, 1st string).

■ **Play the B and E doublestop.** Make a small 1st-finger barre on the top two strings at the 12th fret.

10.1 10.2 10.3 10.4 **10.5** 10.6 10.7 10.8 10.9 10.10

CHAPTER 3

SESSION 10·6 FUNK TRADEMARKS

Funk is primarily rhythm-oriented. It can involve fast sixteenth-note rhythms, or slower triplet-based grooves, but it must encourage people to dance (or at least tap their feet). The guitar's role here is to combine with the drums and bass to work as one precise rhythm machine. Typically, the bass mimics the drummer's bass drum and the guitar complements the hi-hat rhythms. Using a mixture of chords (especially m7, maj7, and sus), the guitarist usually produces a clean tone for short, clipped rhythms or sustained chords. Pentatonic solos do occur—Prince favors them, as does Nile Rodgers—but rhythmic mastery is the mark of a true funk guitarist.

Prince's guitar style mixes all the greats, from Jimi Hendrix to Curtis Mayfield and Nile Rodgers.

ESSENTIAL LISTENING

James Brown *I Feel Good* ◆ *Sex Machine* ◆ *Funky President* ◆ *My Thang* ◆ *The Payback* ◆ *Doing It To Death* ◆ *Funky Drummer*

Chic *Good Times* ◆ *Le Freak* ◆ *Dance Dance Dance* ◆ *Everybody Dance* ◆ *I Want Your Love*

Earth, Wind & Fire *Jupiter* ◆ *Shining Star* ◆ *In The Stone* ◆ *Boogie Wonderland*

Sly and The Family Stone *Dance To The Music* ◆ *I Want To Take You Higher* ◆ *Thank You (Falettinme Be Mice Elf Agin)* ◆ *Stand* ◆ *Family Affair*

Average White Band *Pick Up The Pieces* ◆ *Cut The Cake* ◆ *Let's Go Round Again*

Prince *1999* ◆ *Sign O' The Times* ◆ *Kiss* ◆ *Controversy* ◆ *Sexy MF* ◆ *Gett Off*

KEY TECHNIQUES

Doublestops *See pp.192–93*

Slides *See pp.174–75*

Major 7th chords *See pp.114–15*

Pentatonic notes *See pp.146–47*

Sixteenth-note strumming *See pp.50–51*

CLASSIC EQUIPMENT

Stratocaster Sparkling "chink" sounds for rhythm

Telecaster Biting and soulful for rootsy funk

ES335 Versatile jazz and rock tones for 70s funk

Fender Twin Punchy and clean mid tones

Roland JC120 Powerful and clean sound

CHAPTER 3

EXERCISE 10.6.1 – FUNK RHYTHM

This D Dorian funk groove features two chords (Dm7 and G7) played with precise sixteenth-note rhythms. Keep your picking hand moving fluidly throughout the exercise.

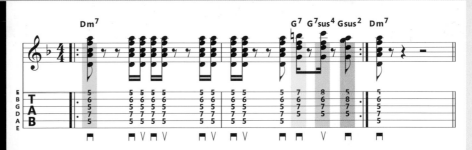

■ **Play the Dm7 chord.** Use your 2nd and 3rd fingers on the 7th and 6th frets, with your 1st finger barring across the 5th fret.

■ **Play the G7 chord.** Use the less common version of the chord (the CAGED D7 shape) with your 1st finger at the 5th fret.

■ **Play the G7sus4 chord.** Retain the fingering of the previous G7 but move your 4th finger up to the 8th fret, 1st string.

■ **Play the Gsus2 chord.** Use a barre across the 5th fret to play this derivative of G7.

EXERCISE 10.6.2 – FUNK LEAD

This prominent funk lead should sound machinelike in its precision. Try it with and without palm muting applied.

■ **Play the D note.** Place your 3rd finger at the 7th fret, 3rd string, for D. Have your 1st finger ready at the 5th fret.

■ **Play the C note.** Lift your 3rd finger off the fretboard to leave the 1st finger at the 5th fret. Pick the C note.

■ **Play the A note.** Use your 3rd finger at the 7th fret, 4th string. Sound the note twice with a down and up pick.

■ **Play the E note.** To close bar 2, place your 3rd finger at the 9th fret, 3rd string. Have your 1st finger in position as shown.

■ **Play the D note.** After playing E, quickly take your 3rd finger off to play D with your 1st finger on the 7th fret, 3rd string.

CHAPTER 3

SESSION 10·7 DVD
REGGAE TRADEMARKS

Reggae is a unique musical style that originated in Jamaica during the mid 1960s. Its roots are in ska, which in turn was influenced by West Indian soca and calypso music. Reggae slowed down ska's rhythms, simplified chord progressions, and made the bass drum and bass guitar more prominent. On the guitar, clipped chords (often using only a few high strings) on each offbeat provide a regular rhythmic lilt. Sometimes the guitar may double the bassline, but an octave higher, making the part more prominent: alternatively, a bubbling single-note line may weave between the other instruments. Wah, phaser, and echo sounds are used, but a clean amp tone is preferred by many.

ESSENTIAL LISTENING

Bob Marley *I Shot The Sheriff* ◆ *No Woman No Cry* ◆ *Wait In Vain* ◆ *Jamming* ◆ *One Love* ◆ *Get Up Stand Up* ◆ *Is This Love?* ◆ *Exodus*

Jimmy Cliff *The Harder They Come* ◆ *Sittin' in Limbo* ◆ *Vietnam*

Desmond Dekker *Israelites* ◆ *Warlock*

Burning Spear *Slavery Days* ◆ *Old Marcus Garvey* ◆ *Dread River*

UB40 *Red Red Wine* ◆ *One in Ten* ◆ *I Got You Babe* ◆ *I Can't Help Falling In Love With You* ◆ *Rat In The Kitchen* ◆ *Breakfast In Bed*

Toots and the Maytals *54–46 That's My Number* ◆ *Funky Kingston* ◆ *Do The Reggay!* ◆ *Pressure Drop* ◆ *Monkey Man*

KEY TECHNIQUES

Clipped chords *See pp.134–35*

Clipped basslines *See pp.86–87*

Slides *See pp.174–75*

Pentatonics *See pp.146–47*

Triplets *See pp.50–51*

CLASSIC EQUIPMENT

Les Paul Junior Clean tones with up strokes

Telecaster Bright and cutting for chords

Stratocaster Broad tonal options

Fender Twin Powerful and loud amplifier

Vox AC30 Adds a little crunch to riffs

Central to Bob Marley's band, the Wailers, guitarist Peter Tosh helped establish the choppy reggae guitar sound.

EXERCISE 10.7.1 – REGGAE RHYTHM

Here you play the basic reggae rhythm—regular clipped chords played on every offbeat. The down strokes (bracketed) are not heard, but the up strokes are.

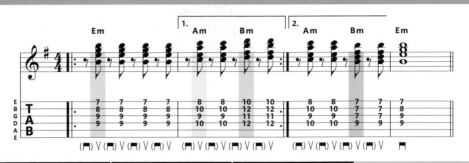

■ **Play the Em chord.** Make a barre at the 7th fret, and play only the top four strings for a very short (clipped) duration.

■ **Play the Am chord.** In bar 2, change to Am based at the 8th fret. Again, use only the top four strings for a clipped sound.

■ **Play the Bm (version 1) chord.** At the end of bar 2, simply move the Am shape up two frets to create Bm.

■ **Play the Bm (version 2) chord.** For added variety and interest, play this alternative Bm down at the 7th fret.

PRACTICE & PROGRESS

Pay attention to chord length when you practice—reggae guitarists often play short, clipped chords in which pitch is hardly detectable, just as if it was a cymbal part. For variety, consider using a phaser pedal (see p.39) for "whooshing" filter effects.

see p.39

CHAPTER 3

EXERCISE 10.7.2 – REGGAE LEAD

This lead part uses E minor pentatonic, shape 1 for a melodic phrase that contrasts with the reggae rhythm. Try it with a clean or slightly overdriven tone.

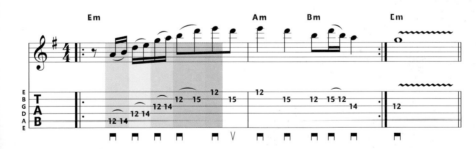

■ **Play A and B.** Use your 1st finger at the 12th fret, 5th string, for A; hammer on with your 3rd finger at the 14th fret for B.

■ **Play D and E.** Use your 1st finger at the 12th fret, 4th string, for D; hammer on with your 3rd finger at the 14th fret for E.

■ **Play G and A.** Use your 1st finger at the 12th fret, 3rd string, for G; hammer on with your 3rd finger at the 14th fret for A.

■ **Play B and D.** Use your 1st finger at the 12th fret, 2nd string, for B; hammer on with your 4th finger at the 15th fret for D.

■ **Play the E note.** Pick the penultimate note in bar 1 with your 1st finger at the 12th fret, 1st string.

SESSION 10·8 DVD
80s POP TRADEMARKS

From the late 1970s onward, music became affected by electronics, with various bands adopting synthesizers, samplers, and electronic drum machines. Many of the biggest bands combined them with guitars, and electronics came to play a considerable part in steering the guitar's role in 80s pop.

The guitar became more machinelike, with single-note and chordal riffs that drew influence from synthesizer sequencer arrangements. This can be heard in music by Madonna (such as *Who's That Girl?*) and Michael Jackson (*Thriller*)—two pop icons of the era. Some bands infused the guitar parts with a funk and/or rock edge, such as Go West (*Don't Look Down*), Level 42 (*Running In The Family*), and Frankie Goes To Hollywood (*Two Tribes*).

Numerous artists found that effects such as chorus, compression, echo, and volume could create impressive results akin to synthesizer "pads," producing big and warm sustaining sounds that evoked orchestral string sections. Two bands that explored these ambient guitar sounds successfully were The Police (especially in *Walking On The Moon*) and U2 (listen to *With Or Without You*).

In the 1980s, players realized that anthemic guitar parts could be achieved using just a few repeating notes. Bands such as U2 and Simple Minds featured simple guitar parts augmented with sound processing to dramatic effect. So next time you look through 80s compilations, listen out for the guitar parts—there's much to enjoy and emulate.

EXERCISE 10.8.1 – 80s POP FUNK RHYTHM

This exercise has a funky machinelike quality, typical of Michael Jackson, Madonna, and Level 42. It is sixteenth note based, and features doublepicked single notes and doublestops. Use light palm muting for a tight sound.

■ **Play the E note.** Place your 2nd finger at the 5th fret, 2nd string. Pick the note using light palm muting.

■ **Play an A and F♯ double-stop.** Use your 1st finger for A (2nd fret, 3rd string) and 3rd finger for F♯ (4th fret, 4th string).

■ **Play the E5 chord.** Use your 1st finger for E (2nd fret, 4th string) and 3rd finger for B (4th fret, 3rd string).

PRACTICE & PROGRESS

Pop guitar doesn't need to involve busy playing and big chords. Often, three-string chords and/or two-note doublestops are enough to get the sound. If you play in a band, try playing rhythmic guitar licks in between keyboard parts. For inspiration, listen to pop guitar masters like David Williams (Madonna, Michael Jackson) and Alan Murphy (Go West, Level 42, Kate Bush).

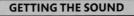

GETTING THE SOUND

The Edge – 80s pop

The chiming guitar sounds of The Edge help define U2's unmistakable sound. Although his playing is often sparse, and rarely includes solos, The Edge puts his stamp on any song. Best known for his unique drone style, enhanced by echo effects, The Edge is a musical innovator and has embraced everything that music technology offers (listen to his sustaining guitar on *With Or Without You*, and the processed filter funk on *Numb*) and revels in rootsy guitar styles such as the Bo-Diddley-type rhythms on *Desire*. Although he is no virtuoso technician, The Edge's guitar style and approach demonstrate considerable musicality and sonic color, making him a true one-of-a-kind guitar legend.

ESSENTIAL TRACKS

Sunday Bloody Sunday
I Will Follow
I Still Haven't Found What I'm Looking For
Where The Streets Have No Name
One
Numb

SIMILAR ARTISTS

Charlie Burchill (Simple Minds)
Matt Bellamy (Muse)
Tom Morello (Rage Against The Machine)
Robert Smith (The Cure)
Mike Scott (The Waterboys)
Billy Duffy (The Cult)

The Edge's bright, chiming, and echo-rich guitar sound and sparse chord voicings have added new dimensions to pop rock guitar.

SESSION 10·9 DVD
JAZZ TRADEMARKS

Jazz is a style that has been primarily driven by instruments such as the piano and the saxophone. It is also a style that numerous guitarists have gravitated towards, due to the wealth of material (classic jazz tunes are often referred to as "standards") and the breadth of melodic and chordal possibilities. While the main melodies to songs—known as the "head"—are fun to play, guitarists revel in improvising before returning to the tune. The hallmark of a great jazz improviser is the mastery of exotic scales and chords all along the fretboard and the confidence to play outside musical convention. Jazz guitarists tend to favor hollow-body guitars fitted with thick-gauge strings.

ESSENTIAL LISTENING

Charlie Christian *Solo Flight* ◆ *Stardust* ◆ *Wholly Cats* ◆ *Swing To Bop*

Joe Pass *Love For Sale* ◆ *Misty* ◆ *All The Things You Are* ◆ *Stella By Starlight*

Django Reinhardt *Nuages* ◆ *Minor Swing* ◆ *Dinah* ◆ *Djangology* ◆ *Sweet Georgia Brown* ◆ *I'll See You In My Dreams*

Wes Montgomery *Tequila* ◆ *Impressions* ◆ *West Coast Blues* ◆ *Four On Six* ◆ *Boss City*

George Benson *Breezin* ◆ *Moody's Mood* ◆ *Oleo* ◆ *Affirmation* ◆ *Sunny* ◆ *L'il Darlin'*

Pat Metheny *James* ◆ *We Live Here* ◆ *Beat 70* ◆ *Third Wind* ◆ *Minuano (Six Eight)* ◆ *Something To Remind You*

KEY TECHNIQUES

Chromatic scale links *See pp.42–43*

7th chords *See pp.114–15*

2-5-1 progressions *See pp.118–19*

Slides *See pp.174–75*

Scale dexterity *See pp.242–43*

CLASSIC EQUIPMENT

Gibson L5 Archtop with warm tone and great depth

Gibson ES175 Adaptable tone for modern jazz

Gibson ES335 Combines woody and biting tones

Polytone Mini Brute Popular for its clean tone

Fender Twin Full, clean tones

George Benson can navigate the most complex of jazz chords. His "scat" singing (singing the same notes as played on guitar) is legendary.

EXERCISE 10.9.1 – JAZZ RHYTHM

This exercise evokes the style of Count Basie's guitarist, Freddie Green, with clipped chords played on each beat. Squeeze the chord on then off to get the effect.

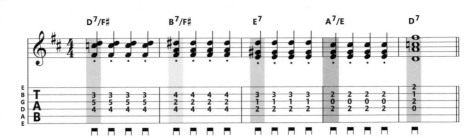

■ **Play D7/F♯.** Fret the chord with the fingering shown then relax soon after sounding the chord so that it doesn't sustain.

■ **Play B7/F♯.** Make this small change in fingering from D7/F♯. The transition to B7/F♯ should sound smooth.

■ **Play E7.** Use your 4th finger at the 3rd fret, 2nd string for the top D note of this chord.

■ **Play A7/E.** Use quick palm muting to stop this chord—which includes an open string—from sustaining.

■ **Play D7.** Finger this familiar D7 chord and let it sustain to finish the exercise.

EXERCISE 10.9.2 – JAZZ LEAD

Jazz lead often involves playing notes one octave apart in a melodic fashion. Watching both fingers is confusing, so try watching the 4th finger as you move around—hopefully your 1st finger will keep up.

■ **Play the D octave.** Place your 4th finger at the 10th fret, 1st string, and your 1st finger at the 7th fret, 3rd string.

■ **Play the C octave.** Place your 4th finger at the 8th fret, 1st string, and your 1st finger at the 5th fret, 3rd string.

■ **Play the A octave.** Place your 4th finger at the 10th fret, 2nd string, and your 1st finger at the 7th fret, 4th string.

PRACTICE & PROGRESS

When playing octaves that span three strings (as here), the middle string needs to be kept quiet. Do this by resting the underside of your 1st finger lightly across the adjacent higher (thinner) string so it's muted.

CHAPTER 3

SESSION 10·10 DVD
JAZZ ROCK TRADEMARKS

Jazz rock arose in the late 1960s and peaked during the 1970s. Sometimes called "fusion," it combines jazz musical vocabulary with the volume, rhythmic drive, and repetition of rock music. For many, the defining album is Miles Davis's *Bitches Brew* (1970); this featured many jazz musicians who later became jazz rock legends.

Since the 1970s, jazz rock has expanded, allowing blues, funk, bluegrass, and reggae into its style. Clean guitar tones are used on solid-body guitars alongside loud amps that offer distortion (pedals offer similar sounds). A thorough knowledge of scales and chords is essential, along with a few rock guitar techniques such as tapping and sweeping.

John McLaughlin set the bar for jazz rock virtuosity: fast picking, exotic chords and scales, odd note groupings, and rock-based riffing.

ESSENTIAL LISTENING

John McLaughlin *Meeting Of The Spirits* ◆ *Birds Of Fire* ◆ *Lotus Feet* ◆ *My Foolish Heart* ◆ *Blue In Green*

Al Di Meola *Mediterranean Sundance* ◆ *Race With Devil On Spanish Highway* ◆ *Egyptian Danza* ◆ *Electric Rendezvous*

Mike Stern *Upside Downside* ◆ *Mood Swings* ◆ *After You* ◆ *Play* ◆ *Tipitina's*

Allan Holdsworth *Fred* ◆ *Proto Cosmos* ◆ *Pud Wud* ◆ *Low Levels High Stakes* ◆ *Joshua*

John Scofield *Wabash* ◆ *Fat Lip* ◆ *So Sue Me* ◆ *Kool* ◆ *Big Top* ◆ *Carlos* ◆ *Chang*

Larry Carlton *Room 335* ◆ *Point It Up* ◆ *Don't Give It Up* ◆ *Last Nite* ◆ *Emotions Wound Us So*

KEY TECHNIQUES

Fast picking See pp.252–53

Odd note groupings See pp.254–55

Big note jumps See pp.242–43

String bending See pp.238–39

Modes See pp.226–31

CLASSIC EQUIPMENT

ES335 Combines woody and biting tones

Les Paul A thick rock tone

Mesa Boogie Mark 1 Thick, sustaining distortion

Chorus pedal Provides swirling chorus effects

Fender Twin Clean tone

EXERCISE 10.10.1 – JAZZ ROCK RHYTHM

Rock power chords and a riff based in F♯ minor pentatonic drive this example of a jazz rock rhythm part.

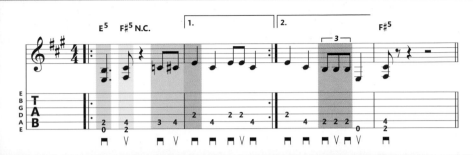

■ **Play the E5 chord.** Use your 1st finger for the higher B note (2nd fret, 5th string) of this chord, which opens the exercise.

■ **Play the F♯5 chord.** Use your 1st finger for F♯ (2nd fret, 6th string) and your 3rd finger for C♯ (4th fret, 5th string).

■ **Play the C and C♯ notes.** On the 5th string, use your 2nd finger at the 3rd fret for C, and 3rd finger at the 4th fret for C♯.

■ **Play the E note.** Begin bar 2 with an E, fretted with your 1st finger at the 2nd fret, 4th string.

■ **Play the B note.** Use your 1st finger at the 2nd fret, 5th string, for the B note in the triplet rhythm.

EXERCISE 10.10.2 – JAZZ ROCK LEAD

This lead part high up the fretboard spells out F♯ Mixolydian (spot the A♯: the major third). Get familiar with the change between two notes per beat and three (triplets) in bar 2.

■ **Play the B note.** Place your 3rd finger at the 16th fret, 3rd string. Have your 2nd finger ready for the next note.

■ **Play the A♯ note.** With your 2nd finger already in place at the 15th fret, 3rd string, play the note with an up pick.

■ **Play the F♯ note.** Use your 3rd finger at the 16th fret, 4th string. Have your 1st finger ready for the next note.

■ **Play the E note.** With your 1st finger already in place at the 14th fret, 4th string, play the E note.

PRACTICE & PROGRESS

Switching between a two- and three-notes-per-beat rhythm within one bar can be tricky. Try setting a regular beat on a metronome; say "ap-ple" on each two beats (two syllables per beat) then switch to "straw-ber-ry" for the next two beats.

CHAPTER 3

"Inspiration can come from the most unlikely places ...
keep your head on and your ears open ..."

BILLY GIBBONS, ZZ TOP

BECOMING AN
ARTIST

4

COVERING SONGS AND WRITING ORIGINAL MATERIAL

Whatever your preferred musical genre, knowing how to play a few cover versions of classic songs is a useful skill—and one that's likely to make you popular with an audience. Developing an ear for hallmark chord progressions and song structures by playing covers is also a strong foundation for writing your own material. Knowing the established "rules" will allow you to break them in a creative but informed way.

Words and music
Bob Dylan's lyrics have a poetic quality, and are brought fully to life through his distinctive voice and music.

COVERING SONGS

Finding music to play is easy: music publishers produce notation and tab versions of a huge variety of classic songs, often with solos as well as chords. There are also many collections of songs by celebrated artists that are selected for their suitability for unaccompanied acoustic guitar. Visit your local music shop or search online and you'll find a wealth of material.

A more satisfying option is to use your chord knowledge and your ear to work out how your favorite recordings are played. Although this can be frustrating at first—requiring you to listen to a piece many times over to follow what's going on—it is a good discipline. It will tune your ear to common chord progressions and help to reveal details that are sometimes missed by the books. When learning this way, try watching footage of performances by guitarists who have tackled the same song—it may enable you to work out some of the finer fingering details by eye or inspire you to produce your own arrangements of classic tracks.

WRITING LYRICS

The are no fixed rules when it comes to writing song lyrics. You can build a song around the mood of lyrics that you have already written, or compose a winning chord progression, then write lyrics to fit over the top. Something to remember is that song lyrics don't have to be strictly literary in their use of language. While artists like Bob Dylan and Joni Mitchell effectively set poems or short stories to music, many of the best rock and pop lyrics are impressionistic and almost wilfully obscure.

WRITING ORIGINAL MATERIAL

If you want to write songs for solo performance, a great way to start is to play around with chord progressions and melodies with a notepad or recording device on hand. Try fitting them into a verse/chorus structure and adding new sections like a classic "middle eight" (*see below*). Add a little sophistication in the form of alternative voicings of common chords and some passing notes and embellishments, and you'll be well on your way to penning an accomplished song. If you record at home (*see pp.288–89*), try using fragments of your guitar playing looped or treated with effects as the basis for composition.

If you want to write for a band (*see pp.286–87*), you can try the collaborative approach. Develop an interesting phrase or riff and take it to a practice session; allow the group members to develop their own accompaniments, which can then be used as the starting point for a song structure.

RHYTHMIC VARIETY

When writing original songs, it's all too easy to stick to formulaic "four on the floor" (4/4) rhythms with the emphasis on the first beat. Why not experiment by playing your chord progression to an alternative rhythm or time signature (*see pp.50–51*), such as a reggae beat (*see pp.272–73*) or a 3/4 waltz rhythm? You may discover that doing this gives your song a "feel" that you like even better than your original idea.

Switching rhythms within a song structure can also be extremely effective and is often overlooked as a musical device. Songs such as *A Day in the Life* by The Beatles demonstrate how effective this technique can be at creating drama and variation.

SONG STRUCTURE IN POPULAR MUSIC

Just as a good story has a beginning, middle, and end, memorable songs in popular music tell a story through their structure. They link together sections—intro, verse, chorus, bridge, and middle eight—that each have a distinct character, creating a sense of direction. This is something we all instinctively understand and respond to when we hear well-structured songs.

Intro The intro of a song must grab the listener's attention and establish the song's personality. Some do this by launching straight into the chorus minus the lyric (try *Song 2* by Blur), or by slowly building tension (for example, Marvin Gaye's *I Heard It Through The Grapevine*).

Verse This sets up a regular pattern of chords on which the melody and lyrical narrative can be built. A verse —a unit of, say, eight bars—can either be repeated to allow the "story'" of the song to develop further (think of *Scarborough Fair* and other strongly narrative folk songs), or lead seamlessly into a bridge or chorus.

Chorus This is the most stirring, climactic part of the song, where all the tension and interest created up to that point gets released. It is typically made up of a triumphant, liberating progression of chords. Many songs end with a repeat chorus, sometimes with a key change for extra "lift"—as in Bon Jovi's *Livin' On A Prayer*.

Bridge The bridge acts as an energizing link between the calm of the verse and the release of the chorus—rather like shifting up a gear in a car—and is is typically between two and eight bars long. Some songs have a "pre chorus" motif that is instantly recognizable—for example the morse-codelike single note in David Bowie's *Starman*.

Middle eight This songwriting device is often found in ballads, to convey a "twist" in the tale before the song's story ends. As the name suggests it is typically eight bars long and often contains a key change. A classic example can be heard in *Tequila Sunrise* by the Eagles.

EXAMPLES OF SONG STRUCTURES

Balancing interest
A successful pop song, such as *I Want To Hold Your Hand* by The Beatles, mixes repetition with points of musical interest. Repetition quickly builds familiarity and helps fix the song in the listener's mind.

FURTHER EXAMPLES

Since U Been Gone: Kelly Clarkson
Verse ▸ Verse ▸ Bridge ▸ Chorus ▸ Verse ▸ Bridge ▸ Chorus ▸ Middle Eight ▸ Chorus ▸ Chorus

Livin' On A Prayer: Bon Jovi
Intro ▸ Verse ▸ Verse ▸ Bridge ▸ Chorus ▸ Verse ▸ Verse ▸ Bridge ▸ Chorus ▸ Solo ▸ Chorus ▸ Chorus (with key change)

CHAPTER 4

PLAYING IN PUBLIC

Impressing a live audience is at the top of the list for many aspiring guitarists. Before you start your live career, you'll need to consider many practicalities—transportation, equipment, and finding the right place to play, for example—and spend some time developing your performance. This is not just about improving your sound, but about presenting yourself and your music to an audience effectively, so you'll grow in confidence and they'll want more.

GETTING YOUR FIRST GIGS

The easiest place to make your debut is an open mic night. These are usually held at small music venues and offer local acts a chance to perform two or three numbers in front of a live audience. You'll usually need to book a slot with venue staff, but it may be possible to simply show up on the night, especially if you are a solo performer. It's very unlikely you'll get paid, but you will gain valuable experience.

If you are aiming to secure a paid gig, you'll usually need to record a demo and provide it to the venue manager for approval. Three tracks on a CD should be sufficient; alternatively, upload your songs (or videos of previous performances) to the Internet and simply give the details of the website to the venue staff. Try asking if you can take a support slot at a forthcoming gig. You may end up opening to an empty room early in the evening, but it will help to establish your name on the circuit of regular players.

Working an audience Many bands start their set with a few of their strongest numbers to pull in the crowd before moving on to new, or experimental, material.

BE PREPARED

Rehearse your material thoroughly before a gig, so you can focus on your performance and your audience. Do some research, too, before stepping on stage.

- Visit the venue in advance, checking the size and position of the stage, lighting, access to power, and equipment available for your use.
- Ask if the venue has its own PA system—you may need to bring your own—and check on volume restrictions (some venues have automatic volume-limiting systems that can unexpectedly curtail your performance).
- Check where and when you are expected to unload and set up your gear and what time you will start and finish.
- Be prepared—take a couple of packs of strings, spare picks, leads, and fresh batteries (if needed) to your performance. Never expect extension cords to be available at a venue—bring your own.

STAGECRAFT AND PERFORMANCE

While it's fine to take to the stage and let your songs do the talking, engaging the crowd fully is about more than the music. You can grab attention through some visuals—flamboyant costumes, hair, and makeup are fun when they emphasize the character of your music—and adding some physical energy to your act will fire up interest. If your music is downbeat, you might want to do the opposite: stillness can be powerful in the right setting, and with the right music. Above all, immerse yourself in the music you are playing. An act that locks "into the groove" and plays it to the hilt will always be compelling to watch and listen to. Excitement is infectious and your performance is the engine for that excitement. Write down a set list before you perform so you don't have to pause to decide what to play next at the end of each number—or, worse, let the audience wait while you debate it with other band members. Make intervals between songs reasonably brief and remarks to the audience concise and pithy. Put the music first and your ego second, and you won't go too far wrong.

PRO TIP
PLAY, DON'T PAY

You probably won't get rich playing local bars, but you should avoid "pay to play" venues. Typically, such venues will set a target number for gig attendance and charge you for any shortfall on that figure on the night. Remember that you are providing a service, so you shouldn't have to pay for the privilege of doing so, regardless of whether you're packing them in or playing to an empty house. Look elsewhere for venues that love music and deal fairly with musicians.

Stage presence There are many ways to impose your presence on an audience. The bold graphics and energy at a Gorillaz gig (*above right*) are a world away from the bluesy, homespun charm of festival favorite Seasick Steve (*right*).

FORMING A BAND

Nothing beats the adrenaline rush of performing with a full band. Playing in a band is not only great fun but creative collaboration will probably take your musicianship to the next level quicker than solo practice—and get you noticed as a musician. Getting a band together can be exciting, but keeping it together requires tact, compromise, and some careful thought about who you recruit.

PUTTING PEOPLE TOGETHER

Bands usually begin casually, with a couple of friends setting out to play gigs in local venues. When you begin, it's likely you'll need to seek out one or two musicians outside your immediate circle to fill key positions in the band (*see box, right*). Once you start getting inquiries you should hold auditions to meet the candidates and establish if they will be a good fit musically and socially. Auditions can take the form of jamming on a piece that you all know, or sending the candidates a piece of your music in advance and seeing how they deal with and interpret your own music.

RECRUITING BAND MEMBERS

A band made up of close friends or even family members has advantages—getting together for practice sessions is easy, and you already have an established rapport. Most new bands have to recruit at least one stranger, however, and in some cases you'll all have to get to know each other from scratch.

- Start by emailing friends and fellow music fans on social networking sites; find out if anyone can put you in touch with musicians who fit the bill.
- Visit local music venues and practice rooms to place and read posted advertisements.
- Make use of the many free websites that help you find available players in your area.
- Consider taking out classified advertisements in music magazines or their websites if you are prepared to invest some money to find the best possible personnel.

PLANNING REHEARSALS

To get ready for any performance you'll need a repertoire of well-practiced songs. Garages and the like are fine venues for small practice sessions, but you'll get better results by renting purpose-built rehearsal rooms—and stand a better chance of staying on good terms with your neighbors.

Most towns have rehearsal space that is available for hire by the hour. These rooms usually come equipped with PA systems for vocalists, plus a guitar and bass amp. Quality rehearsal spaces will often rent out specialized or vintage equipment for an additional fee, and many sell useful kits such as strings, straps, and leads.

Make sure that all band members are happy to pay their fair share toward each session and ensure everyone turns up on time to set up their equipment and begin the rehearsal promptly. Give some structure to your rehearsals by setting out loose goals for each one—such as practicing five new songs, or perfecting a difficult section of a song you already know. Beware of slipping into the habit of just jamming aimlessly for an hour or two unless that's all you really want to do.

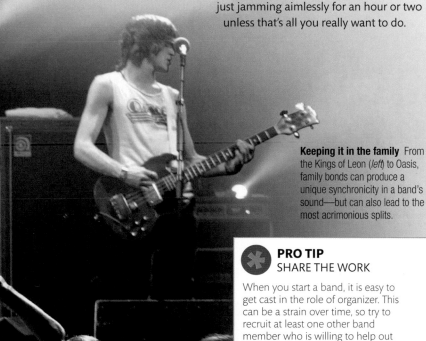

Pacing rehearsal time Use expensive practice room time for focused full band rehearsals in which you work on weaker songs.

Keeping it in the family From the Kings of Leon (*left*) to Oasis, family bonds can produce a unique synchronicity in a band's sound—but can also lead to the most acrimonious splits.

> ✳ **PRO TIP**
> SHARE THE WORK
>
> When you start a band, it is easy to get cast in the role of organizer. This can be a strain over time, so try to recruit at least one other band member who is willing to help out with logistics, bookings, and transportation as the weeks go by.

PERFECTING YOUR SOUND

Your band's first gig at an established venue will, hopefully, introduce you to an exciting new collaborator—the sound engineer. His or her job is to operate the venue's public address (PA) system, which amplifies inputs from the instruments and microphones, and mixes them together into a balanced sound.

- Work closely with the engineer to get the most from your performance: always be courteous and punctual.
- Perform a soundcheck to balance the sound sources. Typically, you'll run through one or two songs a few hours before the performance. Follow the engineer's advice if he or she asks you to adjust the settings of your amp and effects.
- Confer with the engineer about the mix. Not all of your equipment needs to pass through the mixing desk: the engineer may allow "back line" equipment, such as guitar and bass amps, to project their own sound.
- Make sure the levels are right for what the band itself hears on stage via the monitors (the wedge-shaped speakers on stage). Ask the engineer to adjust the monitor levels if, for example, vocals are not clearly audible on stage.

Sound wizardry A mixing desk and a professional engineer can take your band's sound to another level.

HOME RECORDING

With the advent of powerful computers, accessible recording software, and tumbling equipment prices, it is now possible to make highly professional recordings in a home studio. There are many recording techniques available—the path you choose depends on your budget, the space you have available, your technical proficiency, and the sound you wish to achieve.

CHOOSING A LOCATION

To get the best possible sound from your recordings, you must give some thought to where you set up your equipment. The ideal location is a quiet room that is not in continual use and which is isolated from interfering sounds, such as extractor fans and traffic noise. Make sure the area is dry and well ventilated, and has plenty of power outlets available. Avoid rooms with poor acoustics—bare walls, exposed windows, and other hard surfaces will reflect sound waves, causing them to bounce around, to the detriment of your recordings. Rooms that are exactly square have notoriously poor acoustics, although you can take measures to improve acoustic qualities (*see box, right*).

DIGITAL SOLUTIONS

At the heart of most modern home recording setups is a PC or Mac loaded with a Digital Audio Workstation (DAW) program, such as Ableton Live, Cubase, and Logic, to name just a few. This captures sounds digitally, and allows you to record different elements of a song (solo, main riff, and bassline) on separate tracks so they can be edited separately but played back simultaneously, and usually features built-in effects such as reverb and delay. Alternatively, digital multitrack recorders offer a robust, hardware-based alternative to a DAW setup and boast many of the same recording capabilities in a compact package.

IMPROVING ACOUSTICS

A few simple measures will improve the acoustic qualities and make it easier to achieve high-quality recordings.

- Fit thick curtains on windows and place microphone stands on a rug to deaden unwanted vibrations.
- Place monitoring speakers on stands away from the corners of the room.
- Consider lining the room with acoustic tiles to dampen unwanted "early reflections"—high-frequency echoes that are heard as a ringing sound when you clap your hands in an empty room.

USING MONITORS

Once you have made a recording, you need to listen to it critically. The most convenient option is to connect your computer and DAW to active monitors—these are studio-grade loudspeakers that feature integral amplifiers. There are affordable entry-level models available, but be sure to listen to their output before buying.

Listening in Artists—here the Rolling Stones—use headphones during a recording. Headphones let you listen to the processed sound output of your guitar while you record, without causing feedback.

CAPTURING AND MIXING SOUND

How you get the signal from your guitar into your recording system determines the quality of the sound and how much control you have over your recording. Today's technology allows for many options, a selection of which are set out below.

It is possible to simply connect the guitar to the "line in" socket of your computer's sound card; however, this will give you a poor-quality signal. At the very least, you should invest in an inexpensive mixer that will allow you to blend sound sources—such as your guitar and vocals. Mixers typically have inputs for guitar leads, hi-fi audio leads, and three-pin (XLR) microphone leads and allow you to adjust the levels of each input before the overall signal is fed into your sound card. An alternative is to use an outboard audio interface instead of a mixer. This compact box performs the key functions of a sound card and mixer in one unit and plugs in to your computer via the USB or firewire port.

If recording an acoustic guitar or sound produced by a "real" amp (rather than software emulation in the DAW), you will need to use a microphone—often teamed with a multitrack recorder.

RECORDING OPTIONS

Direct recording With the guitar plugged directly into your computer's sound card (through an adapter plug) the weak signal is processed by the sound card, usually giving disappointing results.

Guitar   Computer

Using a mixer or audio interface This offers a robust way to feed a high-quality signal into your DAW and to control EQ (balance of frequencies) of the inputs and set gain. The "clean" guitar sound captured can then be processed using the effects and amp-emulation software within the DAW.

Guitar   Audio interface   Computer

Using a multitrack recorder This is a good alternative to recording on computer. Packed with effects and editing functions, multitrack recorders are almost as versatile and less prone to glitches than DAWs. They lend themselves to microphone-based recordings (*see below*).

Guitar   Amplifier   Microphone   Multitrack recorder

Adding effects If using a multitrack recorder that lacks onboard effects, you may wish to place an effects pedal into the signal chain to record your desired sound direct. Be aware that, doing things this way, the sound of the effect cannot be removed or adjusted after recording.

Guitar   Effects unit   Amplifier   Microphone   Multitrack recorder

CHAPTER 4

RECORDING WITH MICROPHONES

To record a variety of guitar sounds using microphones (mics), you will ideally need one dynamic microphone and one condenser microphone. Dynamic mics are ruggedly built and designed to handle the high sound pressures associated with amplified guitars and vocals; condenser mics are more delicate and sensitive.

To record amplified guitar, try placing the mic about 1in (2cm) from the speaker's grill cloth, pointing at a spot midway between the center of the speaker cone and its rim. Adjust the output level of your mixer or audio interface and the input level of your recording software before recording. For more nuanced

Condenser microphone More often seen in the studio than on stage, these mics are capable of capturing nuanced tones.

sound, try a twin-mic setup with a dynamic mic close to the speaker cone, and a condenser mic on a stand 3–6ft (1–2m) away to record the sound of the room. Many amps sound at their best at, or near, full volume, so consider investing in a low-wattage (5–20 watt) valve amp if you want to get great sounds without irritating the neighbors.

To record an acoustic guitar, place a condenser microphone about 6in (15cm) away from the strings, pointing at a spot near the 14th fret. If the sound you produce seems too boomy or harsh, try moving the microphone head further away from the soundhole. Adjust the levels and record.

GETTING YOUR MUSIC OUT THERE

Once you have a few successful gigs under your belt and your live act is attracting some attention, how do you take it further? There are many "cheap and cheerful" ways to develop your following, but more serious thought and decisions are needed to take you into the professional music industry.

GAINING SUPPORT

Be prepared to put some work into building up your fan base (*see below*). With a strong fan base, you will be in a far stronger position to obtain bookings at larger venues and attract the attention of record companies. You can use many of the same techniques to ensure your recordings are not only widely available, but will be heard in the right places.

PLAYING FESTIVALS

One of the best ways to get in front of larger audiences in new areas is to apply to perform at festivals. Even the major commercial festivals usually have slots for unsigned bands, but will want some reassurance that you'll deliver a good performance; some require you to have won a regional music contest, for example. Being able to demonstrate that you have a healthy local or online following always helps.

Applications to perform at major festivals can usually be made online, so having an up-to-date web presence is important as it will allow organizers to check out your abilities during the application process.

If bookings at the big festivals prove hard to pin down, try starting with smaller regional festivals; there are also events specially created to promote unsigned acts.

BUILDING A FANBASE

Good communication with your fans is key to success: you need to let them know what you're doing and where to see you next. The Internet is a powerful tool but don't overlook traditional methods of self promotion.

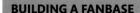

Online A MySpace page has become a near-essential tool for gigging bands—and it allows you to showcase new material with the site's built-in media player. If you have the resources, consider building a dedicated website, which gives you more flexibility about how you present yourselves online.

Merchandise A great time to reach your fans is at gigs. Branded postcards, badges, or even custom-printed picks are inexpensive take-home items that can be distributed for free at live shows: make sure to add your website address to all these items. Consider running off a batch of CDs of your music to give away (or sell) as people leave the gig. This merchandise not only raises your profile, but builds lots of goodwill with your existing fans.

Information Ask a friend to run a merchandise stall at your gigs and ask them to take down email addresses of audience members who express an interest in hearing regular news on your activities. This information can easily be converted into an electronic database and used to generate mailing lists for social media, mass emails, and even printed publications. You must, however, store this information in accordance with national legal requirements for data security.

Showcase Try uploading your work to international music-sharing sites such as Soundcloud, which allows listeners to follow your work online, at no cost, using advanced playback software.

Online phenomenon English rock band Arctic Monkeys (*left*) were one of the first acts to come to public attention largely via the Internet.

MANAGERS AND AGENTS

A good manager can help you sharpen the band's identity, deal with promotion, secure bookings, handle the administrative and financial side of band life, and broker deals with record companies and promoters.

To find a suitable manager in your area, do some research on the Internet: find out who they already have on their books and how well they are represented. Always agree terms (a manager's cut is typically 20 percent of earnings) and begin with a three-month trial, allowing either party to walk away if the relationship proves difficult.

Another option is to consider using booking agents. They use their contacts to get you gigs at good venues but will typically ask for exclusive rights for an agreed period, plus a cut of between 10 and 15 percent of the band's earnings.

Sign here Brian Epstein (*below left*) famously managed The Beatles, securing them a recording contract with the Parlophone label after they had been rejected elsewhere.

GETTING RECORD DEALS

Often seen as the ultimate proof of having "arrived" as a musician, getting a record deal actually marks the start of an ongoing and sometimes complex commercial relationship in which you (the artist) are a key stakeholder, rather than sole decision maker.

Major label deals generally offer you an advance (lump sum) on signing for an initial period, during which you will be expected to make a recording. A contract will typically grant the company options to retain your band for further recordings, plus worldwide rights to your work. Deals offered by smaller, independent labels may be different. Typically, you will receive a smaller (or no) advance on signing but will earn a bigger cut of the royalties than in a major label deal. It is normal for labels to expect the artist to recoup the cost of their advance and other expenditures from record sales before paying royalties.

If you specialize in songwriting, you could try another route—a publishing deal. This will typically grant a publishing company rights to administer requests to use your songs commercially (in commercials or for cell phone ringtones, for example) for a fixed term of 10 years or more. You then take a varying cut of the proceeds, according to the way each song is used.

"My guitar is not a thing.
It is an extension of myself. It is who I am."

JOAN JETT

GUITAR
MAINTENANCE

5

CHOOSING AND FITTING STRINGS

Professional musicians fit a fresh set of strings before each performance or recording to ensure their sound is as rich as possible, and also to reduce the risk of breakages during play. While casual players do not need to change strings quite so frequently, putting on a fresh set every couple of months or so will keep your guitar sounding at its best.

TYPES OF STRING

Different types of guitars require different types of strings. Classical and flamenco guitars have nylon strings, from which they derive some of their soft, percussive sound. The treble strings are made of pure nylon, while the bass strings are silver-plated wire around a polymer core.

Other acoustic guitars require steel strings, which offer brighter tone and greater sustain than nylon strings. These guitars use a mixture of stainless steel (for the treble) and bronzed steel strings (for the bass).

Electric and semi-acoustic guitars must be fitted with steel strings for their magnetic pickups to work. Strings for electrics are typically of lighter gauge (*see right*) than those for acoustic guitars and may be made of pure steel, or nickel-coated steel: the coating increases durability at the cost of some treble-rich twang. You may also encounter flat-wound strings with smooth windings; these offer reduced handling noise at the expense of a somewhat muted treble response. They are therefore suited mainly to studio work and jazz styles. All guitar strings, except classical sets and those for double-locking tremolos (*see p.297*), feature a ball end that enables you to securely anchor the lower end of each string to the guitar.

CHANGING STRINGS

As your strings are used they will gradually lose their brightness and intonation. They may develop visible physical defects, such as notches in the windings where the frets have worn into the string, or patches of discoloration. All these symptoms are indicators that you should replace your strings with a new set. The procedure for changing strings varies between types of guitar but the general guidelines are shown opposite and overleaf.

STRING GAUGES

Light-gauge strings are thin and supple, and they typically offer ease of playability but at the expense of tone and strength. Heavy strings, by contrast, produce a rich, sustained sound and are highly durable, but they can be hard on the fingers.

When you buy a set of strings, the packaging will indicate the gauge of the lightest string (the 1st string) in the pack, or that of the lightest and the heaviest (the 6th string). The table below offers a guide to the terminology used when referring to string gauges for steel-string acoustic and electric guitars.

ACOUSTIC	1st	2nd	3rd	4th	5th	6th
Extra light	.010	.013	.017	.026	.036	.046
Light	.012	.016	.020	.032	.042	.054
Medium/heavy	.013	.017	.026	.036	.046	.056
ELECTRIC	1st	2nd	3rd	4th	5th	6th
Extra light	.009	.011	.016	.024	.032	.042
Light	.010	.013	.017	.026	.036	.046
Medium	.011	.014	.018	.028	.038	.048
Heavy	.012	.016	.020	.032	.042	.054
Extra heavy	.013	.017	.026	.036	.046	.056

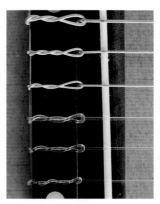

Nylon strings Classical guitars are strung with nylon strings tied onto the bridge.

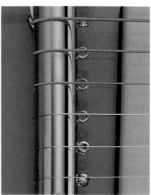

Steel strings These strings are fitted with a ball at one end that is used to secure them at the bridge.

CHANGING STRINGS ON AN ACOUSTIC GUITAR

Replace old strings for new one at a time, rather than all together, to maintain tension on the neck throughout the process. The instructions on this page show how to replace the low E string, but the same process applies to all strings.

Bridge with pins

1 **Slacken the string** you wish to replace by turning its tuning key clockwise.

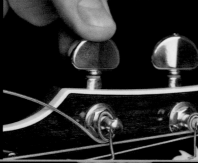

2 **A pin holds** the other end of the string at the bridge. Remove this from its hole using a purpose-made tool. Do not use pliers, which could damage the pin or the wood of the bridge.

3 **Loosen the string** again at the headstock end, by turning the tuning key until the string becomes completely free of the machine post. Pull the string free of the hole in the tuning post and discard it.

4 **Insert the ball-** end of the new string into the string hole in the bridge.

5 **Replace the pin** by gently pushing it wtih your finger, making sure the fluted hollow in its edge aligns with the string. Pull the string gently upward so it sits snugly against the bottom of the pin.

6 **Guide the string** along the fretboard and then thread it through the hole on the post, which should be aligned at 60° to the neck. Thread the string through the hole in the post, from the inside toward the outside.

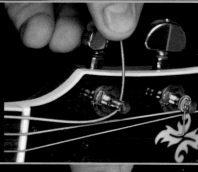

7 **Wind the end** of the string round the top of the post and under the length of string you first passed through the tuning post. Pull the string up and across it to it cinch it up tightly against the post.

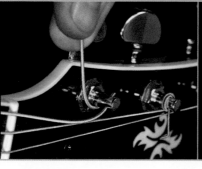

8 **Hold the string** while turning the tuning key to tighten and tune the string. Make sure the windings do not overlap and that the string beds into its slot in the nut as it tightens. Trim off any excess string with wire cutters.

CHAPTER 5

RESTRINGING ELECTRIC GUITARS

The method of restringing depends on the type of guitar. Nonvibrato electric guitars (*see below*) and those fitted with basic Fender-style vibratos are simpler to restring than those with a double-locking tremolo, or whammy bar (*see opposite*). Before you start, make sure you have read and understood the manufacturer's instructions.

PRO TIP
TUNING UP AFTER RESTRINGING

Tune each string progressively up to its correct pitch, rather than slackening the string down to pitch. If you tune the string too sharp (high) on your first attempt, simply slacken the string and tune it up to pitch again.

CHANGING STRINGS ON AN ELECTRIC GUITAR

Electric guitar strings usually need changing more often than strings on acoustic instruments. As with an acoustic guitar, always change one string at a time rather than removing all the strings.

Bridge

1 Loosen the string by turning its tuning key clockwise. Eventually the string will be completely slack and can be pulled free of the post.

2 Grasp the string's ball end (anchored at the rear of the bridge or in a ferrule on the back of the guitar) and pull the string completely free of the instrument.

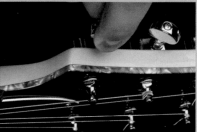

3 Thread the replacement string through the same hole from which you removed the old string (*i.e.*, at the bridge or the ferrules at the back of the guitar).

4 Rotate the tuning key of the appropriate machine head so the hole in the tuning post is at 60° to the neck.

5 Thread the end of the string through the hole on the inside of the post, leaving a small amount of slack free to be taken up as you tune to pitch.

6 Wind the end of the string around the top of the post and back under the length of string you first passed through the post.

7 Pull the string up and across itself to it cinch it up tightly against the post.

8 Hold the string while turning the tuning key to tighten and tune the string. Make sure the windings do not overlap and that the string beds into its slot in the nut as it tightens.

CHANGING STRINGS ON AN ELECTRIC GUITAR WITH A DOUBLE-LOCKING TREMOLO

The basic technique for fitting strings to a standard electric guitar applies to models fitted with a double-locking tremolo but a few extra procedures are required.

Nut lock

Saddle lock

1 **Use a 3mm** Allen key to loosen the relevant locking nut from the trio at the base of the headstock.

2 **Slacken the string** by rotating the appropriate tuning key clockwise.

3 **Using the Allen** key, loosen the locking saddle mechanism (found behind the bridge, in line with the string). This will release the string from the clamp holding it in place.

4 **Pull the old string** out of the bridge and through the looseneed locking nut at the top of the neck. Discard the old string.

5 **Using a pair of** wire-cutting pliers, remove the ball end from the replacement string, cutting just above the twisted section.

6 **Insert the freshly cut** end of the string into the locking mechanism at the bridge, just in front of the square metal clamp; push it in until it stops.

7 **Tighten the locking** saddle mechanism using the Allen key.

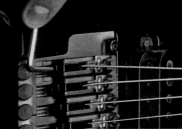

8 **Pass the string** through the relevant locking nut at the top of the neck, and push it through the hole of the post (from inside to outside). Leave a small amount of slack on the string.

9 **Wind the end** of the string round the top of the post and under itself, then pull it up and across to cinch it tightly against the post. Tune to pitch using the tuning keys.

10 **Give the string** a few light tugs to stretch it, then retune it to pitch. Finally, tighten the locking nut using the Allen key.

CHAPTER 5

CLEANING AND STORING GUITARS

Dusty instruments with corroded strings are unresponsive and uninspiring, both to play and hear. A regular wipe down and an occasional, more intensive clean and polish will ensure that your instrument sounds its best every time you pick it up. Storing your guitar properly will minimize the effort you'll need to put into regular maintenance, and also protect your instrument from accidental damage.

CLEANING YOUR GUITAR

Most guitars have a high-gloss polyurethane finish, although many vintage models and some modern custom-made guitars are finished with nitrocellulose lacquer. The fretboard may have the same finish, or may be an oiled wood. The best day-to-day cleaning regime is to give the guitar a wipe down with a soft, dry cloth after playing, to remove grease and moisture before they can blemish or corrode components. Strings can be degreased and protected from premature corrosion by light applications of specialist non oil-based products.

Buffing up Ensuring your guitar is clean can become a pre or post-performance ritual, as it was for a young George Harrison (above).

CLEANING THE BODY

For an intensive cleaning, you'll need to remove the strings (*see pp.294–97*) from your guitar, so time it for when you plan to replace the strings anyway. Lay the guitar on a level surface covered with a towel or rubber mat, to protect the guitar from scratches while you work, and clean and polish the body as below. Then, clean the fretboard following the instructions opposite.

1 Support the neck of the guitar with a rolled up towel or a cloth-wrapped block. This will help to immobilize the guitar and prevent accidental damage.

2 Dab a little guitar polish onto a soft cloth, then use a gentle circular motion to rub it over the surfaces of the guitar's body. Work from area to area, until each has acquired a high gloss.

3 Turn over the guitar and polish the rear surfaces and the back of the neck in the same way. Then give all of the areas you've polished a final buff with a dry cloth.

4 On an electric guitar, work the cloth carefully around the pickups and switchgear, removing all accumulated dust without dislodging wiring or fittings.

CLEANING THE FRETBOARD

How you clean the fretboard depends on whether it is made from maple, rosewood, or ebony. Maple is usually polyurethane-finished in the same way as the body, and can be cleaned using the same polish. Rosewood and ebony must be cleaned with lemon oil or another suitable commercial fretboard cleaner. Oil tends to soften the wood, so only use it every 4–6 months.

❶ Moisten a soft cloth with a little polish or oil, and rub the pad down the fretboard. Leave the oil to soak in for a few minutes. Buff off any excess with a side-to-side motion.

❷ Use the tip of your finger or a thumbnail to run the cloth along the edges of the fretwires where buildup of dirt is thickest.

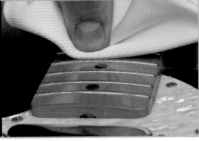

CLEANING THE HARDWARE

Inspect the guitar's metal hardware, including the bridge. Look for any signs of corrosion on adjustable metal parts, such as saddles. Clean any nickel-plated metal parts with chrome cleaners or burnishing cream, and gold-plated parts with nothing more than a soft cloth.

❶ Free any stiff components and clean up any signs of corrosion with a soft, lint-free cloth moistened with a little Teflon®-enhanced penetrating oil such as WD40.

❷ Use a clean corner of the cloth to rub off the excess along with any dirt loosened by the oil.

STORAGE AND TRANSPORTATION

Folding (soft) guitar stands are useful in environments where you will be using the guitar frequently, but it is best to store the guitar in a case during transport or when not in use. This will help to keep it blemish-free and minimize its exposure to heat and humidity changes that may warp the wood. Both soft cases ("gig bags") and hard cases have their pros and cons (*see below*) and your choice will depend on your budget and how often, and where, you carry your guitar around. At the top of the range are foam-lined flight cases, which are expensive but protect your guitar from all but the most violent accidental blows. If you are planning to store your guitar for a long period, place it—in its case—in a cool, dry location that is not subject to significant temperature or humidity fluctuations.

GUITAR CASE CHOICES

SOFT CASE	HARD CASE
Pros Light and inexpensive; allows you to sling your guitar across your back for carrying ease, and is cheap to replace if mislaid.	**Pros** Offers much more protection from damage and temperature and humidity changes; includes useful storage spaces.
Cons Minimal protection from jars and knocks: the slightly more expensive padded versions are worth the extra cost.	**Cons** Heavier and more expensive, and with its suitcase-style handle is more cumbersome to carry.

Hard cases
These cases may be contoured to the shape of the guitar, or rectangular with a molded interior.

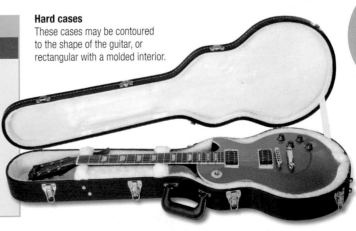

CHAPTER 5

SETTING UP YOUR GUITAR

Over the years, guitar components have become increasingly adjustable. These innovations have improved the accuracy and stability of the tuning, and made guitars easier to play. For example, on most guitars, the height the strings sit at above the fretboard can be adjusted to suit your playing style. The height of the strings and other settings is known as the "setup"—this determines how the guitar feels to play.

Playing compromise On electric guitars, the interplay between bridge height and truss rod settings creates a compromise between ease of playing and tone.

ADJUSTING THE SETUP

On electric guitars, you can raise or lower the saddles or bridge to alter the string height. You can also alter the amount of neck relief (the slight concave bow in the neck that allows the strings to vibrate freely) by adjusting the truss rod. The degree of accuracy to which an electric guitar can be tuned, known as its intonation, can be adjusted on guitars fitted with specially adjustable saddles or bridges. Setup options on acoustic guitars are fewer; they have fixed saddle and bridge components, so intonation and string height cannot be altered without professional help.

Adjustable components
Guitar setup is determined chiefly by string-height settings at the bridge and adjustment of the truss rod.

SOLVING SETUP PROBLEMS

In most cases, it is not necessary to adjust the action or intonation of a guitar, if it holds a standard tuning and feels easy to play. But if you have a new instrument that has been badly set up at the factory, or a used guitar that has suffered some wear and tear, you may wish to consider fine-tuning its setup.

PROBLEM	ACOUSTIC SOLUTION	ELECTRIC SOLUTION
The guitar won't hold a standard tuning	Tuning problems in an acoustic guitar must be referred to a skilled technician.	You may need to improve the guitar's intonation by adjusting the position of the instrument's bridge or individual saddles (*see opposite*).
You find fretting difficult and tiring	Truss rod adjustment is necessary to lower the action on an acoustic guitar (*see p.303*).	The strings may be set too high for comfort; try lowering the action by reducing string height or neck relief (*see p.302*).
The guitar is producing excessive fret buzz	Truss rod adjustment is necessary to raise the action on an acoustic guitar (*see p.303*).	The action may be set too low; try increasing string height and/or neck relief (*see p.302*).

BRIDGE AND SADDLES

Intonation (tuning accuracy) problems in electric guitars can often be corrected by making small adjustments to the position of the saddles or bridge. The guitar's bass strings tend to be very stiff at their extremities, next to the nut and bridge, so cannot vibrate freely along their full length to produce sound. This prevents them from being tuned precisely to their intended pitch, but the problem can be solved by increasing the distance between nut and bridge ("scale length"), so many bridges on electric guitars feature adjustable saddles. These can be moved forward or backward by a few millimeters to establish the correct effective scale length for each string. This is called "setting the intonation."

Curved fretboard Strings can be raised or lowered to alter ease of playing, but any alteration must take account of the curve of the fretboard.

The bridge String height and intonation can be adjusted at the bridge. Even small adjustments can make a significant difference to the sound of the instrument.

INTONATION ON AN ELECTRIC GUITAR

The basic process for adjusting your guitar's intonation is shown below. On many designs of electric guitar bridge, such as Fender's synchronized tremolo unit, this process is completed by adjusting individual saddle screws. On guitars with wraparound bridges, such as some Les Paul Juniors, the saddles cannot be moved. Intonation is changed by turning two screws located at either end of of the bridge, which allows some adjustment of the outer strings. The angled placement of the unit ensures approximately correct intonation for the middle strings.

1 **Tune the open** low E string to pitch using a digital tuner.

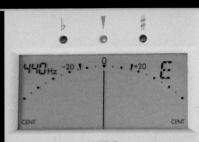

2 **Play a harmonic** (see p.106) at the 12th fret of the low E string by gently plucking the string. This should also register as being in tune.

3 **Depress the string** at the 12th fret with your finger. If this is also correctly in tune, the intonation of this string is set correctly. If not, go to the next step.

4 **If the note** produced is sharp, move the saddle backward. If the note is flat, adjust the saddle so it moves forward. Then repeat the process on the other strings.

CHAPTER 5

ADJUSTING THE ACTION

When musicians talk about a guitar's "action" they are—in general terms—referring to how high the strings sit above the fretboard. A guitar with a high action has a large gap between the fretboard and strings. Instruments set up this way may be difficult for beginners to play, but they produce clear, ringing notes when handled correctly. By contrast, a guitar with a low action, where the strings sit close to the fretboard, is easier to play rapidly and fluently, but the proximity of the strings to the frets beneath makes fret buzz more likely. Fret buzz occurs when a freely vibrating string makes glancing contact with one of the frets beneath it, stifling its sound.

PLAYER'S PREFERENCES

The guitar's neck has an edge-to-edge curve known as its "radius," and adjusting the height of individual strings to conform with that curve makes the guitar easier to play, by creating the most comfortable amount of clearance between strings and fretboard. The amount of clearance is measured at the 12th fret. Personal preference plays a big part in how high a guitar's action should be. For most purposes, a good all-around action is one in which the strings are set high enough above the fretboard to avoid buzzing, but low enough for you to fret comfortably at all points of the neck. However, you might want to change the action to suit your playing style; slide guitarists, for instance, usually prefer a high action.

The wraparound bridge A few guitars feature a bridge with strings wrapped around it. The action on these guitars is altered by turning the screws at either end.

CHANGING STRING HEIGHT

Using a steel ruler, measure the height of the bass E string at the 12th fret. Adjust the saddle until you have a gap of around 0.1in between the top of the fret and the bottom of the string. Do the same on the high E string, but aim for a gap of 0.06in. The strings between should graduate from 0.1 to 0.06in, from bass to treble. On some stopbar-type bridges (*see below*), string height is altered by raising or lowering the whole bridge. Adjustment is made by rotating bolts at either end of the bridge.

On most guitars, you can alter the height of individual strings by turning the saddle screws; usually, you turn clockwise to raise the strings.

You can make string-height adjustments on guitars with stopbar-tailpiece bridges by adjusting the overall bridge height.

Bridge height Adjusting the height of the bridge and the amount of neck relief (*see opposite*) determines the overall action of the guitar.

NECK RELIEF ADJUSTMENT

Adjusting the string height aids playability, while adjusting neck relief determines how bowed the neck will be; the more neck relief, the greater the gap between the fretboard and strings in the middle, or most bowed, part of the neck. String height is not adjustable at the bridge on acoustic guitars, so neck relief adjustment is the only way to alter the clearance between strings and fretboard.

TRUSS ROD ADJUSTMENT

String tension tends to pull a guitar's neck into a concave bow. The extent to which the neck is bowed is called neck relief; some relief is necessary because the vibratory motion of the strings is most pronounced in the middle of their span. A slight bow allows the strings to work freely in this area without hitting the tops of frets. The truss rod (*see below*) allows you to adjust how much relief your neck has, either for personal preference or because changes in humidity or to the strings have altered the amount of relief in your guitar neck. Incorrect adjustment of the truss rod can damage your guitar's neck, so always check first whether adjustment is really necessary (*see right*). If you have any doubts about your ability to take on this job yourself, leave it to a professional technician.

CHECKING NECK RELIEF

Use a feeler gauge to check string height. Readings of 0.08–0.010in indicate a usable amount of neck relief; lower readings increase the likelihood of fret buzz, and any greater than 0.010in suggest a slightly high action. The simplest way to check neck relief is described below.

❶ To check neck relief, fit a capo at the first fret, close to the first fret bar.

❷ Using your right hand, depress the 3rd (G) string at the 14th fret and hold it down.

❸ Using a feeler gauge, measure the gap between the top of the fret and the bottom of the string at the 7th, 8th, and 9th frets to establish neck relief.

ADJUSTING THE TRUSS ROD

Truss rod adjustment is a delicate job, and should only be performed in accordance with the manufacturer's instructions and with the supplied Allen key. Never force a truss rod that seems unyielding, and proceed by small steps to your ideal setting.

On certain electric guitars, the truss rod is accessed at the body-end of the neck; some of these have a recess in the body that allows access to the rod, but those that don't require neck removal for rod adjustment and must be taken to a professional.

ACOUSTIC GUITARS

The truss rod is usually accessed just inside the sound hole. Slacken the strings slightly before you begin, and make only very small incremental adjustments, turning clockwise for less neck relief (lowering the strings), and counterclockwise for more. Retune, then check the neck relief again.

Truss rod access point

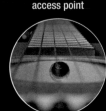

ELECTRIC GUITARS

The truss rod bolt is usually located just above the nut beneath a plastic cover. Make tiny adjustments to this bolt, using quarter-turns of the Allen key. Turn clockwise for less neck relief (lowering the strings), and counterclockwise for more. Leave to settle for a short time, then recheck the neck relief.

Truss rod access point

CUSTOMIZING AND UPGRADING YOUR GUITAR

No matter what the name on the headstock, most instruments are built to a price, and adding high-specification components can give your favorite guitar a lift and a fresh sound. But it is not all about tone, of course. If you want to make a bigger visual impact on stage, you may also wish to change the appearance of your guitar.

Guitar modifications If you decide to replace any of the components of your guitar, keep the originals and store them safely—so you'll be able to pass them on should you decide to sell the guitar.

STRAP LOCKS

High-grade strap locks are designed to stop your guitar from falling to the floor should the strap accidentally slip off the strap buttons: an inexpensive and worthwhile investment.

BRIDGE

Retro-fit bridges with fully adjustable saddles can give more accurate intonation. Some can be fitted quite easily using basic tools.

PICKUPS

New pickups can add extra character to your sound. A popular move is to replace a standard bridge pickup with a high-output model, for a fatter, hotter lead tone.

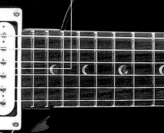

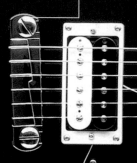
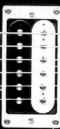

SWITCHES

Plastic bobbins on the end of pickup selector switches are vulnerable to being dislodged, but replacements are easy to find and fit. Leave the replacement of any electrical parts to a professional.

TONE CONTROLS

You can easily replace tone and volume controls for a different look, or if they have suffered damage and no longer function correctly.

SCRATCHPLATE

Replacement scratchplates are available in a variety of styles. If you do decide to replace the guitar's original scratchplate, be sure to keep the original safe for future owners.

COSMETIC MODIFICATIONS

While refinishing a guitar is a job for the professionals, fitting external parts, such as a new scratchplate, can really change its look and can be undertaken at home using basic tools. A wide variety of custom scratchplate designs is available. You can even buy yellowed, aged parts designed to evoke a vintage look.

UPGRADING YOUR HARDWARE

If your guitar suffers from inaccurate intonation or poor tuning stability, you may want to consider upgrading components such as the bridge or machine heads. For example, the original wraparound bridges found on some early Gibsons cannot be finely adjusted for intonation (see p.301), and an upgrade would permit this adjustment. Likewise, fitting high-quality locking machine heads may resolve problems with tuning stability and smoothness of operation. Such items are best fitted by professionals.

FITTING NEW PICKUPS

Fitting high quality pickups can remedy bothersome problems with your sound, such as excessive feedback. If you like the way your guitar looks and plays but are looking for a different tone, new pickups may provide the answer. Brands such as Seymour Duncan, DiMarzio, and EMG all make reliably good replacement pickups, typically designed either to replicate the tones of classic vintage models, offer

high-gain modern sounds, or introduce special features such as hum-canceling capability. Pickups can either be bought in sets to replace all of the standard pickups on your guitar or as individual units for neck, middle, or bridge positions.

Ask store staff to advise you on the best model for your needs or consult manufacturers' websites. Many such sites offer the chance to hear the pickup in action—just remember that the design of your guitar and its other hardware also influences the final tone (see pp.26–29).

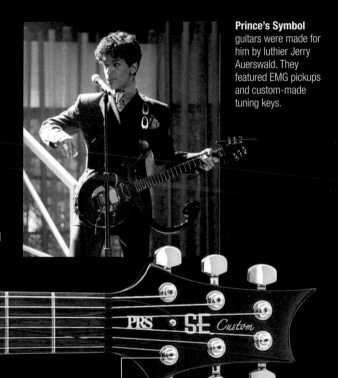

Prince's Symbol guitars were made for him by luthier Jerry Auerswald. They featured EMG pickups and custom-made tuning keys.

PRS • SE Custom

CUSTOMIZING AND RESALE VALUE

If you do decide to customize your guitar, bear in mind that modified instruments can lose a lot of their resale value. This is especially true of vintage instruments; the perfect retro vibe of an all-original 1950s guitar can't be brought back once it has been lost. On the other hand, well-chosen upgrades can improve the performance of most ready-made instruments. If you do decide to replace any components on your guitar, store the original parts safely so you can pass them on to a new owner if you decide to sell; this allows them to choose whether or not to return the guitar to its original spec.

MACHINE HEADS

If you're suffering from string slippage, consider retro-fitting locking machine heads that clamp the string in place at the base of the tuning post.

"Every time you pick up your guitar
to play, play as if it's the last time."

USEFUL
RESOURCES

6

CHORD DIRECTORY

In this directory, you will find the fundamental chord shapes for major and minor chords and 7th-based chords, plus a few selected "spicy" chords in all 12 keys. Each major, minor, and 7th chord type is shown in its five different CAGED-based shapes.

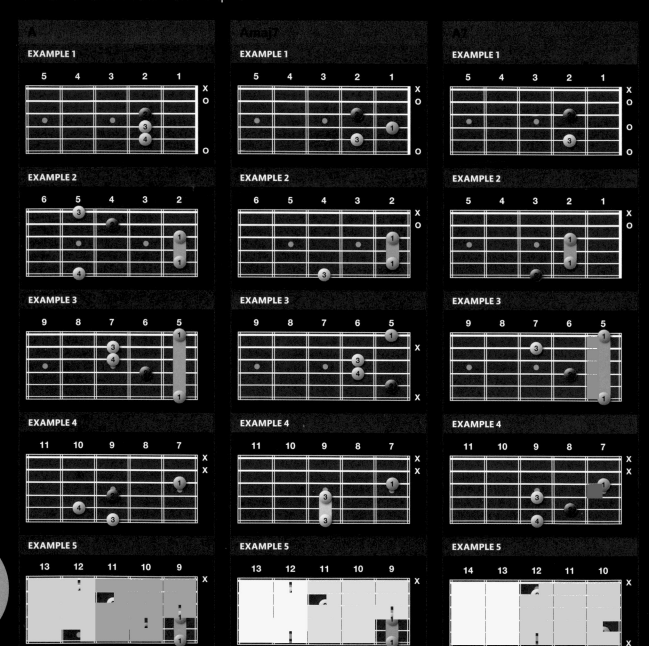

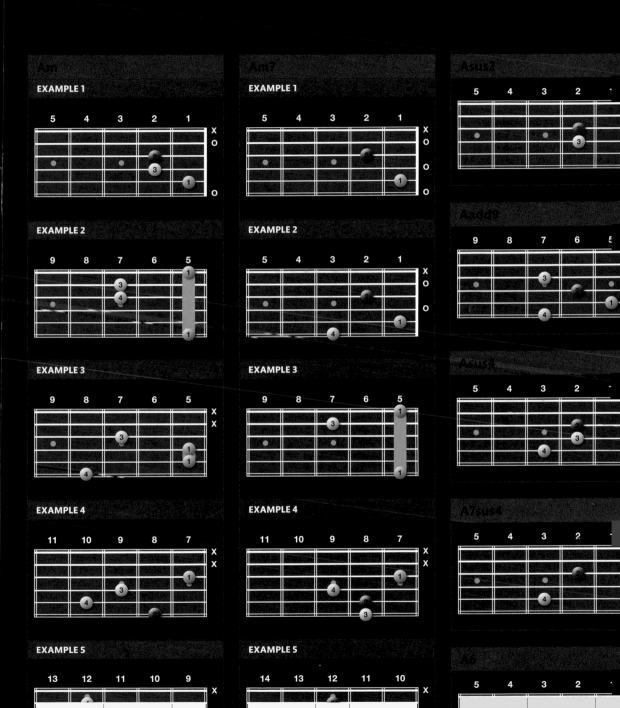

Am

EXAMPLE 1

EXAMPLE 2

EXAMPLE 3

EXAMPLE 4

EXAMPLE 5

Am7

EXAMPLE 1

EXAMPLE 2

EXAMPLE 3

EXAMPLE 4

EXAMPLE 5

Asus2

Aadd9

Asus4

A7sus4

A6

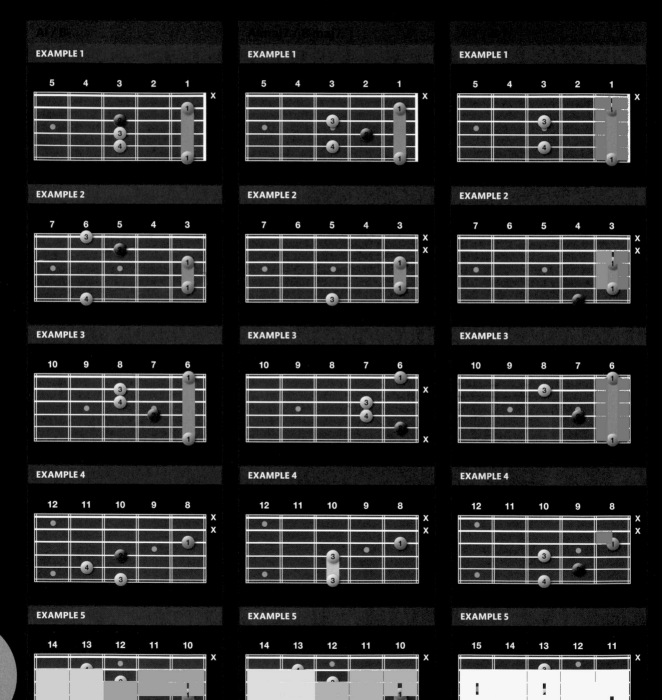

A♯m / B♭m

EXAMPLE 1

EXAMPLE 2

EXAMPLE 3

EXAMPLE 4

EXAMPLE 5

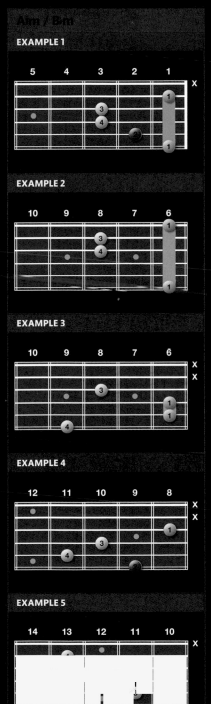

A♯m7 / B♭m7

EXAMPLE 1

EXAMPLE 2

EXAMPLE 3

EXAMPLE 4

EXAMPLE 5

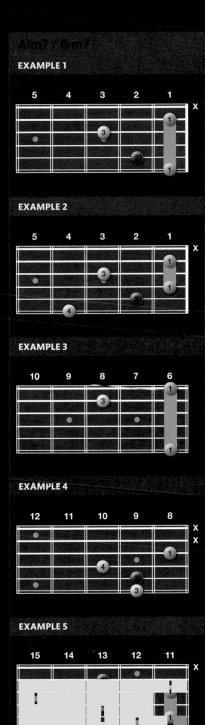

A♯sus2 / B♭sus2

A♯add9 / B♭add9

A♯sus4 / B♭sus4

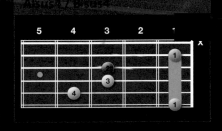

A♯7sus4 / B♭7sus4

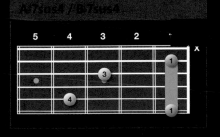

A♯6 / B♭6

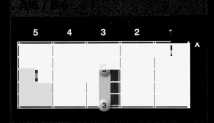

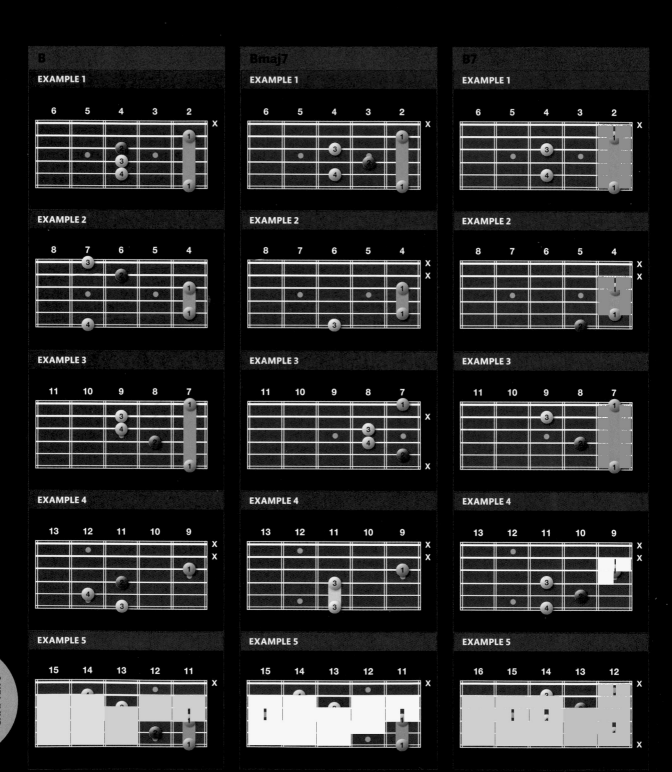

Bm

EXAMPLE 1

6	5	4	3	2	
					X

EXAMPLE 2

11	10	9	8	7

EXAMPLE 3

11	10	9	8	7

EXAMPLE 4

13	12	11	10	9

EXAMPLE 5

15	14	13	12	11

Bm7

EXAMPLE 1

6	5	4	3	2	
					X

EXAMPLE 2

6	5	4	3	2	
					X

EXAMPLE 3

11	10	9	8	7

EXAMPLE 4

13	12	11	10	9

EXAMPLE 5

16	15	14	13	12

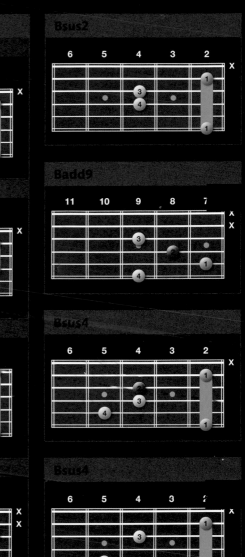

Bsus2

6	5	4	3	2	
					X

Badd9

11	10	9	8	7

Bsus4

6	5	4	3	2	
					X

Bsus4

6	5	4	3	2	
					X

B6

6	5	4	3	2	
					X

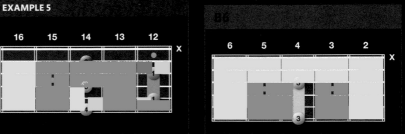

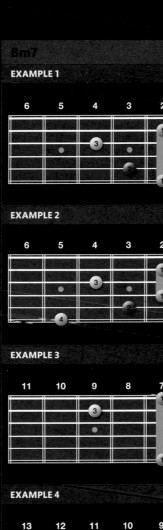

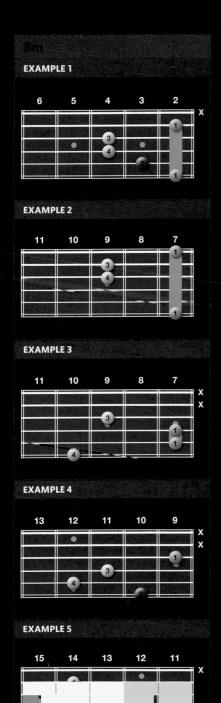

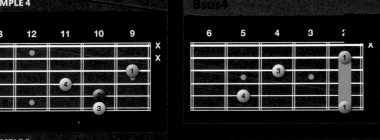

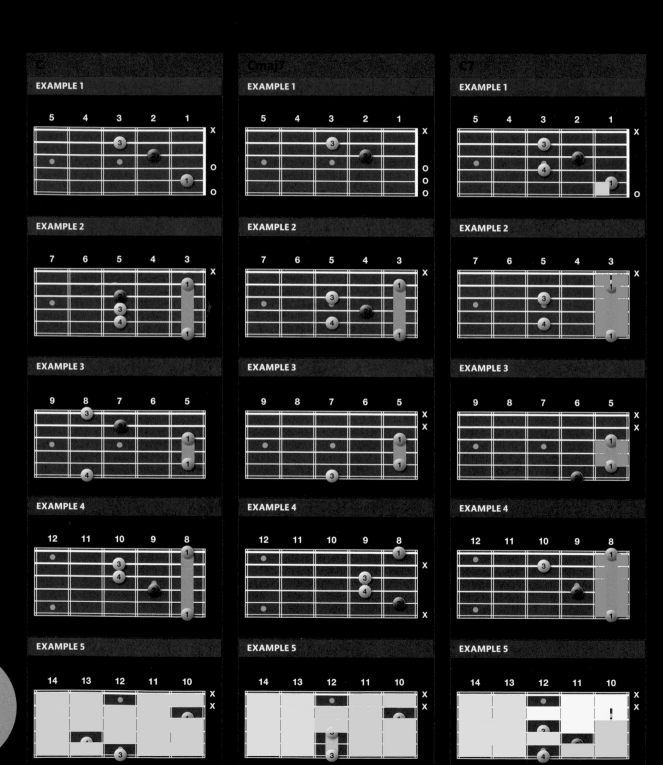

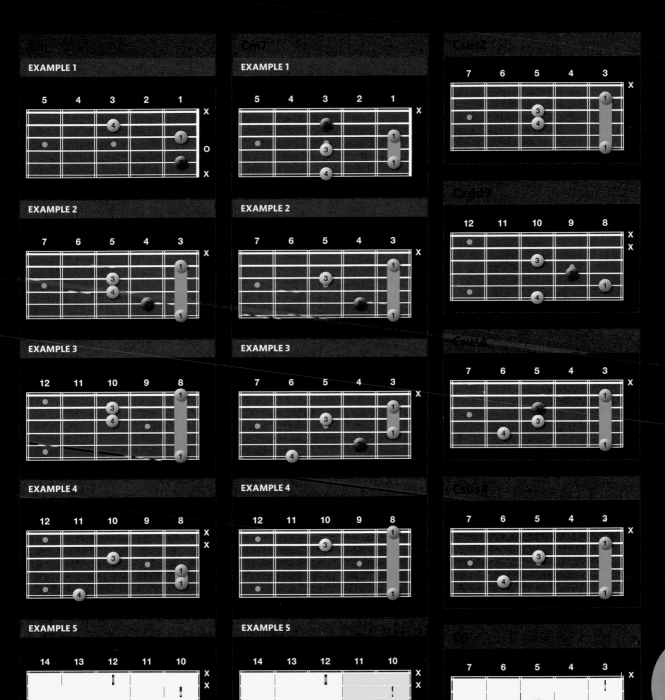

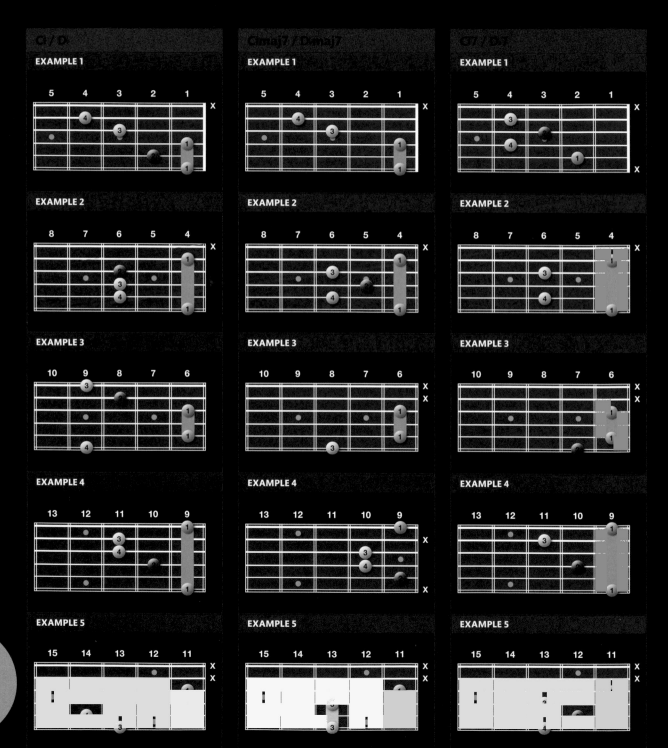

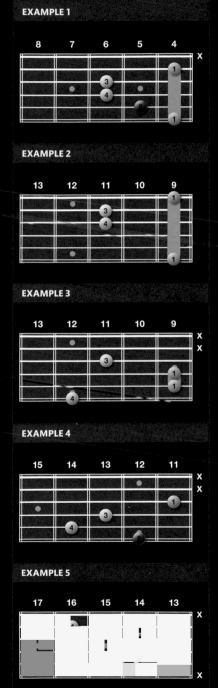

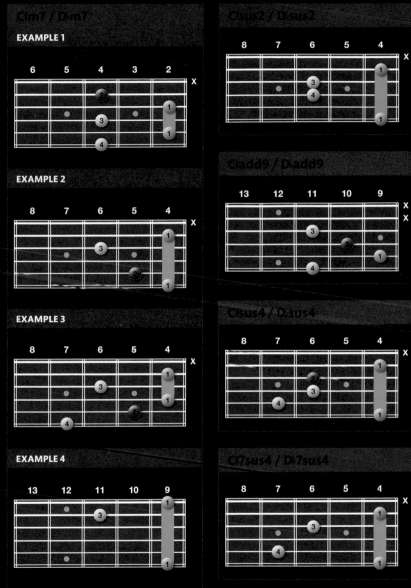

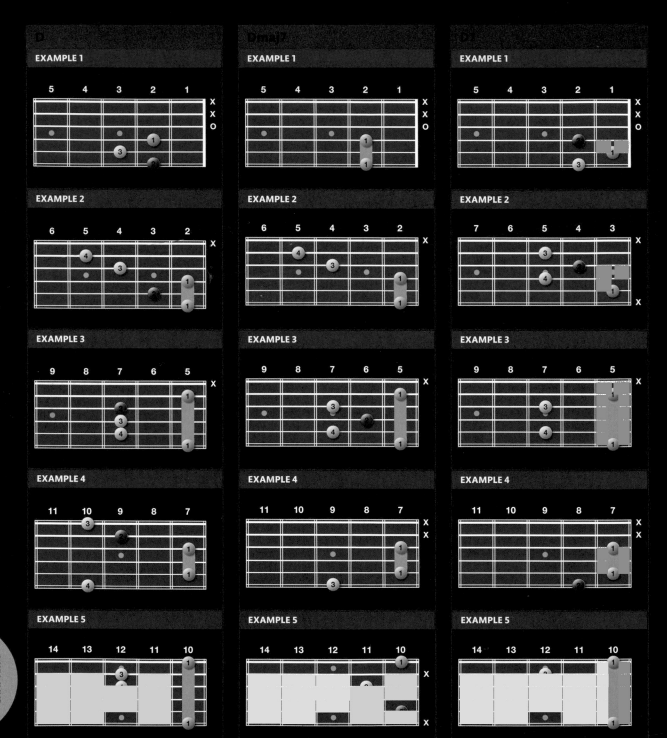

Dm

EXAMPLE 1

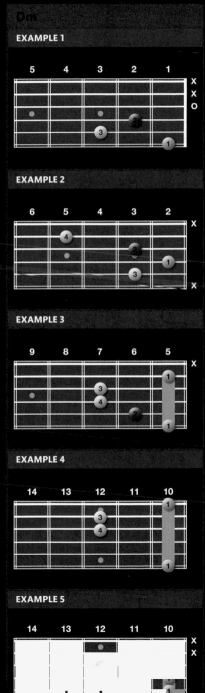

EXAMPLE 2

EXAMPLE 3

EXAMPLE 4

EXAMPLE 5

Dm7

EXAMPLE 1

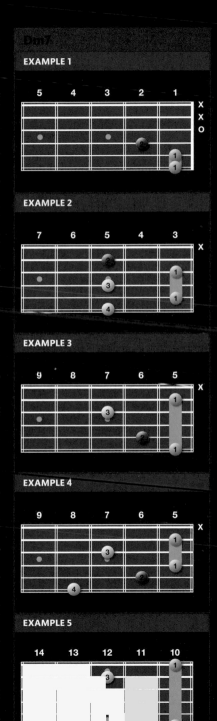

EXAMPLE 2

EXAMPLE 3

EXAMPLE 4

EXAMPLE 5

Dsus2

Dadd9

Dsus4

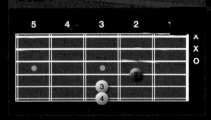

D7sus4

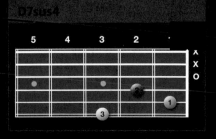

D6

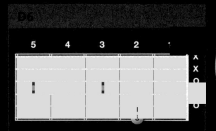

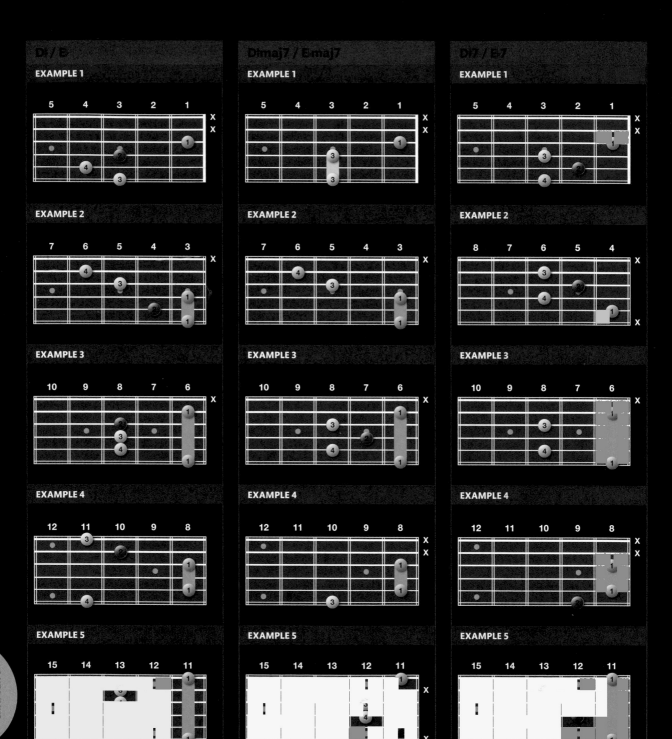

D♯m / E♭m

EXAMPLE 1

EXAMPLE 2

EXAMPLE 3

EXAMPLE 4

EXAMPLE 5

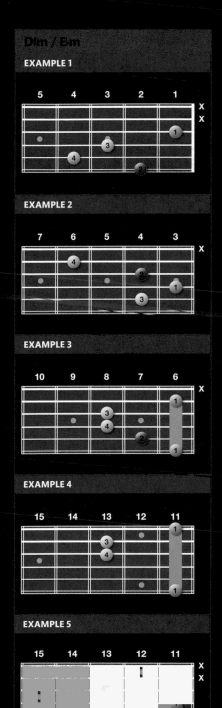

D♯m7 / E♭m7

EXAMPLE 1

EXAMPLE 2

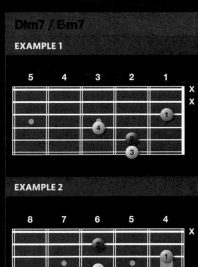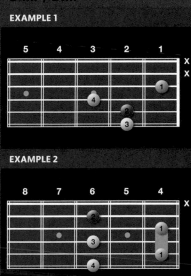

EXAMPLE 3

EXAMPLE 4

EXAMPLE 5

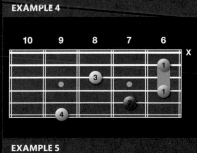

D♯sus2 / E♭sus2

D♯add9 / E♭add9

D♯sus4 / E♭sus4

D♯7sus4 / E♭7sus4

D♯6 / E♭6

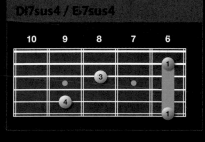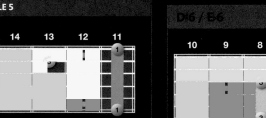

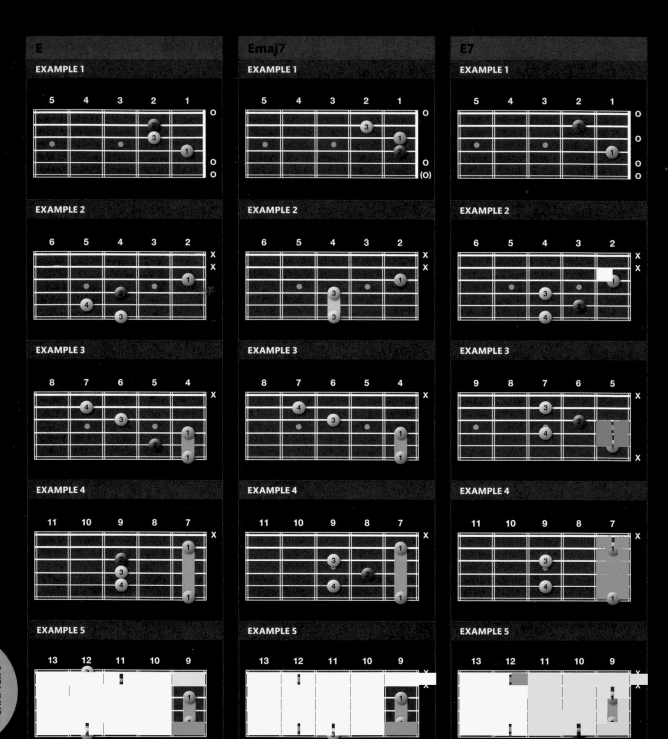

E

EXAMPLE 1
EXAMPLE 2
EXAMPLE 3
EXAMPLE 4
EXAMPLE 5

Emaj7

EXAMPLE 1
EXAMPLE 2
EXAMPLE 3
EXAMPLE 4
EXAMPLE 5

E7

EXAMPLE 1
EXAMPLE 2
EXAMPLE 3
EXAMPLE 4
EXAMPLE 5

Em

EXAMPLE 1

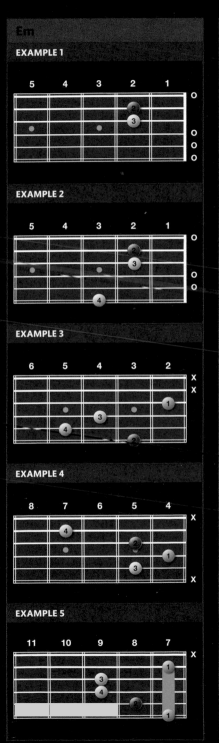

EXAMPLE 2

EXAMPLE 3

EXAMPLE 4

EXAMPLE 5

Em7

EXAMPLE 1

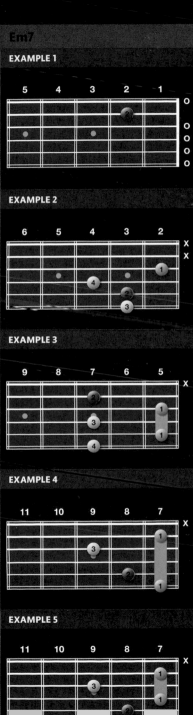

EXAMPLE 2

EXAMPLE 3

EXAMPLE 4

EXAMPLE 5

Esus2

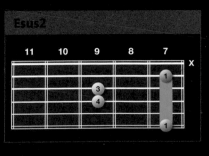

Eadd9

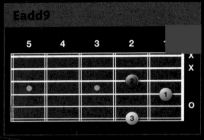

Esus4

E7sus4

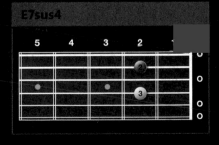

E6

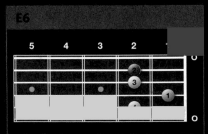

F

EXAMPLE 1

EXAMPLE 2

EXAMPLE 3

EXAMPLE 4

EXAMPLE 5

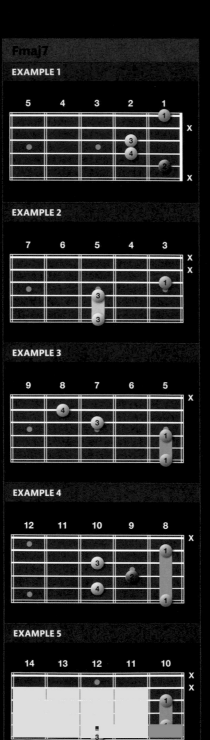

Fmaj7

EXAMPLE 1

EXAMPLE 2

EXAMPLE 3

EXAMPLE 4

EXAMPLE 5

F7

EXAMPLE 1

EXAMPLE 2

EXAMPLE 3

EXAMPLE 4

EXAMPLE 5

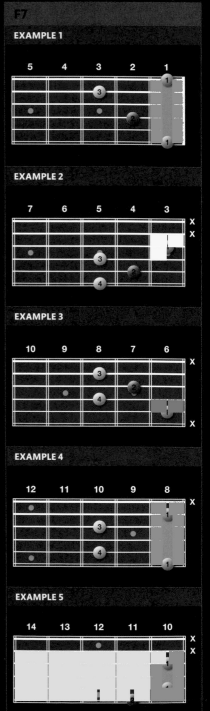

Fm

EXAMPLE 1

EXAMPLE 2

EXAMPLE 3

EXAMPLE 4

EXAMPLE 5

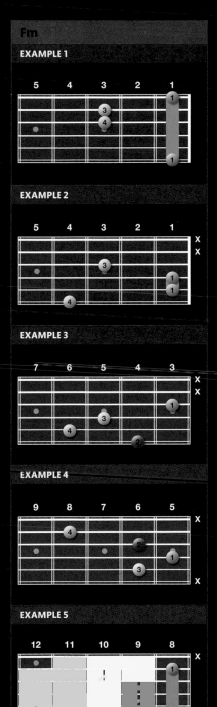

Fm7

EXAMPLE 1

EXAMPLE 2

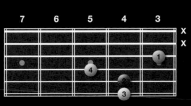

EXAMPLE 3

EXAMPLE 4

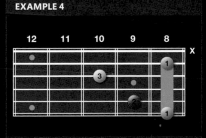

EXAMPLE 5

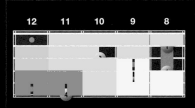

Fsus2

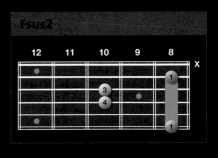

Fadd9

Fsus4

F7sus4

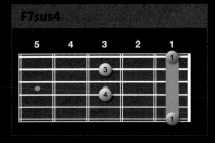

F6

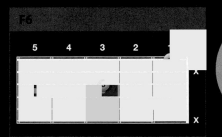

CHAPTER 6

F♯ / G♭

EXAMPLE 1

EXAMPLE 2

EXAMPLE 3

EXAMPLE 4

EXAMPLE 5

F♯maj7 / G♭maj7

EXAMPLE 1

EXAMPLE 2

EXAMPLE 3

EXAMPLE 4

EXAMPLE 5

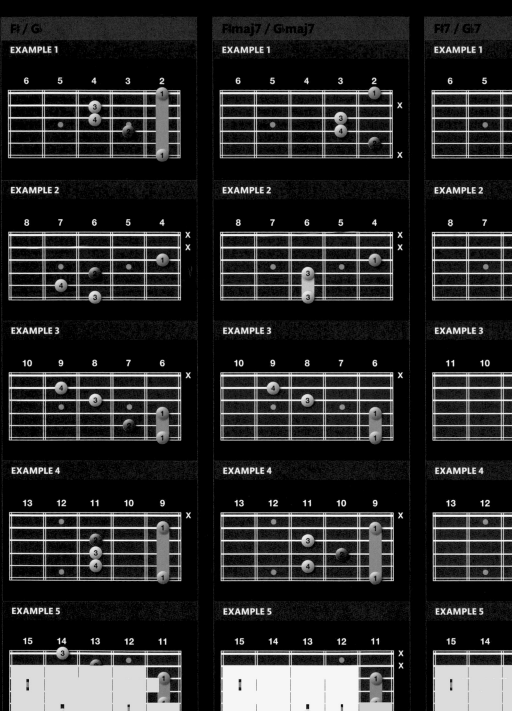

F♯7 / G♭7

EXAMPLE 1

EXAMPLE 2

EXAMPLE 3

EXAMPLE 4

EXAMPLE 5

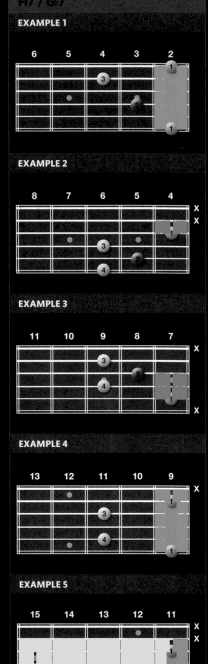

F♯m / G♭m

EXAMPLE 1

EXAMPLE 2

EXAMPLE 3

EXAMPLE 4

EXAMPLE 5

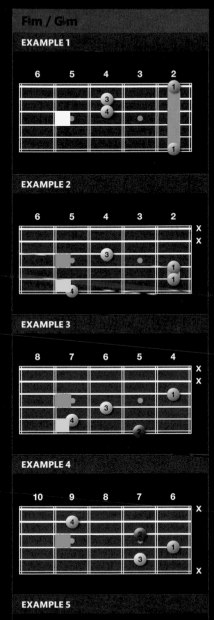

F♯m7 / G♭m7

EXAMPLE 1

EXAMPLE 2

EXAMPLE 3

EXAMPLE 4

EXAMPLE 5

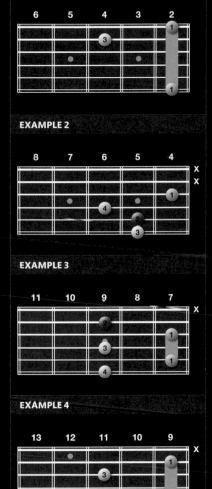

F♯sus2 / G♭sus2

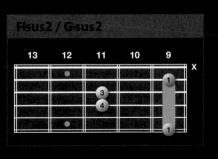

F♯add9 / G♭add9

F♯sus4 / G♭sus4

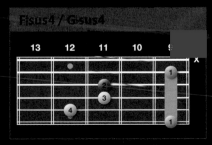

F♯7sus4 / G♭7sus4

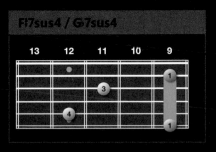

F♯6 / G♭6

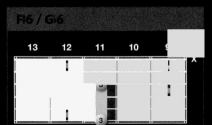

G

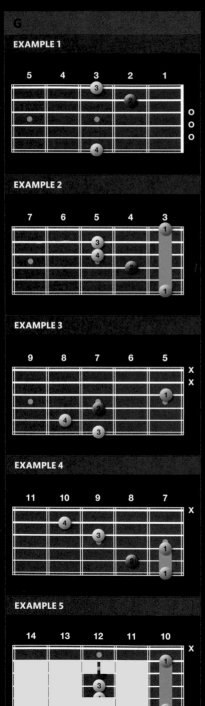

Gmaj7

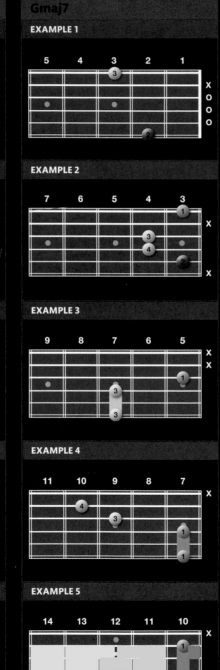

G7

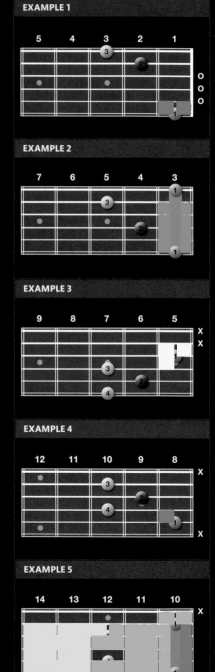